Learning Perl

Other Perl resources from O'Reilly

Related titles Advanced Perl Programming   Perl in a Nutshell
Intermediate Perl   Perl Testing: A Developer's
Perl Best Practices   Notebook™
Perl Cookbook™   Practical mod_perl
Perl Debugger Pocket   Perl 6 and Parrot Essentials
Reference

**Perl Books
Resource Center**
perl.oreilly.com is a complete catalog of O'Reilly's books on Perl and related technologies, including sample chapters and code examples.

Perl.com is the central web site for the Perl community. It is the perfect starting place for finding out everything there is to know about Perl.

Conferences
O'Reilly brings diverse innovators together to nurture the ideas that spark revolutionary industries. We specialize in documenting the latest tools and systems, translating the innovator's knowledge into useful skills for those in the trenches. Visit *conferences.oreilly.com* for our upcoming events.

Safari Bookshelf (*safari.oreilly.com*) is the premier online reference library for programmers and IT professionals. Conduct searches across more than 1,000 books. Subscribers can zero in on answers to time-critical questions in a matter of seconds. Read the books on your Bookshelf from cover to cover or simply flip to the page you need. Try it today for free.

FOURTH EDITION

Learning Perl

Randal L. Schwartz, Tom Phoenix, and brian d foy

O'REILLY®

Beijing · Cambridge · Farnham · Köln · Paris · Sebastopol · Taipei · Tokyo

Learning Perl, Fourth Edition

by Randal L. Schwartz, Tom Phoenix, and brian d foy

Published by O'Reilly Media, Inc., 1005 Gravenstein Highway North, Sebastopol, CA 95472.

O'Reilly books may be purchased for educational, business, or sales promotional use. Online editions are also available for most titles (*safari.oreilly.com*). For more information, contact our corporate/insti-tutional sales department: (800) 998-9938 or *corporate@oreilly.com*.

Editors:	Tatiana Apandi and Allison Randal
Production Editor:	Matt Hutchinson
Production Services:	GEX, Inc.
Cover Designer:	Edie Freedman
Interior Designer:	David Futato

Printing History:

November 1993:	First Edition.
July 1997:	Second Edition.
July 2001:	Third Edition.
July 2005:	Fourth Edition.

 This book uses RepKover™, a durable and flexible lay-flat binding.

ISBN: 0-596-10105-8

[M]

Table of Contents

Preface

Welcome to the fourth edition of *Learning Perl*.

If you're looking for the best way to spend your first 30 to 45 hours with the Perl programming language, you've found it. In the pages that follow, you'll find a carefully paced introduction to the language that is the workhorse of the Internet, as well as the language of choice for system administrators, web hackers, and casual programmers around the world.

We can't give you all of Perl in just a few hours. The books that promise this are probably fibbing a bit. Instead, we've carefully selected a useful subset of Perl for you to learn, good for programs from one to 128 lines long, which end up being about 90% of the programs in use out there. And when you're ready to go on, you can get the Alpaca book, which picks up where this book leaves off. We've also included a number of pointers for further education.

Each chapter is small enough so you can read it in an hour or two. Each chapter ends with a series of exercises to help you practice what you've learned, with the answers in Appendix A for your reference. Thus, this book is ideally suited for a classroom "Introduction to Perl" course. We know this because the material for this book was lifted almost word-for-word from our flagship "Learning Perl" course delivered to thousands of students around the world. However, we've designed the book for self-study as well.

Perl lives as the "toolbox for Unix," but you don't have to be a Unix guru or a Unix user to use this book. Unless otherwise noted, everything we're saying applies equally well to Windows ActivePerl from ActiveState and most other modern implementations of Perl.

Though you don't need to know about Perl to begin reading this book, we recommend that you have familiarity with basic programming concepts such as variables, loops, subroutines, and arrays, and the all-important "editing a source code file with your favorite text editor." We don't spend any time explaining those concepts. We're pleased that we've had many reports of people successfully picking up *Learning Perl* and grasping Perl as their first programming language, but we can't promise the same results for everyone.

History of This Book

For the curious, here's how Randal tells the story of how this book came about:

After I had finished the first *Programming Perl* book with Larry Wall (in 1991), I was approached by Taos Mountain Software in Silicon Valley to produce a training course. This included having me deliver the first dozen or so courses and train its staff to continue offering the course. I wrote the course for the company* and delivered it as promised.

On the third or fourth delivery of that course (in late 1991), someone came up to me and said, "You know, I really like *Programming Perl*, but the way the material is presented in this course is so much easier to follow. You oughtta write a book like this course." It sounded like an opportunity to me, so I started thinking about it.

I wrote to Tim O'Reilly with a proposal based on an outline that was similar to the course I was presenting for Taos, though I had rearranged and modified a few of the chapters based on observations in the classroom. I think that was my fastest proposal acceptance in history; I got a message from Tim within 15 minutes saying, "We've been waiting for you to pitch a second book—*Programming Perl* is selling like gangbusters." That started the effort over the next 18 months to finish the first edition of *Learning Perl*.

During that time, I was starting to see an opportunity to teach Perl classes outside Silicon Valley,† so I created a class based on the text I was writing for *Learning Perl*. I gave a dozen classes for various clients (including my primary contractor, Intel Oregon), and used the feedback to fine-tune the book draft even further.

The first edition hit the streets on the first day of November 1993‡ and became a smashing success, frequently even outpacing *Programming Perl* book sales.

The back-cover jacket of the first book said "written by a leading Perl trainer." Well, that became a self-fulfilling prophesy. Within a few months, I was starting to get email from people all over the United States asking me to teach at their site. During the following seven years, my company became the leading worldwide on-site Perl

---

* In the contract, I retained the rights to the exercises, hoping someday to reuse them in some other way, like in the magazine columns I was writing at the time. The exercises are the only things that leapt from the Taos course to the book.

† My Taos contract had a no-compete clause, so I had to stay out of Silicon Valley with any similar courses, which I respected for many years.

‡ I remember that date well, because it was also the day I was arrested at my home for computer-related activities around my Intel contract, a series of felony charges for which I was later convicted. See *http://www.lightlink.com/fors/* for details.

training company, and I had personally racked up (literally) a million frequent-flier miles. It didn't hurt that the Web started taking off about then, and the webmasters and webmistresses picked Perl as the language of choice for content management, interaction through CGI, and maintenance.

For two years, I worked closely with Tom Phoenix in his role as lead trainer and content manager for Stonehenge, giving him charter to experiment with the "Llama" course by moving things around and breaking things up. When we had come up with what we thought was the best major revision of the course, I contacted O'Reilly and said "it's time for a new book!" And that became the third edition.

Two years after writing the third edition of the Llama, Tom and I decided it was time to push our follow-on "advanced" course out into the world as a book for people writing programs that are "100 to 10,000 lines of code." And together we created the first Alpaca book, released in 2003.

But fellow instructor brian d foy was just getting back from the conflict in the Gulf, and he had noticed that we could use some rewriting in both books because our courseware needed to track the changing needs of the typical student. So, he pitched the idea to O'Reilly to take on rewriting both the Llama and the Alpaca one final time before Perl 6 (we hope). This edition of the Llama reflects those changes. brian has been the lead writer here, working with my occasional guidance, and has done a brilliant job of the usual "herding cats" that a multiple-writer team generally feels like.

Some of the differences you may notice from prior editions:

- The text has been updated for the latest version of Perl, Perl 5.8.
- We've combined some chapters, and renumbered others. We've beefed up the regular expression chapters and introduced filehandles sooner.
- We've added a chapter on CPAN, which has become much more important to beginners.

Typographical Conventions

The following font conventions are used in this book:

Constant width
> Is used for method names, function names, variables, and attributes. It is also used for code examples.

Constant width bold
> Is used to indicate user input.

Constant width italic
> Is used to indicate a replaceable item in code (e.g., *filename*, where you are supposed to substitute an actual filename).

Italic

> Is used for filenames, URLs, hostnames, important words on first mention, and emphasis.

Footnotes

> Are used to attach parenthetical notes that you *should not* read on your first (or perhaps second or third) reading of this book. Sometimes lies are spoken to simplify the presentation, and the footnotes restore the lie to truth. Often the material in the footnote will be advanced material not discussed anywhere else in the book.

Using Code Examples

This book is here to help you get your job done. In general, you may use the code in this book in your programs and documentation. You do not need to contact us for permission unless you're reproducing a significant portion of the code. For example, writing a program that uses several chunks of code from this book does not require permission. Selling or distributing a CD-ROM of examples from O'Reilly books *does* require permission. Answering a question by citing this book and quoting example code does not require permission. Incorporating a significant amount of example code from this book into your product's documentation *does* require permission.

We appreciate, but do not require, attribution. An attribution usually includes the title, author, publisher, and ISBN. For example: "*Learning Perl*, Fourth Edition, by Randal L. Schwartz, Tom Phoenix, and brian d foy. Copyright 2005 O'Reilly Media, Inc., 0-596-10105-8."

How to Contact Us

We have tested and verified all the information in this book to the best of our abilities, but you may find that features have changed or that we have let errors slip through the production of the book. Please let us know of any errors that you find, as well as suggestions for future editions, by writing to:

> O'Reilly Media, Inc.
> 1005 Gravenstein Highway North
> Sebastopol, CA 95472
> (800) 998-9938 (in the U.S. or Canada)
> (707) 829-7000 (international/local)
> (707) 829-0104 (fax)

You can also send messages electronically. To be put on our mailing list or to request a catalog, send email to:

> *info@oreilly.com*

To ask technical questions or to comment on the book, send email to:

bookquestions@oreilly.com

We have a web site for the book, where we'll list examples, errata, and any plans for future editions. It also offers a downloadable set of text files (and a couple of Perl programs) that are useful, but not required, when doing some of the exercises. You can access this page at:

http://www.oreilly.com/catalog/lperl4/

For more information about this book and others, see the O'Reilly web site:

http://www.oreilly.com

Safari Enabled

 When you see a Safari® enabled icon on the cover of your favorite technology book, that means the book is available online through the O'Reilly Network Safari Bookshelf.

Safari offers a solution that's better than e-books. It's a virtual library that lets you easily search thousands of top tech books, cut and paste code samples, download chapters, and find quick answers when you need the most accurate, current information. Try it free at *http://safari.oreilly.com*.

Acknowledgments

Thanks to our reviewers David H. Adler, Dave Cross, Chris Devers, Paul Fenwick, Stephen Jenkins, Matthew Musgrove, and Wil Wheaton for providing comments on the draft of this book.

Thanks to our many students who have let us know what parts of the course material have needed improvement over the years. It's because of you that we're all so proud of it today.

Thanks to the many Perl Mongers who have made us feel at home as we've visited your cities. Let's do it again sometime.

And finally, our sincerest thanks to our friend Larry Wall, for having the wisdom to share his cool and powerful toys with the rest of the world so that we can all get our work done just a little bit faster, easier, and with more fun.

From Randal

I want to thank the Stonehenge trainers past and present (Joseph Hall, Tom Phoenix, Chip Salzenberg, brian d foy, and Tad McClellan) for their willingness to go out and teach in front of classrooms week after week and to come back with their notes about what's working so we could fine-tune the material for this book. I especially want to single out my coauthor and business associate, Tom Phoenix, for having spent many hours working to improve Stonehenge's Llama course and to provide the wonderful core text for most of this book. And brian d foy for being the lead writer of the fourth edition, including taking that eternal to-do item out of my inbox so that it would finally happen.

I want to thank everyone at O'Reilly, especially our very patient editor and overseer, Allison Randal (no relation, but she has a nicely spelled last name), and Tim O'Reilly for taking a chance on me in the first place with the Camel and Llama books.

I am also indebted to the thousands of people who have purchased the past editions of the Llama so that I could use the money to stay "off the streets and out of jail," and to those students in my classrooms who have trained me to be a better trainer, and to the stunning array of Fortune 1000 clients who have purchased our classes in the past and will continue to do so into the future.

As always, a special thanks to Lyle and Jack, for teaching me nearly everything I know about writing. I won't ever forget you guys.

From Tom

I've got to echo Randal's thanks to everyone at O'Reilly. For the third edition of this book Linda Mui was our editor, and I still thank her for her patience in pointing out which jokes and footnotes were most excessive while pointing out that she is in no way to blame for the ones that remain. She and Randal have guided me through the process of writing, and I am grateful. In the present edition, Allison Randal has stepped in as editor, and my thanks go to her as well.

And another echo with regard to Randal and the other Stonehenge trainers, who hardly ever complained when I unexpectedly updated the course materials to try a new teaching technique. You folks have contributed many different viewpoints on teaching methods that I would never have seen.

For many years, I worked at the Oregon Museum of Science and Industry (OMSI), and I'd like to thank the folks there for letting me hone my teaching skills as I learned to build a joke or two into every activity, explosion, or dissection.

To the many folks on Usenet who have given me your appreciation and encouragement for my contributions there, thanks. As always, I hope this helps.

To my many students, who have shown me with their questions (and befuddled looks) when I needed to try a new way of expressing a concept. I hope that the present edition helps to relieve any remaining puzzlement.

Of course, deep thanks are due especially to my coauthor, Randal, for giving me the freedom to try various ways of presenting the material in the classroom and here in the book, as well as for the push to make this material into a book in the first place.

And without fail, I must say that I am indeed inspired by your ongoing work to ensure no one else becomes ensnared by the legal troubles that have stolen so much of your time and energy; you're a fine example.

To my wife, Jenna, thanks for being a cat person, and everything thereafter.

From brian

I have to thank Randal first since I learned Perl from the first edition of this book and then had to learn it again when he asked me to start teaching for Stonehenge in 1998. Teaching is often the best way to learn. Since then, Randal has mentored me in Perl and several other things he thought I needed to learn, like the time he decided that we could use Smalltalk instead of Perl for a demonstration at a web conference. I'm always amazed at the breadth of his knowledge. He's the one who told me to start writing about Perl. Now I'm helping out on the book where I started. I'm honored, Randal.

I'd probably only seen Tom Phoenix for fewer than two weeks in the entire time I've worked for Stonehenge, but I'd been teaching his version of our Learning Perl course for years. That version turned into the third edition of this book. By teaching Tom's new version, I found new ways to explain almost everything and learned even more corners of Perl.

When I convinced Randal that I should help out on the Llama update, I was anointed as the maker of the proposal to the publisher, the keeper of the outline, and the version control wrangler. Our editor, Allison Randal, helped me get all of those set up and endured my frequent emails without complaining.

Special non-Perl thanks to Stacey, Buster, Mimi, Roscoe, Amelia, Lila, and everyone else who tried to distract me while I was busy but still talked to me even though I couldn't come out to play.

## CHAPTER 1

Introduction

Welcome to the Llama book!

This is the fourth edition of a book that has been enjoyed by half a million readers since 1993. At least, we hope they've enjoyed it. It's a sure thing that we've enjoyed writing it.*

Questions and Answers

You probably have some questions about Perl, and maybe some about this book, especially if you've already flipped through the book to see what's coming. So, we'll use this chapter to answer them.

Is This the Right Book for You?

If you're anything like us, you're probably standing in a bookstore right now,† wondering whether you should get this Llama book and learn Perl or maybe that book over there and learn some language named after a snake, or a beverage, or a letter of the alphabet.‡ You've got about two minutes before the bookstore manager comes over to tell you that this isn't a library,§ and you need to buy something or get out. Maybe you want to use these two minutes to see a quick Perl program, so you'll

---

* To be sure, the first edition was written by Randal L. Schwartz, the second by Randal and Tom Christiansen, the third by Randal and Tom Phoenix, and now the fourth by Randal, Tom Phoenix, and brian d foy. So, whenever we say "we" in this edition, we mean that last group. Now, if you're wondering how we can say that we've *enjoyed* writing it (in the past tense) when we're still on the first page, that's easy: we started at the end, and worked our way backward. It sounds like a strange way to do it, we know. But, honestly, once we finished writing the index, the rest was easy.

† Actually, if you're like us, you're standing in a library, not a bookstore. But we're tightwads.

‡ Before you write to tell us that it's a comedy troupe, not a snake, we should really explain that we're dyslexically thinking of CORBA.

§ Unless it *is*.

know something about how powerful Perl is and what it can do. In that case, you should check out the whirlwind tour of Perl later in this chapter.

Why Are There So Many Footnotes?

Thank you for noticing. There are a lot of footnotes in this book. Ignore them. They're needed because Perl is full of exceptions to its rules. This is a good thing, as real life is full of exceptions to rules.

But it means we can't honestly write, "The fizzbin operator frobnicates the hoozistatic variables" without a footnote giving the exceptions.* We're pretty honest, so we have to write the footnotes. But you can be honest without reading them. (It's funny how that works out.)

Many of the exceptions have to do with portability. Perl began on Unix systems, and it still has deep roots in Unix. But wherever possible, we've tried to show when something may behave unexpectedly whether the cause is running on a non-Unix system, or some other reason. We hope that readers who know nothing about Unix will find this book a good introduction to Perl. (And they'll learn a little about Unix along the way at no extra charge.)

And many of the other exceptions have to do with the old "80/20" rule. By that, we mean that 80% of the behavior of Perl can be described in 20% of the documentation, and the other 20% of the behavior takes up the other 80% of the documentation. To keep this book small, we'll talk about the most common, easy-to-talk-about behavior in the main text and hint in the direction of the other stuff in the footnotes (which are in a smaller font, so we can say more in the same space).† Once you've read the book all the way through without reading the footnotes, you'll probably want to look back at some sections for reference. At that point, or if you become unbearably curious along the way, go ahead and read the notes. A lot of them are just computer jokes anyway.

What About the Exercises and Their Answers?

The exercises are at the end of each chapter because, between the three of us, we've presented this same course material to several thousand students.‡ We have carefully crafted these exercises to give you the chance to make mistakes as well.

---

* Except on Tuesdays, during a power outage, when you hold your elbow at a funny angle during the equinox, or when use integer is in effect inside a loop block being called by a prototyped subroutine prior to Perl Version 5.6.

† We even discussed doing the entire book as a footnote to save the page-count, but footnotes on footnotes started to get a bit crazy.

‡ Not all at once.

It's not that we want you to make mistakes, but you need to have the chance. That's because you are going to make most of these mistakes during your Perl programming career, and it may as well be now. Any mistake that you make while reading this book you won't make again when you're writing a program on a deadline. And we're always here to help you out if something goes wrong; Appendix A has our answer for each exercise and a little text to go with it that explains the mistakes you made and a few you didn't. Check out the answers when you're done with the exercises.

Don't peek at the answer until you've given the problem a good try. You'll learn better if you figure it out than if you read about it. Don't knock your head repeatedly against the wall if you don't figure out a solution. Move on to the next chapter and don't worry too much about it.

Even if you never make any mistakes, you should look at the answers when you're done. The accompanying text will point out some details of the program that might not be obvious at first.

What Do Those Numbers Mean at the Start of the Exercise?

Each exercise has a number in square brackets in front of the exercise text, looking something like this:

> [2] What does the number 2 inside square brackets mean when it appears at the start of an exercise's text?

That number is our (very rough) estimate of how many minutes you can expect to spend on that particular exercise. It's rough, so don't be too surprised if you're done (with writing, testing, and debugging) in half that time or not done in twice that long. On the other hand, if you're really stuck, we won't tell anyone that you peeked at Appendix A to see what our answer looked like.

What if I'm a Perl Course Instructor?

If you're a Perl instructor who has decided to use this as your textbook (as many have over the years), you should know that we've tried to make each set of exercises short enough that most students could do the whole set in 45 minutes to an hour with a little time left over for a break. Some chapters' exercises should be quicker, and some may take longer. That's because, once we wrote all of those little numbers in square brackets, we discovered that we don't know how to add. (Luckily, we know how to make computers do it for us.)

What Does "Perl" Stand For?

Perl is sometimes called the "Practical Extraction and Report Language" though it has been called a "Pathologically Eclectic Rubbish Lister" among other expansions.

It's a retronym, not an acronym since Larry Wall, Perl's creator, came up with the name first and the expansion later. That's why "Perl" isn't in all caps. There's no point in arguing which expansion is correct; Larry endorses both.

You may also see "perl" with a lowercase p in some writing. In general, "Perl" with a capital P refers to the language and "perl" with a lowercase p refers to the interpreter that compiles and runs your programs.

Why Did Larry Create Perl?

Larry created Perl in the mid-1980s when he wanted to produce some reports from a Usenet news-like hierarchy of files for a bug-reporting system, and *awk* ran out of steam. Larry, being the lazy programmer that he is,* decided to overkill the problem with a general-purpose tool that he could use in at least one other place. The result was Perl Version zero.

Why Didn't Larry Just Use Some Other Language?

There's no shortage of computer languages, is there? But, at the time, Larry didn't see anything that met his needs. If one of the other languages of today had been available back then, perhaps Larry would have used one of those. He needed something with the quickness of coding available in shell or *awk* programming and with some of the power of more advanced tools like *grep*, *cut*, *sort*, and *sed*,† without having to resort to a language like C.

Perl fills the gap between low-level programming (such as in C or C++ or assembly) and high-level programming (such as "shell" programming). Low-level programming is usually hard to write and is ugly but fast and unlimited; it's hard to beat the speed of a well-written low-level program on a given machine. There, you can do almost anything. High-level programming, at the other extreme, tends to be slow, hard, ugly, and limited; there are many things you can't do with the shell or batch programming if there's no command on your system that provides the needed functionality. Perl is easy, nearly unlimited, mostly fast, and kind of ugly.

Let's take another look at those four claims we made about Perl:

First, Perl is easy. As you'll see, though, this means it's easy to use. It's not especially easy to learn. If you drive a car, you spent many weeks or months learning that, and

---

* We're not insulting Larry by saying he's lazy; laziness is a virtue. The wheelbarrow was invented by someone who was too lazy to carry things; writing was invented by someone who was too lazy to memorize. Perl was invented by someone who was too lazy to get the job done without inventing a whole new computer language.

† Don't worry if you don't know what these are. All that matters is that they were the programs Larry had in his Unix toolbox, but they weren't up to the tasks at hand.

now it's easy to drive. When you've been programming Perl for about as many hours as it took you to learn to drive, Perl will be easy for you.*

Perl is nearly unlimited. There are few things you can't do with Perl. You wouldn't want to write an interrupt-microkernel-level device driver in Perl (though that's been done), but most things that ordinary folks need most of the time are good tasks for Perl from quick little one-off programs to major industrial-strength applications.

Perl is mostly fast. That's because nobody is developing Perl who doesn't also use it, so we all want it to be fast. If someone wants to add a feature that would be cool, but it would slow down other programs, Larry is almost certain to refuse the new feature until we find a way to make it quick enough.

Perl is kind of ugly. This is true. O'Reilly's symbol for Perl is the camel, the animal on the cover of the venerable Camel book (also known as *Programming Perl*), a cousin of this Llama (and her sister, the Alpaca). Camels are kind of ugly, too. But they work hard, even in tough conditions. Camels get the job done despite all difficulties even when they look bad and smell worse and sometimes spit at you. Perl is a little like that.

Is Perl Easy or Hard?

Perl is easy to use, but sometimes hard to learn. This is a generalization, of course. In designing Perl, Larry made many trade-offs. When he's had the chance to make something easier for the programmer at the expense of being more difficult for the student, he's decided in the programmer's favor nearly every time. That's because you'll learn Perl only once, but you'll use it again and again.† Perl has any number of conveniences that let the programmer save time. For example, most functions will have a default; frequently, the default is the way you'll want to use the function. So, you'll see lines of Perl code like these:‡

```
while (<>) {
  chomp;
  print join("\t", (split /:/)[0, 2, 1, 5] ), "\n";
}
```

Written out in full, without using Perl's defaults and shortcuts, that snippet would be roughly ten or twelve times longer, so it would take longer to read and write. It would be harder to maintain and debug, too, with more variables. If you know some Perl, and you don't see the variables in that code, that's part of the point. They're all

---

* But we hope you'll crash less often with the car.

† If you're going to use a programming language for only a few minutes each week or month, you'd prefer one that is easier to learn since you'll have forgotten nearly all of it from one use to the next. Perl is for people who are programmers for at least twenty minutes per day and probably most of that in Perl.

‡ We won't explain it all here, but this example pulls some data from an input file or files in one format and writes some of the data out in another format. All of its features are covered in this book.

being used by default. But to have this ease at the programmer's tasks means paying the price when you're learning; you have to learn those defaults and shortcuts.

A good analogy is the proper and frequent use of contractions in English. Sure, "will not" means the same as "won't." But most people say "won't" rather than "will not" because it saves time and because everybody knows it and it makes sense. Similarly, Perl's "contractions" abbreviate common "phrases" so that they can be "spoken" quicker and understood by the maintainer as a single idiom, rather than a series of unrelated steps.

Once you become familiar with Perl, you may find yourself spending less time getting shell quoting (or C declarations) right, and more time surfing the Web, because Perl is a great tool for leverage. Perl's concise constructs allow you to create some cool one-up solutions or general tools (with minimal fuss). You can drag those tools along to your next job because Perl is highly portable and readily available, so you'll have even more time to surf.

Perl is a high-level language. That means that the code is dense; a Perl program may be around a quarter to three-quarters as long as the corresponding program in C. This makes Perl faster to write, read, debug, and maintain. It doesn't take much programming before you realize that when the entire subroutine is small enough to fit on-screen all at once, you don't have to keep scrolling back and forth to see what's going on. Since the number of bugs in a program is roughly proportional to the length of the source code* (rather than being proportional to the program's functionality), the shorter source in Perl will mean fewer bugs on average.

Like any language, Perl can be "write-only" in that it's possible to write programs impossible to read. But with proper care, you can avoid this common accusation. Yes, sometimes Perl looks like line noise to the uninitiated, but to the seasoned Perl programmer, it looks like the notes of a grand symphony. If you follow the guidelines of this book, your programs should be easy to read and maintain, and they probably won't win The Obfuscated Perl Contest.

How Did Perl Get to Be So Popular?

After playing with Perl a bit, adding stuff here and there, Larry released it to the community of Usenet readers, commonly known as "the Net." The users on this ragtag fugitive fleet of systems around the world (tens of thousands of them) gave him feedback, asking for ways to do this, that, or the other thing, many of which Larry had never envisioned his little Perl handling.

As a result, Perl kept growing. It grew in features. It grew in portability. What was once a little language available on only a couple of Unix systems has grown to have

---

* With a sharp jump when any one section of the program exceeds the size of your screen.

thousands of pages of free online documentation, dozens of books, several mainstream Usenet newsgroups (and a dozen newsgroups and mailing lists outside the mainstream) with an uncountable number of readers and implementations on nearly every system in use today. And don't forget this Llama book as well.

What Is Happening with Perl Now?

Larry doesn't write the code these days, but he still guides the development and makes the big decisions. Perl is mostly maintained by a hardy group of people called the Perl 5 Porters. You can follow their work and discussions on the *perl5-porters@perl.org* mailing list.

As we write this (March 2005), a lot is happening with Perl. For the past few years, many people have been working on the next major version of Perl: Perl 6.

Don't throw away your Perl 5, which is still the current and stable version of Perl. We don't expect a stable version of Perl 6 for a while yet. Perl 5 won't disappear when Perl 6 shows up, and people may end up using both for several years. The Perl 5 Porters maintain Perl 5 just like they always have and some of the good ideas from Perl 6 have made it into Perl 5.

In 2000, Larry Wall first proposed the next major release of Perl as the Perl community's rewrite of Perl. In the years that followed, a new interpreter called Parrot came to life, but not much else happened for average users. This year, Autrijus Tang started playing with Pugs (Perl User Golfing System) as a "featherweight" implementation of Perl 6 in Haskell. Developers from the Perl and Haskell sides of the world ran to help. We can't say what will happen since they are still working on it, but you can write simple Perl 6 programs in Pugs. You can see more about Perl 6 at *http://dev.perl.org/perl6* and *http://www.pugscode.org/* to get more information.

What Is Perl Good For?

Perl is good for quick-and-dirty programs that you whip up in three minutes. Perl is also good for long and extensive programs that take a dozen programmers three years to finish. Of course, you'll probably find yourself writing many programs that take you less than an hour to complete, from the initial plan to the fully tested code.

Perl is optimized for problems that are about 90% working with text and about 10% everything else. That description seems to fit most programming tasks that pop up these days. In a perfect world, every programmer could know every language; you'd always be able to choose the best language for each project. Most of the time, you'd choose Perl.* Though the Web wasn't even a twinkle in Tim Berners-Lee's eye when

---

* Don't take our word for it, though. If you want to know if Perl is better than language X, learn them both and try to see which one you use most often. That's the one that's best for you. In the end, you'll understand Perl better because of your study of language X, and vice versa, so it will be time well spent.

Larry created Perl, it was a marriage made on the Net. Some claim the deployment of Perl in the early 1990s permitted people to move lots of content into HTML format rapidly, and the Web couldn't exist without content. Of course, Perl is the darling language for small CGI scripting (programs run by a web server) as well, so much so that many of the uninformed still make statements like "Isn't CGI just Perl?" or "Why would you use Perl other than for CGI?" We find those statements amusing.

What Is Perl Not Good For?

So, if it's good for so many things, what is Perl not good for? Well, you shouldn't choose Perl for making an *opaque binary*. That's a program that you could give away or sell to someone who then can't see your secret algorithms in the source, and thus can't help you to maintain or debug your code. When you give people your Perl program, you'll normally be giving them the source and not an opaque binary.

If you're wishing for opaque binaries, though, we have to tell you that they don't exist. If people can install and run your program, they can turn it back into source code in any language. Granted, this won't necessarily be the same source that you started with, but it will be some kind of source code. The real way to keep your secret algorithm a secret is, alas, to apply the proper number of attorneys; they can write a license that says, "You can do *this* with the code, but you can't do *that*. And if you break our rules, we've got the proper number of attorneys to ensure that you'll regret it."

How Can I Get Perl?

You probably already have it. At least, we find Perl wherever we go. It ships with many systems, and system administrators often install it on every machine at their site. If you can't find it on your system, you can get it free.

Perl is distributed under two different licenses. For most people who use Perl, either license is adequate. If you'll be modifying Perl, however, you'll want to read the licenses more closely because of the small restrictions on distributing the modified code. For people who won't modify Perl, the licenses say, "It's free—have fun with it."

So, it's free and runs rather nicely on nearly everything that calls itself Unix and has a C compiler. You download it, type a command or two, and it starts configuring and building itself. Better yet, get your system administrator to type those two commands and install it for you.* Besides Unix and Unix-like systems, people have become

---

* If system administrators can't install software, what good are they? If you have trouble convincing your admin to install Perl, offer to buy a pizza. We've never met a sys admin who could say no to a free pizza, or at least counteroffer with something as easy to get.

addicted enough to Perl to port it to other systems, like the Macintosh,* VMS, OS/2, MS/DOS, every modern species of Windows, and probably more by the time you read this.† Many of these ports of Perl come with an installation program that's easier to use than the process for installing Perl on Unix. Check for links in the "ports" section on CPAN.

What Is CPAN?

CPAN is the Comprehensive Perl Archive Network, your one-stop shopping for Perl. It has the source code for Perl itself, ready-to-install ports of Perl to all sorts of non-Unix systems,‡ examples, documentation, extensions to Perl, and archives of messages about Perl. In short, CPAN is comprehensive.

CPAN is replicated on hundreds of mirror machines around the world. Start at *http://search.cpan.org/* or *http://kobesearch.cpan.org/* to browse or search the archive. If you don't have access to the Net, you might find a CD-ROM or DVD-ROM with all of the useful parts of CPAN on it. Check with your local technical bookstore. Look for a recently minted archive, though, since CPAN changes daily. An archive from two years ago is an antique. Better yet, get a kind friend with Net access to burn you one with today's CPAN.

How Can I Get Support for Perl?

Well, you get the complete source, so you get to fix the bugs yourself.

That doesn't sound so good, does it? But it is a good thing. Since there's no "source code escrow" on Perl, anyone can fix a bug. In fact, by the time you've found and verified a bug, someone else will probably have a fix for it. There are thousands of people around the world who help to maintain Perl.

Now, we're not saying that Perl has a lot of bugs, but it's a program, and every program has at least one bug. To see why it's so useful to have the source to Perl, imagine that instead of using Perl, you licensed a programming language called Forehead from a giant, powerful corporation owned by a zillionaire with a bad haircut. (This is all hypothetical. Everyone knows there's no such programming language as Forehead.) Now think of what you can do when you find a bug in Forehead. First, you can report it. Second, you can hope—hope—that they fix the bug, hope that they fix it soon, and hope that they won't charge too much for the new version. You can hope

---

* MacPerl runs under the "classic" Mac OS. If you have Mac OS X, which is a Unix-based system, you have mainstream Perl.

† And no, as we write this, it won't fit in your Palm handheld. It's just too darn big, even stripped down. We've heard rumors that it runs on WinCE, though.

‡ It's nearly always better to compile Perl from the source on Unix systems. Other systems may not have a C compiler or other tools needed for compilation, so CPAN has binaries for these.

the new version doesn't add new features with new bugs, and hope that the giant company doesn't get broken up in an anti-trust lawsuit.

But with Perl, you've got the source. In the rare and unlikely event you can't get a bug fixed any other way, you can hire a programmer or ten and get to work. For that matter, if you buy a new machine that Perl doesn't run on yet, you can port it yourself. Or, if you need a feature that doesn't exist yet, well, you know what to do.

Are There Any Other Kinds of Support?

Sure. One of our favorites is the Perl Mongers. This is a worldwide association of Perl users' groups; see *http://www.pm.org/* for more information. There's probably a group near you with an expert or someone who knows an expert. If there's no group, you can start one.

Of course, for the first line of support, you shouldn't neglect the documentation. Besides the manpages,* you can find the documentation on the CPAN, *http://www.cpan.org*, as well as other sites, such as *http://perldoc.perl.org* that has HTML and PDF versions of the Perl documentation, *http://www.perldoc.com* that lets you search multiple versions of the documentation, or *http://faq.perl.org/* that has the latest version of the perlfaq.

Another authoritative source is O'Reilly's book *Programming Perl*, commonly called "the Camel book" because of its cover animal. (This book is known as "the Llama book.") The Camel book contains the complete reference information, some tutorial stuff, and a bunch of miscellaneous information about Perl. There's also a separate pocket-sized *Perl 5 Pocket Reference* by Johan Vromans (O'Reilly) that's handy to keep at hand (or in your pocket).

If you need to ask a question, there are newsgroups on Usenet and any number of mailing lists.† At any hour of the day or night, there's a Perl expert awake in some time zone answering questions on Usenet's Perl newsgroups; the sun never sets on the Perl empire. This means that if you ask a question, you'll often get an answer within minutes. If you didn't check the documentation and FAQ first, you'll get flamed within minutes.

The official Perl newsgroups on Usenet are located in the *comp.lang.perl.** part of the hierarchy. As of this writing, there are five of them, but they change from time to time. You (or whoever is in charge of Perl at your site) should generally subscribe to *comp.lang.perl.announce*, which is a low-volume newsgroup with important announcements

---

* The term *manpages* is a Unix-ism meaning documentation. If you're not on a Unix system, the manpages for Perl should be available via your system's native documentation system.

† Many mailing lists are listed at *http://lists.perl.org*.

about Perl, including especially any security-related announcements. Ask your local expert if you need help with Usenet.

A few web communities have sprung up around Perl discussions. One popular one, known as The Perl Monastery (*http://www.perlmonks.org*) has seen quite a bit of participation from many Perl book and column authors, including at least two of the authors of this book. You can also check out *http://learn.perl.org/* and its associated mailing list, *beginners@perl.org*.

If you find yourself needing a support contract for Perl, a number of firms are willing to charge as much as you'd like. Most other support avenues will take care of you free.

What if I Find a Bug in Perl?

The first thing to do when you find a bug is to check the documentation* again.† Perl has so many special features and exceptions to rules that you may have discovered a feature and not a bug. Check that you don't have an older version of Perl; maybe you found something that's been fixed in a more recent version.

When you're almost certain that you've found a real bug, ask around. Ask someone at work, at your local Perl Mongers' meeting, or at a Perl conference. Chances are, it's still a feature and not a bug.

Once you're certain you've found a real bug, cook up a test case. (What, you haven't done so already?) The ideal test case is a tiny self-contained program that any Perl user could run to see the same (mis-)behavior as you've found. Once you've got a test case that clearly shows the bug, use the *perlbug* utility (which comes with Perl) to report the bug. That will normally send email from you to the Perl developers, so don't use *perlbug* until you've got your test case ready.

Once you've sent off your bug report, if you've done everything right, you may get a response within minutes. Typically, you can apply a simple patch and get right back to work. Of course, you may (at worst) get no response at all since the Perl developers are under no obligation to even read your bug reports. But all of us love Perl, so nobody likes to let a bug escape our notice.

How Do I Make a Perl Program?

It's about time you asked (even if you didn't). Perl programs are text files; you can create and edit them with your favorite text editor. (You don't need any special

---

* Even Larry admits to consulting the documentation from time to time.

† Maybe even twice or three times. Many times, we've gone into the documentation looking to explain a particular unexpected behavior and found some new nuance that ends up on a slide or in a column.

development environment, though some commercial ones are available from various vendors. We've never used any of these enough to recommend them.)

You should generally use a programmers' text editor, rather than an ordinary editor. What's the difference? Well, a programmers' text editor will let you do things that programmers need, like indent or unindent a block of code or to find the matching closing curly brace for a given opening curly brace. On Unix systems, the two most popular programmers' editors are *emacs* and *vi* (and their variants and clones). BBEdit and Alpha are good editors for Mac OS X, and a lot of people have said nice things about UltraEdit and Programmer's Favorite Editor (PFE) on Windows. The `perlfaq2` manpage lists several other editors, too. Ask your local expert about text editors on your system.

For the simple programs you'll write for the exercises in this book, none of which should be more than about twenty or thirty lines of code, any text editor will be fine.

A few beginners try to use a word processor instead of a text editor. We recommend against this because it's inconvenient at best and impossible at worst. But we won't try to stop you. Be sure to tell the word processor to save your file as "text only"; the word processor's own format will almost certainly be unusable. Most word processors will probably tell you that your Perl program is spelled incorrectly and should use fewer semicolons.

In some cases, you may need to compose the program on one machine and transfer it to another to run it. If you do this, be sure that the transfer uses "text" or "ASCII" mode and not "binary" mode. This step is needed because of the different text formats on different machines. Without that, you may get inconsistent results. Some versions of Perl abort when they detect a mismatch in the line endings.

A Simple Program

According to the oldest rule in the book, any book about a computer language that has Unix-like roots has to start with showing the "Hello, world" program. So, here it is in Perl:

```
#!/usr/bin/perl
print "Hello, world!\n";
```

Let's imagine that you've typed that into your text editor. (Don't worry yet about what the parts mean and how it works. We'll see about those in a moment.) You can generally save that program under any name you wish. Perl doesn't require any special kind of filename or extension, and it's better to use no extension at all.* But some

---

* Why is it better to have no extension? Imagine that you've written a program to calculate bowling scores and you've told all of your friends that it's called *bowling.plx*. One day you decide to rewrite it in C. Do you still call it by the same name, implying that it's still written in Perl? Or do you tell everyone that it has a new name? (And don't call it *bowling.c*, please!) The answer is that it's none of their business what language it's written in if they're merely *using* it. So, it should have simply been called *bowling* in the first place.

systems may require an extension like *.plx* (meaning PerL eXecutable); see your system's release notes for more information.

You may need to do something so your system knows it's an executable program (that is, a command). What you'll do depends upon your system; maybe you won't have to do anything more than to save the program in a certain place. (Your current directory will generally be fine.) On Unix systems, you mark a program as being executable by using the chmod command, perhaps like this:

```
$ chmod a+x my_program
```

The dollar sign (and space) at the start of the line represents the shell prompt, which will probably look different on your system. If you're used to using chmod with a number like 755 instead of a symbolic parameter like a+x, that's fine, too. Either way, it tells the system that this file is now a program.

Now you're ready to run it:

```
$ ./my_program
```

The dot and slash at the start of this command mean to find the program in the current working directory. That's not needed in all cases, but you should use it at the start of each command invocation until you fully understand what it's doing.* If everything worked, it's a miracle. More often, you'll find that your program has a bug. Edit and try again, but you don't need to use chmod each time since that should "stick" to the file. (Of course, if the bug is that you didn't use chmod correctly, you'll probably get a "permission denied" message from your shell.)

What's Inside That Program?

Like other "free-form" languages, Perl generally lets you use insignificant whitespace (like spaces, tabs, and newlines) at will to make your program easier to read. Most Perl programs use a fairly standard format though, much like most of what we show here. We strongly encourage you to indent your programs properly since that makes your program easier to read; a good text editor will do most of the work for you. Good comments make a program easier to read. In Perl, comments run from a pound sign (#) to the end of the line. (There are no "block comments" in Perl.)† We don't use many comments in the programs in this book because the surrounding text explains their workings, but you should use comments as needed in your own programs.

---

* In short, it's preventing your shell from running another program (or shell built-in) of the same name. A common mistake among beginners is to name their first program test. Many systems have a program (or shell built-in) with that name; that's what the beginners run instead of their program.

† But there are a number of ways to fake them. See the FAQ (accessible with *perldoc perlfaq* on most installations).

So another way (a strange way, it must be said) to write that same "Hello, world" program might be like this:

```
#!/usr/bin/perl
    print    # This is a comment
"Hello, world!\n"
  ;    # Don't write your Perl code like this!
```

That first line is a special comment. On Unix systems,* if the first two characters on the first line of a text file are "#!", then what follows is the name of the program that executes the rest of the file. In this case, the program is stored in the file */usr/bin/perl*.

This #! line is the least portable part of a Perl program because you'll need to find out what goes there for each machine. Fortunately, it's almost always */usr/bin/perl* or */usr/local/bin/perl*. If that's not it, you'll have to find where your system is hiding perl and use that path. On Unix systems, you might use a shebang line that finds perl for you:

```
#!/usr/bin/env perl
```

If perl isn't in any of the directories in your search path, you might have to ask your local system administrator or somebody using the same system as you.

On non-Unix systems, it's traditional (and even useful) to make the first line say #!perl. If nothing else, it tells your maintenance programmer as soon as he or she gets ready to fix it that it's a Perl program.

If that #! line is wrong, you'll generally get an error from your shell. This may be something unexpected, like "file not found." It's not your program that's not found though; it's */usr/bin/perl* that wasn't where it should have been. We'd make the message clearer, but it's not coming from Perl; it's the shell that's complaining. (By the way, you should be careful to spell it *usr* and not *user* because the folks who invented Unix were lazy typists, so they omitted a lot of letters.)

Another problem you could have is if your system doesn't support the #! line at all. In that case, your shell (or whatever your system uses) will probably run your program by itself, with results that may disappoint or astonish you. If you can't figure out what some strange error message is telling you, search for it in the *perldiag* manpage.

The "main" program consists of all of the ordinary Perl statements (not including anything in subroutines, which you'll see later). There's no "main" routine, as there is in languages like C or Java. In fact, many programs don't have routines (in the form of subroutines).

---

* Most modern ones, anyway. The "shebang" mechanism pronounced "sheh-bang," as in "the whole she-bang" was introduced somewhere in the mid-1980s, and that's pretty ancient, even on the extensively long Unix timeline.

There's no required variable declaration section as there is in some other languages. If you've always had to declare your variables, you may be startled or unsettled by this at first. But it allows us to write quick-and-dirty Perl programs. If your program is only two lines long, you don't want to have to use one of those lines just to declare your variables. If you want to declare your variables, that's a good thing; you'll see how to do that in Chapter 4.

Most statements are an expression followed by a semicolon. Here's the one you've seen a few times so far:

```
print "Hello, world!\n";
```

As you may have guessed by now, this line prints the message Hello, world!. At the end of that message is the shortcut \n, which is probably familiar to you if you've used another language like C, C++, or Java; it means a newline character. When that's printed after the message, the print position drops down to the start of the next line, allowing the following shell prompt to appear on a line of its own rather than being attached to the message. Every line of output should end with a newline character. We'll see more about the newline shortcut and other so-called backslash escapes in the next chapter.

How Do I Compile Perl?

Just run your Perl program. The perl interpreter compiles and then runs your program in one user step.

```
$ perl my_program
```

When you run your program, Perl's internal compiler first runs through your entire source, turning it into internal *bytecode*, which is an internal data structure representing the program. Perl's bytecode engine takes over and runs the bytecode. If there's a syntax error on line 200, you'll get that error message before you start running line two.* If you have a loop that runs 5,000 times, it's compiled once; the loop can then run at top speed. And there's no runtime penalty for using as many comments and as much whitespace as you need to make your program easy to understand. If you use calculations involving only constants the result will be a constant computed once as the program is beginning, not each time through a loop.

To be sure, this compilation does take time. It's inefficient to have a voluminous Perl program that does one small quick task (out of many potential tasks, say) and then exits because the runtime for the program will be dwarfed by the compile time. But the compiler is fast; normally the compilation will be a tiny percentage of the runtime.

An exception might be if you were writing a program run as a CGI script, where it may be called hundreds or thousands of times every minute. (This is a high usage

---

* Unless line two happens to be a compile-time operation, like a BEGIN block or a use invocation.

rate. If it were called a few hundreds or thousands of times per day, like most programs on the Web, we probably wouldn't worry too much about it.) Many of these programs have short runtimes, so the issue of recompilation may become significant. If this is an issue for you, you'll want to find a way to keep your program in memory between invocations. The mod_perl extension to the Apache web server *http://perl.apache.org* or Perl modules like `CGI::Fast` can help you.

What if you could save the compiled bytecode to avoid the overhead of compilation? Or, even better, what if you could turn the bytecode into another language, like C, and then compile that? Well, both of these things are possible in some cases, but they probably won't make most programs any easier to use, maintain, debug, or install, and they may make your program slower. Perl 6 should do a lot better in this regard, although it is too soon to tell (as we write this).

A Whirlwind Tour of Perl

So, you want to see a real Perl program with some meat? (If you don't, just play along for now.) Here you are:

```
#!/usr/bin/perl
@lines = `perldoc -u -f atan2`;
foreach (@lines) {
  s/\w<([^>]+)>/\U$1/g;
  print;
}
```

Now, the first time you see Perl code like this, it can seem strange. (In fact, every time you see Perl code like this, it can seem strange.) But let's take it line by line, and see what this example does. (These explanations are brief; this is a whirlwind tour, after all. We'll see all of this program's features in more detail during the rest of this book. You're not really supposed to understand the whole thing until later.)

The first line is the #! line, as you saw before. You might need to change that line for your system, as we discussed earlier.

The second line runs an external command, named within backquotes ("` `"). (The backquote key is often found next to the number 1 on full-sized American keyboards. Be sure not to confuse the backquote with the single quote, "'".) The command we used is `perldoc -u -f atan2`; type that at your command line to see what its output looks like. The `perldoc` command is used on most systems to read and display the documentation for Perl and its associated extensions and utilities, so it should normally be available.* This command tells you something about the trigonometric function atan2;

---

* If perldoc is unavailable, that probably means that your system doesn't have a command-line interface, and your Perl can't run commands (like perldoc) in backticks or via the piped-open, which you'll see in Chapter 14. In that case, you should skip the exercises that use perldoc.

we're using it here as an example of an external command whose output we wish to process.

The output of that command in the backticks is saved in an array variable called @lines. The next line of code starts a loop that processes each one of those lines. Inside the loop, the statements are indented. Though Perl doesn't require this, good programmers do.

The first line inside the loop body is the scariest one; it says s/\w<([^>]+)>/\U$1/g;. Without going into too much detail, we'll just say that this can change any line that has a special marker made with angle brackets (< >), and there should be at least one of those in the output of the perldoc command.

The next line, in a surprise move, prints out each (possibly modified) line. The resulting output should be similar to what perldoc -u -f atan2 would do on its own, but there will be a change where any of those markers appears.

Thus, in the span of a few lines, we've run another program, saved its output in memory, updated the memory items, and printed them out. This kind of program is a fairly common use of Perl, where one type of data is converted to another.

Exercises

Normally, each chapter will end with some exercises, with the answers in Appendix A. But you don't need to write the programs needed to complete this section as they are supplied within the chapter text.

If you can't get these exercises to work on your machine, check your work and then consult your local expert. Remember that you may need to tweak each program a little, as described in the text.

1. [7] Type in the "Hello, world" program and get it to work. (You may name it anything you wish, but a good name might be ex1-1, for simplicity, since it's exercise 1 in Chapter 1.)

2. [5] Type the command perldoc -u -f atan2 at a command prompt and note its output. If you can't get that to work, then find out from a local administrator or the documentation for your version of Perl about how to invoke perldoc or its equivalent. (You'll need this for the next exercise anyway.)

3. [6] Type in the second example program (from the previous section) and see what it prints. (Hint: Be careful to type those punctuation marks exactly as shown.) Do you see how it changed the output of the command?

CHAPTER 2

Scalar Data

In English, as in many other spoken languages, you're used to distinguishing between singular and plural. As a computer language designed by a human linguist, Perl is similar. As a general rule, when Perl has just one of something, that's a *scalar*.[*] A *scalar* is the simplest kind of data that Perl manipulates. Most scalars are a number (like 255 or 3.25e20) or a string of characters (like hello[†] or the Gettysburg Address). Though you may think of numbers and strings as different things, Perl uses them nearly interchangeably.

A scalar value can be acted on with operators (such as addition or concatenation), generally yielding a scalar result. A scalar value can be stored into a scalar variable. Scalars can be read from files and devices, and can be written out as well.

Numbers

Though a scalar is most often either a number or a string, it's useful to look at numbers and strings separately for the moment. We'll cover numbers first and then move on to strings.

All Numbers Have the Same Format Internally

As you'll see in the next few paragraphs, you can specify integers (whole numbers, like 255 or 2001) and floating-point numbers (real numbers with decimal points, like 3.14159, or 1.35×10^{25}). But internally, Perl computes with double-precision

---

[*] This has little to do with the similar term from mathematics or physics in that a scalar is a single thing; there are no vectors in Perl.

[†] If you have been using other programming languages, you may think of hello as a collection of five characters, rather than as a single thing. But in Perl, a string is a single scalar value. Of course, you can access the individual characters when you need to; you'll see how to do that in later chapters.

floating-point values.* This means that there are no integer values internal to Perl. An integer constant in the program is treated as the equivalent floating-point value.† You probably won't notice the conversion (or care much), but you should stop looking for distinct integer operations (as opposed to *floating-point* operations) because they don't exist.‡

Floating-Point Literals

A literal is the way a value is represented in the source code of the Perl program. A literal is not the result of a calculation or an I/O operation; it's data written directly into the source code.

Perl's floating-point literals should look familiar to you. Numbers with and without decimal points are allowed (including an optional plus or minus prefix), as well as attaching a power-of-10 indicator (exponential notation) with E notation.

```
1.25
255.000
255.0
7.25e45   # 7.25 times 10 to the 45th power (a big number)
-6.5e24   # negative 6.5 times 10 to the 24th
          # (a big negative number)
-12e-24   # negative 12 times 10 to the -24th
          # (a very small negative number)
-1.2E-23 # another way to say that - the E may be uppercase
```

Integer Literals

Integer literals are straightforward:

```
0
2001
-40
255
61298040283768
```

That last one is a little hard to read. Perl allows underscores for clarity within integer literals, so you can also write that number like this:

```
61_298_040_283_768
```

---

* A double-precision floating-point value is whatever the C compiler that compiled Perl used for a double declaration. While the size may vary from machine to machine, most modern systems use the IEEE-754 format, which suggests 15 digits of precision and a range of at least 1e-100 to 1e100.

† Well, Perl will sometimes use internal integers in ways invisible to the programmer. That is, the only difference you should generally be able to see is that your program runs faster. And who could complain about that?

‡ Okay, there is the integer pragma. But using that is beyond the scope of this book. And yes, some operations compute an integer from a given floating-point number, as you'll see later. But that's not what we're talking about here.

It's the same value but looks different to us human beings. You might have thought that commas should be used for this purpose, but commas are used for a more important purpose in Perl (as you'll see in the next chapter).

Non-Decimal Integer Literals

Like many other programming languages, Perl allows you to specify numbers in bases other than 10 (decimal). Octal (base 8) literals start with a leading 0, hexadecimal (base 16) literals start with a leading 0x, and binary (base 2) literals start with a leading 0b.* The hex digits A through F (or a through f) represent the conventional digit values of 10 through 15:

```
0377        # 377 octal, same as 255 decimal
0xff        # FF hex, also 255 decimal
0b11111111  # also 255 decimal
```

Though these values look different to us humans, all three are the same number to Perl. It makes no difference to Perl whether you write 0xFF or 255.000, so choose the representation that makes the most sense to you and your maintenance programmer (by which we mean the poor chap who gets stuck trying to figure out what you meant when you wrote your code. Most often, this poor chap is you, and you can't recall why you did what you did three months ago).

When a non-decimal literal is more than about four characters long, it may be hard to read. For this reason, Perl allows underscores for clarity within these literals:

```
0x1377_0B77
0x50_65_72_7C
```

Numeric Operators

Perl provides the typical ordinary addition, subtraction, multiplication, and division operators, and so on:

```
2 + 3      # 2 plus 3, or 5
5.1 - 2.4  # 5.1 minus 2.4, or 2.7
3 * 12     # 3 times 12 = 36
14 / 2     # 14 divided by 2, or 7
10.2 / 0.3 # 10.2 divided by 0.3, or 34
10 / 3     # always floating-point divide, so 3.3333333...
```

Perl also supports a *modulus* operator (%). The value of the expression 10 % 3 is the remainder when 10 is divided by 3, which is 1. Both values are first reduced to their

---

* The "leading zero" indicator works only for literals and not for automatic string-to-number conversion, which you'll see later in this chapter. You can convert a data string that looks like an octal or hex value into a number with oct( ) or hex( ). Though there's no "bin" function for converting binary values, oct( ) can do that for strings beginning with 0b.

integer values, so 10.5 % 3.2 is computed as 10 % 3.* Additionally, Perl provides the FORTRAN-like *exponentiation* operator, which many have yearned for in Pascal and C. The operator is represented by the double asterisk, such as 2**3, which is two to the third power, or eight.† We will introduce other numeric operators as we need them.

Strings

Strings are sequences of characters (like hello). Strings may contain any combination of any characters.‡ The shortest possible string has no characters. The longest string fills all of your available memory, though you wouldn't be able to do much with that. This is in accordance with the principle of "no built-in limits" that Perl follows at every opportunity. Typical strings are printable sequences of letters, digits, and punctuation in the ASCII 32 to ASCII 126 range. However, the ability to have any character in a string means you can create, scan, and manipulate raw binary data as strings and that is something with which many other utilities would have great difficulty. For example, you could update a graphical image or compiled program by reading it into a Perl string, making the change, and writing the result back out.

Like numbers, strings have a literal representation, which is the way you represent the string in a Perl program. Literal strings come in two different flavors: *single-quoted string literals* and *double-quoted string literals*.

Single-Quoted String Literals

A *single-quoted string literal* is a sequence of characters enclosed in single quotes. The single quotes are not part of the string itself but are there to let Perl identify the beginning and the ending of the string. Any character other than a single quote or a backslash between the quote marks (including newline characters, if the string continues onto successive lines) stands for itself inside a string. To get a backslash, put two backslashes in a row; to get a single quote, put a backslash followed by a single quote:

```
'fred'     # those four characters: f, r, e, and d
'barney'   # those six characters
''         # the null string (no characters)
'Don\'t let an apostrophe end this string prematurely!'
'the last character of this string is a backslash: \\'
```

---

* The result of a modulus operator when a negative number (or two) is involved can vary between Perl implementations. Beware.

† You can't normally raise a negative number to a noninteger exponent. Math geeks know that the result would be a complex number. To make that possible, you'll need the help of the Math::Complex module.

‡ Unlike C or C++, there's nothing special about the NUL character in Perl because Perl uses length counting, not a null byte, to determine the end of the string.

```
'hello\n'  # hello followed by backslash followed by n
'hello
there'     # hello, newline, there (11 characters total)
'\'\\'     # single quote followed by backslash
```

The \n within a single-quoted string is not interpreted as a newline but as the two characters backslash and n. Only when the backslash is followed by another backslash or a single quote does it have special meaning.

Double-Quoted String Literals

A *double-quoted string literal* is similar to the strings you may have seen in other languages. Once again, it's a sequence of characters, though this time enclosed in double quotes. But now the backslash takes on its full power to specify certain control characters or any character through octal and hex representations. Here are some double-quoted strings:

```
"barney"         # just the same as 'barney'
"hello world\n" # hello world, and a newline
"The last character of this string is a quote mark: \""
"coke\tsprite"  # coke, a tab, and sprite
```

The double-quoted literal string "barney" means the same six-character string to Perl as does the single-quoted literal string 'barney'. It's like what you saw with numeric literals, where you saw that 0377 was another way to write 255.0. Perl lets you write the literal in the way that makes more sense to you. Of course, if you wish to use a backslash escape (like \n to mean a newline character), you'll need to use the double quotes.

The backslash can precede different characters to mean different things (generally called a *backslash escape*). The nearly complete[*] list of double-quoted string escapes is given in Table 2-1.

Table 2-1. Double-quoted string backslash escapes

Construct	Meaning
\n	Newline
\r	Return
\t	Tab
\f	Formfeed
\b	Backspace
\a	Bell
\e	Escape (ASCII escape character)
\007	Any octal ASCII value (here, 007 = bell)

[*] Recent versions of Perl have introduced Unicode escapes, which we aren't going to show you here.

Table 2-1. Double-quoted string backslash escapes (continued)

Construct	Meaning
\x7f	Any hex ASCII value (here, 7f = delete)
\cC	A "control" character (here, Ctrl-C)
\\	Backslash
\"	Double quote
\l	Lowercase next letter
\L	Lowercase all following letters until \E
\u	Uppercase next letter
\U	Uppercase all following letters until \E
\Q	Quote non-word characters by adding a backslash until \E
\E	End \L, \U, or \Q

Another feature of double-quoted strings is that they are *variable interpolated*, meaning that some variable names within the string are replaced with their current values when the strings are used. You haven't formally been introduced to what a variable looks like yet, so we'll get back to this later in this chapter.

String Operators

String values can be concatenated with the . operator. (Yes, that's a single period.) This doesn't alter either string, any more than 2+3 alters either 2 or 3. The resulting (longer) string is then available for further computation or assignment to a variable:

```
"hello" . "world"       # same as "helloworld"
"hello" . ' ' . "world" # same as 'hello world'
'hello world' . "\n"    # same as "hello world\n"
```

The concatenation must be explicitly requested with the . operator, unlike in some other languages where you merely have to stick the two values next to each other.

A special string operator is the *string repetition* operator, consisting of the single lowercase letter x. This operator takes its left operand (a string) and makes as many concatenated copies of that string as indicated by its right operand (a number):

```
"fred" x 3      # is "fredfredfred"
"barney" x (4+1) # is "barney" x 5, or "barneybarneybarneybarneybarney"
5 x 4           # is really "5" x 4, which is "5555"
```

That last example is worth spelling out. The string repetition operator wants a string for a left operand, so the number 5 is converted to the string "5" (using rules described in detail in the next section), giving a one-character string. This new string is then copied four times, yielding the four-character string 5555. If you had reversed the order of the operands, as 4 x 5, you would have made five copies of the string 4, yielding 44444. This shows that string repetition is not commutative.

The copy count (the right operand) is first truncated to an integer value (4.8 becomes 4) before being used. A copy count of less than one results in an empty (zero-length) string.

Automatic Conversion Between Numbers and Strings

For the most part, Perl automatically converts between numbers and strings as needed. How does it know whether a number or a string is needed? It all depends on the operator being used on the scalar value. If an operator expects a number (as + does), Perl will see the value as a number. If an operator expects a string (like . does), Perl will see the value as a string. You don't need to worry about the difference between numbers and strings; use the proper operators, and Perl will make it all work.

When a string value is used where an operator needs a number (say, for multiplication), Perl automatically converts the string to its equivalent numeric value as if it had been entered as a decimal floating-point value.* So "12" * "3" gives the value 36. Trailing nonnumber stuff and leading whitespace are discarded, so "12fred34" * " 3" will give 36 without any complaints.† At the extreme end of this, something that isn't a number at all converts to zero. This would happen if you used the string "fred" as a number.

Likewise, if a numeric value is given when a string value is needed (say, for string concatenation), the numeric value expands into whatever string would have been printed for that number. For example, if you want to concatenate the string Z followed by the result of 5 multiplied by 7,‡ you can say it this way:

```
"Z" . 5 * 7 # same as "Z" . 35, or "Z35"
```

In other words, you don't have to worry about whether you have a number or a string (most of the time). Perl performs all the conversions for you.§

Perl's Built-in Warnings

Perl can be told to warn you when it sees something suspicious going on in your program. To run your program with warnings turned on, use the -w option on the command line:

```
$ perl -w my_program
```

---

* The trick of using a leading zero to mean a non-decimal value works for literals but never for automatic conversion. Use hex( ) or oct( ) to convert those kinds of strings.

† Unless you request warnings, which we'll discuss in a moment.

‡ You'll see about precedence and parentheses shortly.

§ And if you're worried about efficiency, don't be. Perl generally remembers the result of a conversion so it's done only once.

Or, if you always want warnings, you may request them on the #! line:

```
#!/usr/bin/perl -w
```

That works even on non-Unix systems where it's traditional to write something like this, since the path to Perl doesn't generally matter:

```
#!perl -w
```

With Perl 5.6 and later, you can turn on warnings with a pragma. (Be careful, because it won't work for people with earlier versions of Perl.)[*]

```
#!/usr/bin/perl
use warnings;
```

Now, Perl will warn you if you use '12fred34' as if it were a number:

```
Argument "12fred34" isn't numeric
```

Of course, warnings are generally meant for programmers and not for end-users. If a programmer doesn't see the warning, it probably won't do any good. And warnings won't change the behavior of your program except that now it will emit gripes once in a while. If you get a warning message you don't understand, you can get a longer description of the problem with the diagnostics pragma. The perldiag manpage has the short warning and the longer diagnostic description.

```
#!/usr/bin/perl
use diagnostics;
```

When you add the use diagnostics pragma to your program, it may seem to you that your program now pauses for a moment whenever you launch it. That's because your program has to do a lot of work (and gobble a chunk of memory) in case you want to read the documentation as soon as Perl notices your mistakes, if any. This leads to a nifty optimization that can accelerate your program's launch (and memory footprint) with no adverse impact on users, once you no longer need to read the documentation about the warning messages produced by your program, remove the use diagnostics pragma. (It's even better if you fix your program to avoid causing the warnings. But it's sufficient merely to finish reading the output.)

A further optimization can be had by using one of Perl's command-line options, -M, to load the pragma only when needed instead of editing the source code each time to enable and disable diagnostics:

```
$ perl -Mdiagnostics ./my_program
Argument "12fred34" isn't numeric in addition (+) at ./my_program line 17 (#1)
    (W numeric) The indicated string was fed as an argument to
    an operator that expected a numeric value instead.  If you're
    fortunate the message will identify which operator was so unfortunate.
```

---

[*] The warnings pragma allows lexical warnings, but you'll have to see the perllexwarn manpage to find out about those.

As we run across situations in which Perl will usually be able to warn us about a mistake in your code, we'll point them out. But you shouldn't count on the text or behavior of any warning staying the same in future Perl releases.

Scalar Variables

A *variable* is a name for a container that holds one or more values.* The name of the variable stays the same throughout the program, but the value or values contained in that variable typically change repeatedly throughout the execution of the program.

A scalar variable holds a single scalar value as you'd expect. Scalar variable names begin with a dollar sign followed by what we'll call a *Perl identifier*: a letter or underscore, and then possibly more letters, or digits, or underscores. Another way to think of it is that it's made up of alphanumerics and underscores but can't start with a digit. Uppercase and lowercase letters are distinct: the variable $Fred is a different variable from $fred. And all of the letters, digits, and underscores are significant:

```
$a_very_long_variable_that_ends_in_1
```

The preceding line is different from the following line:

```
$a_very_long_variable_that_ends_in_2
```

Scalar variables in Perl are always referenced with the leading $.† In the shell, you use $ to get the value, but leave the $ off to assign a new value. In *awk* or C, you leave the $ off entirely. If you bounce back and forth a lot, you'll find yourself typing the wrong things occasionally. This is expected. (Most Perl programmers would recommend that you stop writing shell, *awk*, and C programs, but that may not work for you.)

Choosing Good Variable Names

You should generally select variable names that mean something regarding the purpose of the variable. For example, $r is probably not descriptive but $line_length is. A variable used for only two or three lines close together may be called something like $n, but a variable used throughout a program should probably have a more descriptive name.

Similarly, properly placed underscores can make a name easier to read and understand, especially if your maintenance programmer has a different spoken language background than you have. For example, $super_bowl is a better name than $superbowl since that last one might look like $superb_owl. Does $stopid mean

---

* As you'll see, a scalar variable can hold only one value. But other types of variables, such as arrays and hashes, may hold many values.

† This is called a "sigil" in Perlspeak.

$sto_pid (storing a process-ID of some kind?), $s_to_pid (converting something to a process-ID?), or $stop_id (the ID for some kind of "stop" object?) or is it just a stopid misspelling?

Most variable names in our Perl programs are all lowercase like most of the ones you'll see in this book. In a few special cases, uppercase letters are used. Using all caps (like $ARGV) generally indicates that there's something special about that variable. When a variable's name has more than one word, some say $underscores_are_cool while others say $giveMeInitialCaps. Just be consistent.

Of course, choosing good or poor names makes no difference to Perl. You could name your program's three most important variables $OOOOOOOOO, $OOOOOOOO, and $OOOOOOOOO and Perl wouldn't be bothered; in that case, please, don't ask us to maintain your code.

Scalar Assignment

The most common operation on a scalar variable is *assignment*, which is the way to give a value to a variable. The Perl assignment operator is the equals sign (much like other languages), which takes a variable name on the left side and gives it the value of the expression on the right:

```
$fred   = 17;         # give $fred the value of 17
$barney = 'hello';    # give $barney the five-character string 'hello'
$barney = $fred + 3;  # give $barney the current value of $fred plus 3 (20)
$barney = $barney * 2; # $barney is now $barney multiplied by 2 (40)
```

Notice that last line uses the $barney variable twice: once to get its value (on the right side of the equals sign) and once to define where to put the computed expression (on the left side of the equals sign). This is legal, safe, and rather common. In fact, it's so common that you can write it using a convenient shorthand as you'll see in the next section.

Binary Assignment Operators

Expressions such as $fred = $fred + 5 (where the same variable appears on both sides of an assignment) occur frequently enough that Perl (like C and Java) has a shorthand for the operation of altering a variable: the *binary assignment operator*. Nearly all binary operators that compute a value have a corresponding binary assignment form with an appended equals sign. For example, the following two lines are equivalent:

```
$fred   = $fred + 5; # without the binary assignment operator
$fred += 5;          # with the binary assignment operator
```

These are also equivalent:

```
$barney   = $barney * 3;
$barney *= 3;
```

In each case, the operator alters the existing value of the variable in some way rather than overwriting the value with the result of some new expression.

Another common assignment operator is made with the string concatenate operator (.); this gives us an append operator (.=):

```
$str  = $str . " "; # append a space to $str
$str .= " ";        # same thing with assignment operator
```

Nearly all binary operators are valid this way. For example, a *raise to the power of operator* is written as **=. So, $fred **= 3 means "raise the number in $fred to the third power, placing the result back in $fred".

Output with print

It's generally a good idea to have your program produce some output; otherwise, someone may think it didn't do anything. The print( ) operator makes this possible. It takes a scalar argument and puts it out without any embellishment onto standard output. Unless you've done something odd, this will be your terminal display:

```
print "hello world\n"; # say hello world, followed by a newline

print "The answer is ";
print 6 * 7;
print ".\n";
```

You can give print a series of values, separated by commas:

```
print "The answer is ", 6 * 7, ".\n";
```

This is a *list*, but we haven't talked about lists yet, so we'll put that off for later.

Interpolation of Scalar Variables into Strings

When a string literal is double-quoted, it is subject to *variable interpolation*[*] besides being checked for backslash escapes. This means that any scalar variable[†] name in the string is replaced with its current value:

```
$meal   = "brontosaurus steak";
$barney = "fred ate a $meal";    # $barney is now "fred ate a brontosaurus steak"
$barney = 'fred ate a ' . $meal; # another way to write that
```

As you see on the last line above, you can get the same results without the double quotes. But the double-quoted string is often the more convenient way to write it.

---

[*] This has nothing to do with mathematical or statistical interpolation.

[†] And some other variable types, but you won't see those until later.

If the scalar variable has never been given a value,* the empty string is used instead:

```
$barney = "fred ate a $meat"; # $barney is now "fred ate a "
```

Don't bother with interpolating if you have the one lone variable:

```
print "$fred"; # unneeded quote marks
print $fred;   # better style
```

There's nothing wrong with putting quote marks around a lone variable, but the other programmers will laugh at you behind your back.† *Variable interpolation* is also known as *double-quote interpolation* because it happens when double-quote marks (but not single quotes) are used. It happens for some other strings in Perl, which we'll mention as we get to them.

To put a real dollar sign into a double-quoted string, precede the dollar sign with a backslash, which turns off the dollar sign's special significance:

```
$fred = 'hello';
print "The name is \$fred.\n";    # prints a dollar sign
print 'The name is $fred' . "\n"; # so does this
```

The variable name will be the longest possible variable name that makes sense at that part of the string. This can be a problem if you want to follow the replaced value immediately with some constant text that begins with a letter, digit, or underscore.‡ As Perl scans for variable names, it would consider those characters as additional name characters, which is not what you want. Perl provides a delimiter for the variable name in a manner similar to the shell. Enclose the *name* of the variable in a pair of curly braces. Or you can end that part of the string and start another part of the string with a concatenation operator:

```
$what = "brontosaurus steak";
$n = 3;
print "fred ate $n $whats.\n";          # not the steaks, but the value of $whats
print "fred ate $n ${what}s.\n";        # now uses $what
print "fred ate $n $what" . "s.\n";     # another way to do it
print 'fred ate ' . $n . ' ' . $what . "s.\n"; # an especially difficult way
```

Operator Precedence and Associativity

Operator precedence determines which operations in a complex group of operations happen first. For example, in the expression 2+3*4, do you perform the addition first

---

* This is the special undefined value, undef, which you'll see a little later in this chapter. If warnings are turned on, Perl will complain about interpolating the undefined value.

† Well, it may interpret the value as a string, rather than as a number. In rare cases, that may be needed, but nearly always it's just a waste of typing.

‡ There are some other characters that may be a problem as well. If you need a left square bracket or a left curly brace after a scalar variable's name, precede it with a backslash. You may also do that if the variable's name is followed by an apostrophe or a pair of colons, or you could use the curly-brace method described in the main text.

or the multiplication first? If you did the addition first, you'd get 5*4, or 20. But if you did the multiplication first (as you were taught in math class), you'd get 2+12, or 14. Fortunately, Perl chooses the common mathematical definition, performing the multiplication first. Because of this, you say multiplication has a higher precedence than addition.

You can override the default precedence order by using parentheses. Anything in parentheses is completely computed before the operator outside of the parentheses is applied (as you learned in math class). So if you want the addition before the multiplication, you can say (2+3)*4, yielding 20. If you wanted to demonstrate that multiplication is performed before addition, you could add a decorative but unnecessary set of parentheses, as in 2+(3*4).

While precedence is simple for addition and multiplication, you start running into problems when faced with string concatenation compared with exponentiation. The proper way to resolve this is to consult the official, accept-no-substitutes Perl operator precedence chart, shown in Table 2-2.* (Some of the operators have not yet been described and may not appear anywhere in this book, but don't let that scare you from reading about them in the *perlop* manpage.)

Table 2-2. Associativity and precedence of operators (highest to lowest)

Associativity	Operators
left	Parentheses and arguments to list operators
left	->
	++ -- (autoincrement and autodecrement)
right	**
right	\ ! ~ + - (unary operators)
left	=~ !~
left	* / % x
left	+ - . (binary operators)
left	<< >>
	Named unary operators (-X filetests, rand)
	< <= > >= lt le gt ge (the "unequal" ones)
	== != <=> eq ne cmp (the "equal" ones)
left	&
left	| ^
left	&&
left	||

---

* C programmers: Rejoice! The operators that are available in both Perl and C have the same precedence and associativity in both.

Table 2-2. Associativity and precedence of operators (highest to lowest) (continued)

Associativity	Operators
	. . . . .
right	? : (ternary)
right	= += -= .= (and similar assignment operators)
left	, =>
	List operators (rightward)
right	not
left	and
left	or xor

In the chart, any given operator has a higher precedence than all of the operators listed below it and a lower precedence than all of the operators listed above it. Operators at the same precedence level resolve according to rules of associativity instead.

Like precedence, *associativity* resolves the order of operations when two operators of the same precedence compete for three operands:

```
4 ** 3 ** 2 # 4 ** (3 ** 2), or 4 ** 9 (right associative)
72 / 12 / 3 # (72 / 12) / 3, or 6/3, or 2 (left associative)
36 / 6 * 3  # (36/6)*3, or 18
```

In the first case, the ** operator has right associativity, so the parentheses are implied on the right. Comparatively, the * and / operators have left associativity, yielding a set of implied parentheses on the left.

So, should you just memorize the precedence chart? No! Nobody does that. Instead, use parentheses when you don't remember the order of operations or when you're too busy to look in the chart. After all, if you can't remember it without the parentheses, your maintenance programmer is going to have the same trouble. So be nice to your maintenance programmer because you may be that person one day.

Comparison Operators

For comparing numbers, Perl has the logical comparison operators that remind you of algebra: < <= == >= > !=. Each of these returns a true or false value. You'll find out more about those return values in the next section. Some of these may be different than you'd use in other languages. For example, == is used for equality. The single = sign is used for assignment. != is used for inequality testing because <> is used for another purpose in Perl. You'll need >= and not => for "greater than or equal to" because the latter is used for another purpose in Perl. In fact, nearly every sequence of punctuation is used for something in Perl. So, if you get writers' block, let the cat walk across the keyboard and debug what results.

For comparing strings, Perl has an equivalent set of string comparison operators that look like funny little words: lt le eq ge gt ne. These compare two strings character by character to see if they're the same, or if one comes first in standard string sorting order. (In ASCII, the capital letters come before the lowercase letters, so beware.)

The comparison operators (for both numbers and strings) are given in Table 2-3.

Table 2-3. Numeric and string comparison operators

Comparison	Numeric	String
Equal	==	eq
Not equal	!=	ne
Less than	<	lt
Greater than	>	gt
Less than or equal to	<=	le
Greater than or equal to	>=	ge

Here are some example expressions using these comparison operators:

```
35 != 30 + 5           # false
35 == 35.0             # true
'35' eq '35.0'         # false (comparing as strings)
'fred' lt 'barney'     # false
'fred' lt 'free'       # true
'fred' eq "fred"       # true
'fred' eq 'Fred'       # false
' ' gt ''              # true
```

The if Control Structure

Once you can compare two values, you'll probably want your program to make decisions based upon that comparison. Like all similar languages, Perl has an if control structure:

```
if ($name gt 'fred') {
    print "'$name' comes after 'fred' in sorted order.\n";
}
```

If you need an alternative choice, the else keyword provides that as well:

```
if ($name gt 'fred') {
    print "'$name' comes after 'fred' in sorted order.\n";
} else {
    print "'$name' does not come after 'fred'.\n";
    print "Maybe it's the same string, in fact.\n";
}
```

Those block curly braces are required around the conditional code (unlike C, whether you know C or not). It's a good idea to indent the contents of the blocks of code as we show here; that makes it easier to see what's going on. If you're using a programmers' text editor (as discussed in Chapter 1), it'll do most of the work for you.

Boolean Values

You may use any scalar value as the conditional of the if control structure. That's handy if you want to store a true or false value into a variable, like this:

```
$is_bigger = $name gt 'fred';
if ($is_bigger) { ... }
```

But how does Perl decide whether a given value is true or false? Perl doesn't have a separate Boolean data type as some languages have. Instead, it uses a few simple rules:[*]

- If the value is a number, 0 means false; all other numbers mean true.
- If the value is a string, the empty string ('') means false; all other strings mean true.
- If the value is another kind of scalar than a number or a string, convert it to a number or a string and try again.[†]

There's one trick hidden in those rules. Because the string '0' is the same scalar value as the number 0, Perl has to treat them the same. That means that the string '0' is the only nonempty string that is false.

If you need to get the opposite of any Boolean value, use the unary *not* operator, !. If what follows it is a true value, it returns false; if what follows is false, it returns true:

```
if (! $is_bigger) {
  # Do something when $is_bigger is not true
}
```

Getting User Input

At this point, you're probably wondering how to get a value from the keyboard into a Perl program. Here's the simplest way: use the line-input operator, <STDIN>.[‡]

Each time you use <STDIN> in a place where a scalar value is expected, Perl reads the next complete text line from *standard input* (up to the first newline) and uses that string as the value of <STDIN>. Standard input can mean many things; unless you do something uncommon, it means the keyboard of the user who invoked your program (probably you). If there's nothing waiting for <STDIN> to read (typically the case

---

[*] These aren't the rules Perl uses but are rules you can use to get the same result.

[†] This means that undef (which we'll see soon) means false, and all references (which are covered in the Alpaca book) are true.

[‡] This is a line-input operator working on the filehandle STDIN, but we can't tell you about that until we get to filehandles (in Chapter 5).

unless you type ahead a complete line), the Perl program will stop and wait for you to enter some characters followed by a newline (return).*

The string value of <STDIN> typically has a newline character on the end of it.† So, you could do something like this:

```
$line = <STDIN>;
if ($line eq "\n") {
  print "That was just a blank line!\n";
} else {
  print "That line of input was: $line";
}
```

In practice, you don't often want to keep the newline, so you need the chomp operator.

The chomp Operator

The first time you read about the chomp operator, it seems overspecialized. It works on a variable, and the variable has to hold a string. If the string ends in a newline character, chomp can get rid of the newline. That's (nearly) all it does as in this example:

```
$text = "a line of text\n"; # Or the same thing from <STDIN>
chomp($text);                # Gets rid of the newline character
```

It turns out to be so useful, you'll put it into nearly every program you write. As you see, it's the best way to remove a trailing newline from a string in a variable. In fact, there's an easier way to use chomp because of a simple rule: whenever you need a variable in Perl, you can use an assignment instead. Perl does the assignment and then it uses the variable in whatever way you requested. The most common use of chomp looks like this:

```
chomp($text = <STDIN>); # Read the text, without the newline character

$text = <STDIN>;        # Do the same thing...
chomp($text);           # ...but in two steps
```

At first glance, the combined chomp may not seem to be the easy way, especially if it seems more complex. If you think of it as two operations, read a line and chomp it, then it's more natural to write it as two statements. If you think of it as one operation, read just the text and not the newline, it's more natural to write the one statement. Since

---

* To be honest, it's normally your system that waits for the input; Perl waits for your system. Though the details depend upon your system and its configuration, you can generally correct your mistyping with a backspace key before you press return since your system handles that, not Perl itself. If you need more control over the input, get the Term::ReadLine module from CPAN.

† The exception is if the standard input stream somehow runs out in the middle of a line. But that's not a proper text file, of course.

most other Perl programmers are going to write it that way, you may as well get used to it now.

chomp is a function. As a function, it has a return value, which is the number of characters removed. This number is hardly ever useful:

```
$food = <STDIN>;
$betty = chomp $food; # gets the value 1 - but you knew that!
```

As you see, you may write chomp with or without the parentheses. This is another general rule in Perl: except in cases where it changes the meaning to remove them, parentheses are always optional.

If a line ends with two or more newlines,* chomp removes only one. If there's no newline, it does nothing and returns zero.

The while Control Structure

Like most algorithmic programming languages, Perl has a number of looping structures.† The while loop repeats a block of code as long as a condition is true:

```
$count = 0;
while ($count < 10) {
  $count += 2;
  print "count is now $count\n"; # Gives values 2 4 6 8 10
}
```

As always in Perl, the truth value here works like the truth value in the if test. Like the if control structure, the block curly braces are required. The conditional expression is evaluated before the first iteration, so the loop may be skipped completely if the condition is initially false.

The undef Value

What happens if you use a scalar variable before you give it a value? Nothing serious and definitely nothing fatal. Variables have the special undef value before they are first assigned, which is Perl's way of saying "nothing here to look at—move along, move along." If you use this "nothing" as a "numeric something," it will act like zero. If you use it as a "string something," it will act like the empty string. But undef is neither a number nor a string; it's an entirely separate kind of scalar value.

---

* This situation can't arise if you're reading a line at a time, but it can when you have set the input separator ($/) to something other than newline, use the read function, or perhaps have glued some strings together yourself.

† Every programmer eventually creates an infinite loop by accident. If your program keeps running and running, you can generally stop it in the same way you'd stop any other program on your system. Often, typing Ctrl-C will stop a runaway program; check with your system's documentation to be sure.

Because undef automatically acts like zero when used as a number, it's easy to make an numeric accumulator that starts out empty:

```
# Add up some odd numbers
$n = 1;
while ($n < 10) {
  $sum += $n;
  $n += 2; # On to the next odd number
}
print "The total was $sum.\n";
```

This works properly when $sum was undef before the loop started. The first time through the loop, $n is one, so the first line inside the loop adds one to $sum. That's like adding 1 to a variable that already holds zero because you're using undef as if it were a number. Now it has the value 1. After that, since it's been initialized, adding works in the traditional way.

Similarly, you could have a string accumulator that starts out empty:

```
$string .= "more text\n";
```

If $string is undef, this will act as if it already held the empty string, putting "more text\n" into that variable. But if it holds a string, the new text is appended.

Perl programmers frequently use a new variable in this way, letting it act as zero or the empty string as needed.

Many operators return undef when the arguments are out of range or don't make sense. If you don't do anything special, you'll get a zero or a null string without major consequences. In practice, this is hardly a problem. In fact, most programmers rely upon this behavior. But you should know that when warnings are turned on, Perl will typically warn about unusual uses of the undefined value since that may indicate a bug. For example, copying undef from one variable into another isn't a problem, but trying to print it would generally cause a warning.

The defined Function

One operator that can return undef is the line-input operator, <STDIN>. Normally, it returns a line of text. But if there is no more input, such as at end-of-file, it will return undef to signal this.* To tell if a value is undef and not the empty string, use the defined function, which returns false for undef and true for everything else:

```
$madonna = <STDIN>;
if ( defined($madonna) ) {
  print "The input was $madonna";
```

---

* Normally, there's no "end-of-file" when the input comes from the keyboard, but the input may have been redirected to come from a file. Or the user may have pressed the key that the system recognizes to indicate end-of-file.

```
  } else {
    print "No input available!\n";
  }
```

If you'd like to make your own undef values, you can use the obscurely named undef operator:

```
$madonna = undef; # As if it had never been touched
```

Exercises

See Appendix A for answers to the following exercises:

1. [5] Write a program that computes the circumference of a circle with a radius of 12.5. Circumference is 2π times the radius (approximately 2 times 3.141592654). The answer you get should be about 78.5.

2. [4] Modify the program from the previous exercise to prompt for and accept a radius from the person running the program. So, if users enter 12.5 for the radius, they should get the same number as in the previous exercise.

3. [4] Modify the program from the previous exercise so, if the user enters a number less than zero, the reported circumference will be zero, rather than negative.

4. [8] Write a program that prompts for and reads two numbers (on separate lines of input) and prints out the product of the two numbers multiplied together.

5. [8] Write a program that prompts for and reads a string and a number (on separate lines of input) and prints out the string the number of times indicated by the number on separate lines. (Hint: Use the "x" operator.) If the user enters "fred" and "3," the output should be three lines, each saying "fred". If the user enters "fred" and "299792," there may be a lot of output.

CHAPTER 3

Lists and Arrays

If a scalar is the "singular" in Perl, as we described it at the beginning of Chapter 2, the "plural" in Perl is represented by lists and arrays.

A *list* is an ordered collection of scalars. An *array* is a variable that contains a list. In Perl, the two terms are often used as if they're interchangeable. But, to be accurate, the list is the data, and the array is the variable. You can have a list value that isn't in an array, but every array variable holds a list, though that list may be empty. Figure 3-1 represents a list, whether it's stored in an array or not.

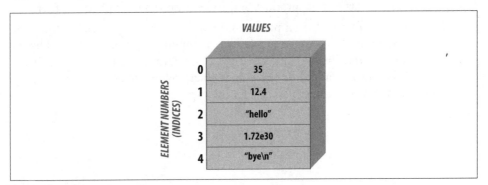

Figure 3-1. A list with five elements

Each *element* of an array or list is a separate scalar variable with an independent scalar value. These values are ordered, that is, they have a particular sequence from the first to the last element. The elements of an array or list are indexed by small integers starting at zero[*] and counting by ones, so the first element of any array or list is always element zero.

---

[*] Array and list indices always start at zero in Perl unlike in some other languages. In early Perl, it was possible to change the starting number of array and list indexing (not for just one array or list but for all of them at once). Larry later realized that this was a misfeature, and its (ab)use is now strongly discouraged. But, if you're terminally curious, look up the $[variable in the *perlvar* manpage.

Since each element is an independent scalar value, a list or array may hold numbers, strings, undef values, or any mixture of different scalar values. Nevertheless, it's most common to have all elements of the same type, such as a list of book titles (all strings) or a list of cosines (all numbers).

Arrays and lists can have any number of elements. The smallest one has no elements, and the largest can fill all of the available memory. Once again, this is in keeping with Perl's philosophy of "no unnecessary limits."

Accessing Elements of an Array

If you've used arrays in another language, you won't be surprised to find Perl provides a way to subscript an array to refer to an element by a numeric index.

The array elements are numbered using sequential integers, beginning at zero and increasing by one for each element, like this:

```
$fred[0] = "yabba";
$fred[1] = "dabba";
$fred[2] = "doo";
```

The array name (in this case, "fred") is from a completely separate namespace than scalars use. You could have a scalar variable named $fred in the same program. Perl treats them as different things and doesn't get confused.* (Your maintenance programmer might be confused though, so don't capriciously make all of your variable names the same.)

You can use an array element like $fred[2] in every place† where you could use any other scalar variable like $fred. For example, you can get the value from an array element or change that value by the same sorts of expressions we used in the previous chapter:

```
print $fred[0];
$fred[2]  = "diddley";
$fred[1] .= "whatsis";
```

Of course, the subscript may be any expression that gives a numeric value. If it's not an integer, it'll automatically be truncated to the next lower integer:

```
$number = 2.71828;
print $fred[$number - 1]; # Same as printing $fred[1]
```

---

* The syntax is always unambiguous; tricky perhaps, but unambiguous.

† Well, almost. The most notable exception is that the control variable of a foreach loop, which you'll see later in this chapter, must be a simple scalar. And there are others, like the "indirect object slot" and "indirect filehandle slot" for print and printf.

If the subscript indicates an element that would be beyond the end of the array, the corresponding value will be undef. This is the same as ordinary scalars; if you've never stored a value into the variable, it's undef.

```
$blank = $fred[ 142_857 ]; # unused array element gives undef
$blanc = $mel;             # unused scalar $mel also gives undef
```

Special Array Indices

If you store in an array an element that is beyond the end of the array, the array is automatically extended as needed. There's no limit on its length as long as there's available memory for Perl to use. If Perl needs to create the intervening elements, it creates them as undef values.

```
$rocks[0]  = 'bedrock';     # One element...
$rocks[1]  = 'slate';       # another...
$rocks[2]  = 'lava';        # and another...
$rocks[3]  = 'crushed rock'; # and another...
$rocks[99] = 'schist';      # now there are 95 undef elements
```

Sometimes you need to find out the last element index in an array. For the array of rocks that we've been using, the last element index is $#rocks.* That's not the same as the number of elements because there's an element number zero.

```
$end = $#rocks;               # 99, which is the last element's index
$number_of_rocks = $end + 1;  # okay, but you'll see a better way later
$rocks[ $#rocks ] = 'hard rock'; # the last rock
```

Using the $#name value as an index, like that last example, happens often enough that Larry has provided a shortcut: negative array indices count from the end of the array. But don't get the idea that these indices "wrap around." If you've got three elements in the array, the valid negative indices are -1 (the last element), -2 (the middle element), and -3 (the first element). In the real world, nobody seems to use any of these except -1, though.

```
$rocks[ -1 ]   = 'hard rock';   # easier way to do that last example
$dead_rock     = $rocks[-100];  # gets 'bedrock'
$rocks[ -200 ] = 'crystal';     # fatal error!
```

List Literals

An *array* (the way you represent a list value within your program) is a list of comma-separated values enclosed in parentheses. These values form the elements of the list:

```
(1, 2, 3)    # list of three values 1, 2, and 3
(1, 2, 3,)   # the same three values (the trailing comma is ignored)
("fred", 4.5) # two values, "fred" and 4.5
```

---

* Blame this ugly syntax on the C shell. Fortunately, you don't have to look at this often in the real world.

```
( )             # empty list - zero elements
(1..100)        # list of 100 integers
```

That last one uses the .. range operator, seen here for the first time, which creates a list of values by counting from the left scalar up to the right scalar by ones:

```
(1..5)           # same as (1, 2, 3, 4, 5)
(1.7..5.7)       # same thing - both values are truncated
(5..1)           # empty list - .. only counts "uphill"
(0, 2..6, 10, 12) # same as (0, 2, 3, 4, 5, 6, 10, 12)
($m..$n)         # range determined by current values of $m and $n
(0..$#rocks)     # the indices of the rocks array from the previous section
```

As you can see from those last two items, the elements of a list literal are not necessarily constants—they can be expressions that will be newly evaluated each time the literal is used:

```
($m, 17)      # two values: the current value of $m, and 17
($m+$o, $p+$q) # two values
```

Of course, a list may have any scalar values, like this typical list of strings:

```
("fred", "barney", "betty", "wilma", "dino")
```

The qw Shortcut

It turns out that lists of simple words (like the previous example) are frequently needed in Perl programs. The qw shortcut makes it easy to generate them without typing a lot of extra quote marks:

```
qw( fred barney betty wilma dino ) # same as above, but less typing
```

qw stands for "quoted words" or "quoted by whitespace," depending upon whom you ask. Either way, Perl treats it like a single-quoted string so, you can't use \n or $fred inside a qw list as you would in a double-quoted string. The whitespace (characters like spaces, tabs, and newlines) will be discarded, and whatever remains becomes the list of items. Since whitespace is discarded, here's another (but unusual) way to write that same list:

```
qw(fred
   barney     betty
wilma dino)  # same as above, but pretty strange whitespace
```

Since qw is a form of quoting, you can't put comments inside a qw list.

The previous two examples have used parentheses as the delimiter, but Perl lets you choose any punctuation character as the delimiter. Here are some of the common ones:

```
qw! fred barney betty wilma dino !
qw# fred barney betty wilma dino #   # like in a comment!
qw( fred barney betty wilma dino )
qw{ fred barney betty wilma dino }
```

```
qw[ fred barney betty wilma dino ]
qw< fred barney betty wilma dino >
```

As those last four show, sometimes the two delimiters can be different. If the opening delimiter is one of those "left" characters, the corresponding "right" character is the proper closing delimiter. Other delimiters use the same character for start and finish.

If you need to include the closing delimiter within the string as one of the characters, you probably picked the wrong delimiter. But if you can't or don't want to change the delimiter, you can include the character using the backslash:

```
qw! yahoo\! google excite lycos ! # include yahoo! as an element
```

As in single-quoted strings, two consecutive backslashes contribute one single backslash to the item.

Though the Perl motto is "There's More Than One Way To Do It," you may well wonder why anyone would need all of those different ways. Well, you'll see later there are other kinds of quoting where Perl uses this same rule, and it can come in handy in many of those. But even here, it could be useful if you were to need a list of Unix filenames:

```
qw{
  /usr/dict/words
  /home/rootbeer/.ispell_english
}
```

That list would be inconvenient to read, write, and maintain if the slash were the only available delimiter.

List Assignment

In much the same way as scalar values, list values may be assigned to variables:

```
($fred, $barney, $dino) = ("flintstone", "rubble", undef);
```

All three variables in the list on the left get new values, as if you did three separate assignments. Since the list is built up before the assignment starts, this makes it easy to swap two variables' values in Perl:[*]

```
($fred, $barney) = ($barney, $fred); # swap those values
($betty[0], $betty[1]) = ($betty[1], $betty[0]);
```

But what happens if the number of variables (on the left side of the equals sign) isn't the same as the number of values (from the right side)? In a list assignment, extra values are silently ignored. Perl figures that if you wanted those values stored somewhere, you

---

[*] As opposed to languages like C, which has no easy way to do this in general. C programmers use an auxiliary swap variable to hold the value temporarily, possibly managed via a macro.

would have told it where to store them. Alternatively, if you have too many variables, the extras get the value undef.*

```
($fred, $barney) = qw< flintstone rubble slate granite >; # two ignored items
($wilma, $dino)  = qw[flintstone];                        # $dino gets undef
```

Now that you can assign lists, you could build up an array of strings with a line of code like this:†

```
($rocks[0], $rocks[1], $rocks[2], $rocks[3]) = qw/talc mica feldspar quartz/;
```

But when you wish to refer to an entire array, Perl has a simpler notation. Just use the at sign (@) before the name of the array (and no index brackets after it) to refer to the entire array at once. You can read this as "all of the," so @rocks is "all of the rocks."‡ This works on either side of the assignment operator:

```
@rocks  = qw/ bedrock slate lava /;
@tiny   = ( );                     # the empty list
@giant  = 1..1e5;                  # a list with 100,000 elements
@stuff  = (@giant, undef, @giant); # a list with 200,001 elements
$dino   = "granite";
@quarry = (@rocks, "crushed rock", @tiny, $dino);
```

That last assignment gives @quarry the five-element list (bedrock, slate, lava, crushed rock, granite) since @tiny contributes zero elements to the list. (In particular, it doesn't put an undef item into the list, but you could do that explicitly as we did with @stuff earlier.) It's also worth noting that an array name is replaced by the list it contains. An array doesn't become an element in the list because these arrays can contain only scalars, not other arrays.§ The value of an array variable that has not yet been assigned is ( ), the empty list. Just as new, empty scalars start out with undef, new, empty arrays start out with the empty list.

When an array is copied to another array, it's still a list assignment. The lists are stored in arrays as in this example:

```
@copy = @quarry; # copy a list from one array to another
```

---

* Well, that's true for scalar variables. Array variables get an empty list as you'll see in a moment.

† We're cheating by assuming that the rocks array is empty before this statement. If there were a value in $rocks[7], say, this assignment wouldn't affect that element.

‡ Larry claims that he chose the dollar and at sign because they can be read as $calar (scalar) and @rray (array). If you don't get that or remember it that way, no big deal.

§ But in the Alpaca book, we'll show you a special kind of scalar called a reference. That lets us make what are informally called "lists of lists" among other interesting and useful structures. In that case, you're still not storing a list into a list; you're storing a reference to an array.

The pop and push Operators

You could add new items to the end of an array by storing them into elements with new, larger indices. But real Perl programmers don't use indices.* So, in the next few sections, we'll present some ways to work with an array without using indices.

One common use of an array is as a stack of information where new values are added to and removed from the right-hand side of the list. (This is the end with the "last" items in the array, the end with the highest index values.) These operations occur often enough to have their own special functions.

The pop operator takes the last element off of an array and returns it:

```
@array  = 5..9;
$fred   = pop(@array);  # $fred gets 9, @array now has (5, 6, 7, 8)
$barney = pop @array;   # $barney gets 8, @array now has (5, 6, 7)
pop @array;             # @array now has (5, 6). (The 7 is discarded.)
```

That last example uses pop "in a void context," which is a fancy way of saying the return value isn't going anywhere. There's nothing wrong with using pop in this way if that's what you want.

If the array is empty, pop leaves it alone (since there is no element to remove) and it returns undef.

You may have noticed that pop may be used with or without parentheses. This is a general rule in Perl: as long as the meaning isn't changed by removing the parentheses, they're optional.† The converse operation is push, which adds an element (or a list of elements) to the end of an array:

```
push(@array, 0);     # @array now has (5, 6, 0)
push @array, 8;      # @array now has (5, 6, 0, 8)
push @array, 1..10;  # @array now has those 10 new elements
@others = qw/ 9 0 2 1 0 /;
push @array, @others; # @array now has those five new elements (19 total)
```

The first argument to push or the only argument for pop must be an array variable: pushing and popping would not make sense on a literal list.

---

* Of course, we're joking, but there's a kernel of truth in this joke. Indexing into arrays is not using Perl's strengths. If you use the pop, push, and similar operators that avoid using indexing, your code will generally be faster than if you use many indices, as well as be more likely to avoid "off-by-one" errors, often called "fencepost" errors. Occasionally, a beginning Perl programmer (wanting to see how Perl's speed compares to C's) will take, say, a sorting algorithm optimized for C (with many array index operations), rewrite it straightforwardly in Perl (again, with many index operations), and wonder why it's so slow. The answer is that using a Stradivarius violin to pound nails should not be considered a sound construction technique.

† A reader from the educated class will recognize that this is a tautology.

The shift and unshift Operators

The push and pop operators do things to the end of an array (the right side of an array or the portion with the highest subscripts, depending upon how you like to think of it). Similarly, the unshift and shift operators perform the corresponding actions on the "start" of the array (the "left" side of an array or the portion with the lowest subscripts). Here are a few examples:

```
@array = qw# dino fred barney #;
$m = shift(@array);        # $m gets "dino", @array now has ("fred", "barney")
$n = shift @array;         # $n gets "fred", @array now has ("barney")
shift @array;              # @array is now empty
$o = shift @array;         # $o gets undef, @array is still empty
unshift(@array, 5);        # @array now has the one-element list (5)
unshift @array, 4;         # @array now has (4, 5)
@others = 1..3;
unshift @array, @others;   # @array now has (1, 2, 3, 4, 5)
```

Analogous to pop, shift returns undef if given an empty array variable.

Interpolating Arrays into Strings

Like scalars, array values may be interpolated into a double-quoted string. Elements of an array are automatically separated by spaces[*] upon interpolation:

```
@rocks = qw{ flintstone slate rubble };
print "quartz @rocks limestone\n";  # prints five rocks separated by spaces
```

There are no extra spaces added before or after an interpolated array; if you want those, you'll have to put them in yourself:

```
print "Three rocks are: @rocks.\n";
print "There's nothing in the parens (@empty) here.\n";
```

If you forget that arrays interpolate like this, you'll be surprised when you put an email address into a double-quoted string. For historical reasons,[†] this is a fatal error at compile time:

```
$email = "fred@bedrock.edu";  # WRONG! Tries to interpolate @bedrock
$email = "fred\@bedrock.edu"; # Correct
$email = 'fred@bedrock.edu';  # Another way to do that
```

However, in versions of Perl 5 soon to be released as we write this, the behavior of an unseen array variable will become similar to an unseen scalar variable, i.e., replaced

---

[*] The separator is the value of the special $" variable, which is a space by default.

[†] Since you asked: Before Version 5, Perl would silently leave uninterpolated an unused array's name in a double-quoted string. So, "fred@bedrock.edu" might be a string containing an email address. This attempt to "Do What I Mean" will backfire when someone adds a variable named @bedrock to the program; now the string becomes "fred.edu" or worse.

with an empty string with a warning if warnings are enabled. The Perl developers apparently figure that 10 years of fatality are enough warning.

A single element of an array will be replaced by its value as you'd expect:

```
@fred = qw(hello dolly);
$y = 2;
$x = "This is $fred[1]'s place";    # "This is dolly's place"
$x = "This is $fred[$y-1]'s place"; # same thing
```

The index expression is evaluated as an ordinary expression, as if it were outside a string. It is not variable interpolated first. In other words, if $y contains the string "2*4", we're still talking about element 1, not element 7, because "2*4" as a number (the value of $y used in a numeric expression) is just plain 2.* If you want to follow a simple scalar variable with a left square bracket, you need to delimit the square bracket so it isn't considered part of an array reference:

```
@fred = qw(eating rocks is wrong);
$fred = "right";               # we are trying to say "this is right[3]"
print "this is $fred[3]\n";    # prints "wrong" using $fred[3]
print "this is ${fred}[3]\n";  # prints "right" (protected by braces)
print "this is $fred"."[3]\n"; # right again (different string)
print "this is $fred\[3]\n";   # right again (backslash hides it)
```

The foreach Control Structure

It's handy to be able to process an entire array or list, so Perl provides a control structure to do that. The foreach loop steps through a list of values, executing one iteration (time through the loop) for each value:

```
foreach $rock (qw/ bedrock slate lava /) {
    print "One rock is $rock.\n";  # Prints names of three rocks
}
```

The control variable ($rock in that example) takes on a new value from the list for each iteration. The first time through the loop, it's "bedrock"; the third time, it's "lava".

The control variable is not a copy of the list element—it actually *is* the list element. That is, if you modify the control variable inside the loop, you'll be modifying the element in the original list, as shown in the following code snippet. This is useful and supported, but it would surprise you if you weren't expecting it.

```
@rocks = qw/ bedrock slate lava /;
foreach $rock (@rocks) {
    $rock = "\t$rock";      # put a tab in front of each element of @rocks
    $rock .= "\n";          # put a newline on the end of each
```

---

* Of course, if you've got warnings turned on, Perl is likely to remind you that "2*4" is a funny-looking number.

```
}
print "The rocks are:\n", @rocks; # Each one is indented, on its own line
```

What is the value of $rock after the loop has finished? It's the same as it was before the loop started. The value of the control variable of a foreach loop is automatically saved and restored by Perl. While the loop is running, there's no way to access or alter that saved value. So after the loop is done, the variable has the value it had before the loop or undef if it didn't have a value. That means that if you want to name your loop control variable "$rock", you don't have to worry that maybe you've used that name for another variable.

Perl's Favorite Default: $_

If you omit the control variable from the beginning of the foreach loop, Perl uses its favorite default variable, $_. This is (mostly) like any other scalar variable, except for its unusual name, as in this example:

```
foreach (1..10) {  # Uses $_ by default
  print "I can count to $_!\n";
}
```

Though this isn't Perl's only default by a long shot, it's Perl's most common default. You'll see many other cases in which Perl automatically uses $_ when you don't tell it to use some other variable or value, thereby saving the programmer from the heavy labor of having to think up and type a new variable name. Not to keep you in suspense, one of those cases is print, which prints $_ if given no other argument:

```
$_ = "Yabba dabba doo\n";
print;  # prints $_ by default
```

The reverse Operator

The reverse operator takes a list of values (which may come from an array) and returns the list in the opposite order. If you were disappointed that the range operator, .., only counts upward, this is the way to fix it:

```
@fred   = 6..10;
@barney = reverse(@fred);  # gets 10, 9, 8, 7, 6
@wilma  = reverse 6..10;   # gets the same thing, without the other array
@fred   = reverse @fred;   # puts the result back into the original array
```

The last line is noteworthy because it uses @fred twice. Perl always calculates the value being assigned (on the right) before it begins the actual assignment.

Remember that reverse returns the reversed list; it doesn't affect its arguments. If the return value isn't assigned anywhere, it's useless:

```
reverse @fred;        # WRONG - doesn't change @fred
@fred = reverse @fred; # that's better
```

The sort Operator

The sort operator takes a list of values (which may come from an array) and sorts them according to the internal character ordering. For ASCII strings, that would be ASCIIbetical order. Of course, ASCII is a strange place where all of the capital letters come before all of the lowercase letters, where the numbers come before the letters, and the punctuation marks are here, there, and everywhere. But sorting in ASCII order is the default behavior; you'll see in Chapter 13 how to sort in whatever order you'd like:

```
@rocks   = qw/ bedrock slate rubble granite /;
@sorted  = sort(@rocks);        # gets bedrock, granite, rubble, slate
@back    = reverse sort @rocks; # these go from slate to bedrock
@rocks   = sort @rocks;         # puts sorted result back into @rocks
@numbers = sort 97..102;        # gets 100, 101, 102, 97, 98, 99
```

As you can see from that last example, sorting numbers as if they were strings may not give useful results. But, of course, any string that starts with 1 has to sort before any string that starts with 9, according to the default sorting rules. And like what happened with reverse, the arguments themselves aren't affected. If you want to sort an array, you must store the result back into that array:

```
sort @rocks;         # WRONG, doesn't modify @rocks
@rocks = sort @rocks; # Now the rock collection is in order
```

Scalar and List Context

This is the most important section in this chapter. In fact, it's the most important section in the entire book. It wouldn't be an exaggeration to say that your entire career in using Perl will depend upon understanding this section. If you've gotten away with skimming the text up to this point, this is where you should pay attention.

That's not to say that this section is in difficult to understand. It's a simple idea: a given expression may mean different things depending upon where it appears. This is nothing new; it happens all the time in natural languages. For example, in English,[*] suppose someone asked you what the word "read"[†] means. It has different meanings depending on how it's used. You can't identify the meaning until you know the context.

---

[*] If you aren't a native speaker of English, this analogy may not be obvious to you. But context sensitivity happens in every spoken language, so you may be able to think of an example in your own language.

[†] Or maybe they were asking what the word "red" means, if they were speaking rather than writing a book. It's ambiguous either way. As Douglas Hofstadter said, no language can express every thought unambiguously, especially this one.

The context refers to where an expression is found. As Perl is parsing your expressions, it always expects a scalar or list value.[*] What Perl expects is called the context of the expression.[†]

```
42 + something # The something must be a scalar
sort something # The something must be a list
```

If something is the exact same sequence of characters, in one case it may give a single, scalar value, and in another, it may give a list.[‡] Expressions in Perl always return the appropriate value for their context. For example, how about the "name"[§] of an array. In a list context, it gives the list of elements. But in a scalar context, it returns the number of elements in the array:

```
@people = qw( fred barney betty );
@sorted = sort @people; # list context: barney, betty, fred
$number = 42 + @people;  # scalar context: 42 + 3 gives 45
```

Even ordinary assignment (to a scalar or a list) causes different contexts:

```
@list = @people; # a list of three people
$n = @people;     # the number 3
```

Don't jump to the conclusion that scalar context always gives the number of elements that would have been returned in list context. Most list-producing expressions[**] return something more interesting than that.

Using List-Producing Expressions in Scalar Context

There are many expressions that would typically be used to produce a list. If you use one in a scalar context, what do you get? See what the author of that operation says about it. Usually, that person is Larry, and usually the documentation gives the whole story. A big part of learning Perl is learning how Larry thinks.[††] Therefore, once you can think like Larry does, you know what Perl should do. But while you're learning, you'll probably need to look into the documentation.

Some expressions don't have a scalar-context value at all. For example, what should sort return in a scalar context? You wouldn't need to sort a list to count its

---

[*] Unless, of course, Perl is expecting something else entirely. There are other contexts that aren't covered here. Nobody knows how many contexts Perl uses; the biggest brains in all of Perl haven't agreed on an answer.

[†] This is no different than what you're used to in human languages. If I make a grammatical mistake, you notice it right away because you expect certain words in certain places. Eventually, you'll read Perl this way, too, but at first you have to think about it.

[‡] The list may be one element long, of course. It could also be empty, or it could have any number of elements.

[§] Well, the true name of the array @people is people. The @ sign is a qualifier.

[**] With regard to the point of this section, there's no difference between a "list-producing" expression and a "scalar-producing" one. Any expression can produce a list or a scalar, depending upon context. So when we say "list-producing expressions," we mean expressions that are typically used in a list context and that might surprise you when they're used unexpectedly in a scalar context (like reverse or @fred).

[††] This is only fair since while writing Perl he tried to think like you do to predict what you would want.

elements, so until someone implements something else, sort in a scalar context always returns undef.

Another example is reverse. In a list context, it gives a reversed list. In a scalar context, it returns a reversed string (or reversing the result of concatenating all the strings of a list, if given one):

```
@backwards = reverse qw/ yabba dabba doo /;
    # gives doo, dabba, yabba
$backwards = reverse qw/ yabba dabba doo /;
    # gives oodabbadabbay
```

At first, it's not always obvious if an expression is being used in a scalar or a list context. But, trust us, it *will* become second nature for you eventually.

Here are some common contexts to start you off:

```
$fred = something;          # scalar context
@pebbles = something;       # list context
($wilma, $betty) = something; # list context
($dino) = something;        # still list context!
```

Don't be fooled by the one-element list; that last one is a list context and not a scalar one. The parentheses are significant here, making the fourth of those different than the first. If you're assigning to a list (no matter the number of elements), it's a list context. If you're assigning to an array, it's a list context.

Let's look at other expressions you've seen and the contexts they provide. First, here are some that provide scalar context to something:

```
$fred = something;
$fred[3] = something;
123 + something
something + 654
if (something) { ... }
while (something) { ... }
$fred[something] = something;
```

Here are some that provide a list context:

```
@fred = something;
($fred, $barney) = something;
($fred) = something;
push @fred, something;
foreach $fred (something) { ... }
sort something
reverse something
print something
```

Using Scalar-Producing Expressions in List Context

Going this direction is straightforward: if an expression doesn't normally have a list value, the scalar value is automatically promoted to make a one-element list:

```
@fred = 6 * 7; # gets the one-element list (42)
@barney = "hello" . ' ' . "world";
```

Well, there's one possible catch:

```
@wilma = undef; # OOPS! Gets the one-element list (undef)
    # which is not the same as this:
@betty = ( );    # A correct way to empty an array
```

Since undef is a scalar value, assigning undef to an array doesn't clear the array. The better way to do that is to assign an empty list.*

Forcing Scalar Context

On occasion, you may need to force scalar context where Perl is expecting a list. In that case, you can use the fake function scalar. It's not a true function because it just tells Perl to provide a scalar context:

```
@rocks = qw( talc quartz jade obsidian );
print "How many rocks do you have?\n";
print "I have ", @rocks, " rocks!\n";        # WRONG, prints names of rocks
print "I have ", scalar @rocks, " rocks!\n"; # Correct, gives a number
```

Oddly enough, there's no corresponding function to force list context. It turns out you never need it. Trust us on this, too.

<STDIN> in List Context

One previously seen operator that returns a different value in an array context is the line-input operator, <STDIN>. As described earlier, <STDIN> returns the next line of input in a scalar context. Now, in list context, this operator returns all of the remaining lines up to the end of file. Each line is returned as a separate element of the list as in this example:

```
@lines = <STDIN>; # read standard input in list context
```

When the input is coming from a file, this will read the rest of the file. But how can there be an end-of-file when the input comes from the keyboard? On Unix and similar systems, including Linux and Mac OS X, you'll normally type a Ctrl-D† to indicate to the system that there's no more input. The special character is never seen by Perl, though it may be echoed to the screen. On DOS/Windows systems, use Ctrl-Z instead.‡ You'll need to check the documentation for your system or ask your local expert if it's different from these.

---

* Well, in most real-world algorithms, if the variable is declared in the proper scope, you will not need to empty it explicitly. This type of assignment is rare in well-written Perl programs. You'll learn about scoping in the next chapter.

† This is merely the default; it can be changed by the stty command. But it's pretty dependable; we've never seen a Unix system where a different character was used to mean end-of-file from the keyboard.

‡ There's a bug affecting some ports of Perl for DOS/Windows where the first line of output to the terminal following the use of Ctrl-Z is obscured. On these systems, you can work around this problem by printing a blank line ("\n") after reading the input.

If the person running the program types three lines and presses the proper keys needed to indicate end-of-file, the array will have with three elements. Each element will be a string that ends in a newline, corresponding to the three newline-terminated lines entered.

Wouldn't it be nice if, having read those lines, you could chomp the newlines all at once? It turns out that if you give chomp an array holding a list of lines, it will remove the newlines from each item in the list as in this example:

```
@lines = <STDIN>; # Read all the lines
chomp(@lines);    # discard all the newline characters
```

But the more common way to write that is with code similar to what we used earlier:

```
chomp(@lines = <STDIN>); # Read the lines, not the newlines
```

Though you're welcome to write your code either way in the privacy of your own cubicle, most Perl programmers will expect the second, more compact notation.

It may be obvious to you that once these lines of input have been read, they can't be re-read.* Once you've reached end-of-file, there's no more input out there to read.

And what happens if the input is coming from a 400 MB log file? The line input operator reads all of the lines, gobbling up lots of memory.† Perl tries not to limit you in what you can do, but the other users of your system (not to mention your system administrator) are likely to object. If the input is large, you should generally find a way to deal with it without reading it all into memory at once.

Exercises

See Appendix A for answers to the following exercises:

1. [6] Write a program that reads a list of strings on separate lines until end-of-input and prints out the list in reverse order. If the input comes from the keyboard, you'll probably need to signal the end of the input by pressing Ctrl-D on Unix or Ctrl-Z on Windows.

2. [12] Write a program that reads a list of numbers (on separate lines) until end-of-input and then prints for each number the corresponding person's name from the list shown below. (Hardcode this list of names into your program. That is, it

---

* Well, yes, if the input is from a source upon which you can seek, then you'll be able to go back and read again. But that's not what we're talking about here.

† Typically, that's more memory than the size of the file, too. That is, a 400 MB file will typically take up at least a full gigabyte of memory when read into an array. This is because Perl will generally waste memory to save time. This is a good tradeoff: if you're short of memory, you can buy more; if you're short on time, you're hosed.

should appear in your program's source code.) For example, if the input numbers were 1, 2, 4, and 2, the output names would be fred, betty, dino, and betty:

```
fred betty barney dino wilma pebbles bamm-bamm
```

3. [8] Write a program that reads a list of strings (on separate lines) until end-of-input. Then it should print the strings in ASCIIbetical order. That is, if you enter the strings fred, barney, wilma, betty, the output should show barney betty fred wilma. Are all of the strings on one line in the output, or on separate lines? Could you make the output appear in either style?

CHAPTER 4
Subroutines

You've seen and used some of the built-in system functions, such as chomp, reverse, and print. But, as other languages do, Perl has the ability to make *subroutines*, which are user-defined functions.* These let us recycle one chunk of code many times in one program.† The name of a subroutine is another Perl identifier (letters, digits, and underscores, but it can't start with a digit) occasionally with an optional ampersand (&) in front. There's a rule about when you can omit the ampersand and when you cannot; you'll see that rule by the end of the chapter. For now, we'll use it every time it's allowed, which is always a safe rule. We'll tell you every place where it's forbidden, of course.

The subroutine name comes from a separate namespace, so Perl won't be confused if you have a subroutine called &fred and a scalar called $fred in the same program, though there's no reason to do that under normal circumstances.

Defining a Subroutine

To define your own subroutine, use the keyword sub, the name of the subroutine (without the ampersand), and the indented block of code (in curly braces)‡ that makes up the body of the subroutine, something like this:

```
sub marine {
  $n += 1;  # Global variable $n
```

---

* In Perl, we don't generally make the distinction that Pascal programmers are used to, i.e., between *functions*, which return a value, and *procedures*, which don't. A *subroutine* is always user-defined, but a *function* may or may not be. That is, the word *function* may be used as a synonym for *subroutine*, or it may mean one of Perl's built-in functions. That's why this chapter is titled *Subroutines*: because it's about the ones you can define and not the built-ins. Mostly.

† The code examples used in this book are recycled from at least 40% post-consumer programming and are at least 75% recyclable into your programs when properly decomposed.

‡ Okay, purists, we admit that the curly braces are part of the block, properly speaking. And Perl doesn't require the indentation of the block, but your maintenance programmer will. So please be stylish.

```
    print "Hello, sailor number $n!\n";
}
```

Subroutine definitions can be anywhere in your program text, but programmers who come from a background of languages such as C or Pascal like to put them at the start of the file. Others may prefer to put them at the end of the file, so the main part of the program appears at the beginning. It's up to you. In any case, you don't normally need any kind of forward declaration.* Subroutine definitions are global; without some powerful trickiness, there are no private subroutines.† If you have two subroutine definitions with the same name, the second one overwrites the first one.‡ That's generally considered bad form or the sign of a confused maintenance programmer.

As you may have noticed in the previous example, you may use any global variables within the subroutine body. In fact, all of the variables you've seen so far are globals; that is, they are accessible from every part of your program. This horrifies linguistic purists, but the Perl development team formed an angry mob with torches and ran them out of town years ago. You'll see how to make private variables in the section "Private Variables in Subroutines" later in this chapter.

Invoking a Subroutine

Invoke a subroutine from within any expression by using the subroutine name (with the ampersand):§

```
&marine;   # says Hello, sailor number 1!
&marine;   # says Hello, sailor number 2!
&marine;   # says Hello, sailor number 3!
&marine;   # says Hello, sailor number 4!
```

Most often, we refer to the invocation as *calling* the subroutine.

Return Values

The subroutine is always invoked as part of an expression even if the result of the expression isn't being used. When we invoked &marine earlier, we were calculating the value of the expression containing the invocation but then throwing away the result.

---

* Unless your subroutine is being particularly tricky and declares a "prototype," which dictates how a compiler will parse and interpret its invocation arguments. This is rare; see the perlsub manpage for more information.

† If you wish to be powerfully tricky, read the Perl documentation about coderefs stored in private (lexical) variables.

‡ A warnable offense, however.

§ And frequently a pair of parentheses, even if empty. As written, the subroutine inherits the caller's @_ value, which we'll be discussing shortly. So don't stop reading here, or you'll be writing code with unintended effects.

Many times, you'll call a subroutine and do something with the result. This means that you'll be paying attention to the *return value* of the subroutine. All Perl subroutines have a return value—there's no distinction between those that return values and those that don't. Not all Perl subroutines have a useful return value, however.

Since all Perl subroutines can be called in a way that needs a return value, it would be a bit wasteful to have to declare special syntax to return a particular value for the majority of the cases. So Larry made it simple. As Perl is chugging along in a subroutine, it is calculating values as part of its series of actions. Whatever calculation is last performed in a subroutine is automatically also the return value.

For example, let's define this subroutine:

```
sub sum_of_fred_and_barney {
  print "Hey, you called the sum_of_fred_and_barney subroutine!\n";
  $fred + $barney;  # That's the return value
}
```

The last expression evaluated in the body of this subroutine is the sum of $fred and $barney, so the sum of $fred and $barney will be the return value. Here's that in action:

```
$fred = 3;
$barney = 4;
$wilma = &sum_of_fred_and_barney;        # $wilma gets 7
print "\$wilma is $wilma.\n";
$betty = 3 * &sum_of_fred_and_barney;  # $betty gets 21
print "\$betty is $betty.\n";
```

That code will produce this output:

```
Hey, you called the sum_of_fred_and_barney subroutine!
$wilma is 7.
Hey, you called the sum_of_fred_and_barney subroutine!
$betty is 21.
```

That print statement is a debugging aid, so you can see you called the subroutine. You'd take it out when the program is finished. But suppose you added another line to the end of the code, like this:

```
sub sum_of_fred_and_barney {
  print "Hey, you called the sum_of_fred_and_barney subroutine!\n";
  $fred + $barney;  # That's not really the return value!
  print "Hey, I'm returning a value now!\n";       # Oops!
}
```

In this example, the last expression evaluated is not the addition; it's the print statement. Its return value will normally be 1, meaning "printing was successful,"* but

---

* The return value of print is true for a successful operation and false for a failure. You'll see how to determine the kind of failure later in the next chapter.

that's not the return value you wanted. So be careful when adding additional code to a subroutine since the last expression evaluated will be the return value.

So, what happened to the sum of $fred and $barney in that second (faulty) subroutine? We didn't put it anywhere, so Perl discarded it. If you had requested warnings, Perl (noticing that there's nothing useful about adding two variables and discarding the result) would likely warn you about something like "a useless use of addition in a void context." The term *void context* is a fancy way of saying that the answer isn't being stored in a variable or used in any other way.

"The last expression evaluated" really means the last expression evaluated, rather than the last line of text. For example, this subroutine returns the larger value of $fred or $barney:

```
sub larger_of_fred_or_barney {
  if ($fred > $barney) {
    $fred;
  } else {
    $barney;
  }
}
```

The last expression evaluated is $fred or $barney, so the value of one of those variables becomes the return value. You won't know if the return value will be $fred or $barney until you see what those variables hold at runtime.

These are all rather trivial examples. It gets better when you can pass different values for each invocation into a subroutine instead of relying on global variables. In fact, that's coming right up.

Arguments

That subroutine called larger_of_fred_or_barney would be much more useful if it didn't force you to use the global variables $fred and $barney. If you wanted to get the larger value from $wilma and $betty, you currently have to copy those into $fred and $barney before you can use larger_of_fred_or_barney. And if you had something useful in those variables, you'd have to first copy those to other variables, say $save_fred and $save_barney. Then, when you're done with the subroutine, you'd have to copy those back to $fred and $barney.

Luckily, Perl has subroutine arguments. To pass an argument list to the subroutine, place the list expression, in parentheses, after the subroutine invocation like this:

```
$n = &max(10, 15);  # This sub call has two parameters
```

The list is *passed* to the subroutine; that is, it's made available for the subroutine to use however it needs to. Of course, you have to store this list somewhere, so Perl automatically stores the parameter list (another name for the argument list) in the special array variable named @_ for the duration of the subroutine. The subroutine can access this variable to determine the number of arguments and the value of those arguments.

This means that the first subroutine parameter is stored in $_[0], the second one is stored in $_[1], and so on. But—and here's an important note—these variables have nothing to do with the $_ variable, any more than $dino[3] (an element of the @dino array) has to do with $dino (a completely distinct scalar variable). The parameter list must be stored into some array variable for the subroutine to use it, and Perl uses the array @_ for this purpose.

Now, you could write the subroutine &max to look a little like the subroutine &larger_of_fred_or_barney, but instead of using $fred, you could use the first subroutine parameter ($_[0]), and instead of using $barney, you could use the second subroutine parameter ($_[1]). And so you could end up with code something like this:

```
sub max {
  # Compare this to &larger_of_fred_or_barney
  if ($_[0] > $_[1]) {
    $_[0];
  } else {
    $_[1];
  }
}
```

Well, as we said, you could do that. But it's pretty ugly with all of those subscripts, and it's hard to read, write, check, and debug, too. You'll see a better way in a moment.

There's another problem with this subroutine. The name &max is nice and short, but it doesn't remind us that this subroutine works properly only if called with exactly two parameters:

```
$n = &max(10, 15, 27);  # Oops!
```

Excess parameters are ignored; since the subroutine never looks at $_[2], Perl doesn't care whether there's something in there or not. Insufficient parameters are also ignored; you simply get undef if you look beyond the end of the @_ array as with any other array. Later in this chapter, you'll see how to make a better &max, which works with any number of parameters.

The @_ variable is private to the subroutine;* if there's a global value in @_, it is saved before the subroutine is invoked and restored to its previous value upon return from the subroutine.† This means that a subroutine can pass arguments to another sub-

---

* Unless there's an ampersand in front of the name for the invocation and no parentheses (or arguments) afterward, in which case the @_ array is inherited from the caller's context. That's generally a bad idea but is occasionally useful.

† You might recognize that this is the same mechanism as used with the control variable of the foreach loop as seen in the previous chapter. In either case, the variable's value is saved and automatically restored by Perl.

routine without fear of losing its own @_ variable. The nested subroutine invocation gets its own @_ in the same way. Even if the subroutine calls itself recursively, each invocation gets a new @_, so @_ is always the parameter list for the current subroutine invocation.

Private Variables in Subroutines

But if Perl can give us a new @_ for every invocation, can't it give us variables for our own use as well? Of course it can.

By default, all variables in Perl are global variables; that is, they are accessible from every part of the program. But you can create private variables called *lexical variables* at any time with the my operator:

```
sub max {
  my($m, $n);        # new, private variables for this block
  ($m, $n) = @_;     # give names to the parameters
  if ($m > $n) { $m } else { $n }
}
```

These variables are private (or *scoped*) to the enclosing block; any other $m or $n is totally unaffected by these two. And that goes the other way, too; no other code can access or modify these private variables by accident or design.* You could drop this subroutine into any Perl program in the world and know that you wouldn't mess up that program's $m and $n (if any).† Inside the if's blocks, there's no semicolon needed after the return value expression. Though Perl allows you to omit the last semicolon in a block, in practice you omit it only when the code is so simple that you can write the block in a single line.

The subroutine in the previous example could be made simpler. Did you notice that the list ($m, $n) was written twice? The my operator can be applied to a list of variables enclosed in parentheses, so it's customary to combine those first two statements in the subroutine:

```
my($m, $n) = @_;  # Name the subroutine parameters
```

That one statement creates the private variables and sets their values, so the first parameter has the easier name $m and the second has $n. Nearly every subroutine will start with a line much like that one, naming its parameters. When you see that line, you'll know that the subroutine expects two scalar parameters, which you'll call $m and $n inside the subroutine.

---

* Advanced programmers will realize that a lexical variable may be accessible by reference from outside its scope but never by name.

† Of course, if that program had a subroutine called &max, you'd mess that up.

Variable-Length Parameter Lists

In real-world Perl code, subroutines are often given parameter lists of arbitrary length. That's because of Perl's "no unnecessary limits" philosophy. Of course, this is unlike many traditional programming languages, which require every subroutine to be strictly typed to permit only a certain, predefined number of parameters of predefined types. It's nice that Perl is so flexible, but (as you saw with the &max routine earlier) that may cause problems when a subroutine is called with a different number of arguments than the author expected.

Of course, the subroutine can easily check that it has the right number of arguments by examining the @_ array. For example, we could have written &max to check its argument list like this:[*]

```
sub max {
  if (@_ != 2) {
    print "WARNING! &max should get exactly two arguments!\n";
  }
  # continue as before...
  .
  .
  .
}
```

That if test uses the "name" of the array in a scalar context to find out the number of array elements, as you saw in Chapter 3.

But in real-world Perl programming, this sort of check is rarely used; it's better to make the subroutine adapt to the parameters.

A Better &max Routine

So let's rewrite &max to allow for any number of arguments:

```
$maximum = &max(3, 5, 10, 4, 6);

sub max {
  my($max_so_far) = shift @_;   # the first one is the largest yet seen
  foreach (@_) {                # look at the remaining arguments
    if ($_ > $max_so_far) {     # could this one be bigger yet?
      $max_so_far = $_;
    }
  }
  $max_so_far;
}
```

---

[*] As soon as you learn about warn in the next chapter, you'll see that you can use it to turn improper usage like this into a proper warning. Or perhaps you'll decide this case is severe enough to warrant using die, described in the same chapter.

This code uses what has often been called the *high-water mark* algorithm: after a flood, when the waters have surged and receded for the last time, the high-water mark shows where the highest water was seen. In this routine, $max_so_far keeps track of our high-water mark, the largest number yet seen.

The first line sets $max_so_far to 3 (the first parameter in the example code) by shifting that parameter from the parameter array, @_. So, @_ now holds (5, 10, 4, 6) since the 3 has been shifted off. The largest number yet seen is the only one yet seen: 3, the first parameter.

Now, the foreach loop will step through the remaining values in the parameter list from @_. The control variable of the loop is, by default, $_. (But, remember, there's no automatic connection between @_ and $_; it's a coincidence that they have similar names.) The first time through the loop, $_ is 5. The if test sees that it is larger than $max_so_far, so $max_so_far is set to 5, which is the new high-water mark.

The next time through the loop, $_ is 10. That's a new record high, so it's stored in $max_so_far as well.

The next time, $_ is 4. The if test fails since that's no larger than $max_so_far, which is 10, so the body of the if is skipped.

The next time, $_ is 6, and the body of the if is skipped again. And that was the last time through the loop, so the loop is done.

Now, $max_so_far becomes the return value. It's the largest number we've seen, and we've seen them all, so it must be the largest from the list: 10.

Empty Parameter Lists

That improved &max algorithm works fine now, even if there are more than two parameters. But what happens if there are none?

At first, it may seem too esoteric to worry about. After all, why would someone call &max without giving it any parameters? But maybe someone wrote a line like this one:

```
$maximum = &max(@numbers);
```

And the array @numbers might sometimes be an empty list; perhaps it was read in from a file that turned out to be empty. So you need to know this: What does &max do in that case?

The first line of the subroutine sets $max_so_far by using shift on @_, the (now empty) parameter array. That's harmless; the array is left empty, and shift returns undef to $max_so_far.

Now the foreach loop wants to iterate over @_, but since that's empty, the loop body is executed zero times.

In short order, Perl returns the value of $max_so_far—undef—as the return value of the subroutine. In some sense, that's the right answer because there is no largest value in an empty list.

Of course, whoever is calling this subroutine should be aware that the return value may be undef, or they could ensure that the parameter list is never empty.

Notes on Lexical (my) Variables

Those lexical variables can be used in any block, not merely in a subroutine's block. For example, they can be used in the block of an if, while, or foreach:

```
foreach (1..10) {
  my($square) = $_ * $_;  # private variable in this loop
  print "$_ squared is $square.\n";
}
```

The variable $square is private to the enclosing block; in this case, that's the block of the foreach loop. If there's no enclosing block, the variable is private to the entire source file. For now, your programs aren't going to use more than one source file, so this isn't an issue. But the important concept is that the scope of a lexical variable's name is limited to the smallest enclosing block or file. The only code that can say $square and mean that variable is the code inside that textual scope. This is a big win for maintainability—if the wrong value is found in $square, the culprit will be found within a limited amount of source code. As experienced programmers have learned (often the hard way), limiting the scope of a variable to a page of code, or to a few lines of code, accelerates the development and testing cycle.

Also, the my operator doesn't change the context of an assignment:

```
my($num) = @_;  # list context, same as ($num) = @_;
my $num  = @_;  # scalar context, same as $num = @_;
```

In the first one, $num gets the first parameter, as a list-context assignment; in the second, it gets the number of parameters, in a scalar context. Either line of code could be what the programmer wanted; you can't tell from that one line alone, so Perl can't warn you if you use the wrong one. (Of course, you wouldn't have both of those lines in the same subroutine since you can't have two lexical variables with the same name declared in the same scope; this is just an example.) When reading code like this, you can always tell the context of the assignment by seeing what the context would be without the word my.

So long as we're discussing using my( ) with parentheses, remember that without the parentheses, my only declares a *single* lexical variable:*

```
my $fred, $barney;          # WRONG! Fails to declare $barney
my($fred, $barney);         # declares both
```

Of course, you can use my to create new, private arrays as well:†

```
my @phone_number;
```

Any new variable will start out empty: undef for scalars or the empty list for arrays.

The use strict Pragma

Perl tends to be a permissive language.‡ But maybe you want Perl to impose a little discipline; that can be arranged with the use strict pragma.

A *pragma* is a hint to a compiler, telling it something about the code. In this case, the use strict pragma tells Perl's internal compiler that it should enforce some good programming rules for the rest of this block or source file.

Why would this be important? Well, imagine that you're composing your program, and you type a line like this one:

```
$bamm_bamm = 3;  # Perl creates that variable automatically
```

Now, you keep typing for a while. After that line has scrolled off the top of the screen, you type this line to increment the variable:

```
$bammbamm += 1;  # Oops!
```

Since Perl sees a new variable name (the underscore is significant in a variable name), it creates a new variable and increments that one. If you're lucky and smart, you've turned on warnings, and Perl can tell you that you used one or both of those global variable names once in your program. But if you're merely smart, you used each name more than once, and Perl won't be able to warn you.

To tell Perl you're ready to be more restrictive, put the use strict pragma at the top of your program (or in any block or file where you want to enforce these rules):

```
use strict; # Enforce some good programming rules
```

---

* As usual, turning on warnings will generally report this abuse of my, or you can call 1-800-LEXICAL-ABUSE and report it yourself. Using the strict pragma, which we'll see in a moment, should forbid it outright.

† Or hashes, which you'll see in Chapter 6.

‡ Bet you hadn't noticed.

Now, among other restrictions,* Perl will insist that you declare every new variable, usually done with my:†

```
my $bamm_bamm = 3;   # New lexical variable
```

If you try to spell it the other way, Perl can complain that you haven't declared any variable called $bammbamm, so your mistake is automatically caught at compile time.

```
$bammbamm += 1;   # No such variable: Compile time fatal error
```

Of course, this applies only to new variables; you don't need to declare Perl's built-in variables, such as $_ and @_.‡ If you add use strict to a previously written program, you'll generally get a flood of warning messages, so it's better to use it from the start when it's needed.

Most people recommend that programs that are longer than a screenful of text generally need use strict. And we agree.

From here on, most (but not all) of our examples will be written as if use strict is in effect even where we don't show it. That is, we'll generally declare variables with my where it's appropriate. Though we don't always do so here, we encourage you to include use strict in your programs as often as possible.

The return Operator

The return operator immediately returns a value from a subroutine:

```
my @names = qw/ fred barney betty dino wilma pebbles bamm-bamm /;
my $result = &which_element_is("dino", @names);

sub which_element_is {
  my($what, @array) = @_;
  foreach (0..$#array) {  # indices of @array's elements
    if ($what eq $array[$_]) {
      return $_;          # return early once found
    }
  }
  -1;                     # element not found (return is optional here)
}
```

This subroutine is being used to find the index of "dino" in the array @names. First, the my declaration names the parameters: there's $what, which is what we're searching for,

---

* To learn about the other restrictions, see the documentation for strict. The documentation for any pragma is filed under that pragma's name, so the command perldoc strict (or your system's native documentation method) should find it for you. In brief, the other restrictions require that strings be quoted in most cases, and that references be true (hard) references. Neither of these restrictions should affect beginners in Perl.

† There are some other ways to declare variables, too.

‡ In some circumstances, you don't want to declare $a and $b because they're used internally by sort. So, if you're testing this feature, use other variable names than those two. The fact that use strict doesn't forbid these two is one of the most frequently reported non-bugs in Perl.

---

and @array, an array of values to search within. That's a copy of the array @names in this case. The foreach loop steps through the indices of @array (the first index is 0, and the last one is $#array, as you saw in Chapter 3).

Each time through the foreach loop, we check to see whether the string in $what is equal* to the element from @array at the current index. If it's equal, we return that index at once. This is the most common use of the keyword return in Perl—to return a value immediately without executing the rest of the subroutine.

What if we never found that element? In that case, the author of this subroutine has chosen to return -1 as a "value not found" code. It would be more Perlish, perhaps, to return undef in that case, but this programmer used -1. Saying return -1 on that last line would be correct, but the word return isn't needed.

Some programmers like to use return every time there's a return value as a means of documenting that it is a return value. For example, you might use return when the return value is not the last line of the subroutine, such as in the subroutine &larger_of_fred_or_barney earlier in this chapter. It's not needed, but it doesn't hurt anything. However, many Perl programmers believe it's just an extra seven characters of typing.

Omitting the Ampersand

A few rules govern when a subroutine call can omit the ampersand. If the compiler sees the subroutine definition before invocation or if Perl can tell from the syntax that it's a subroutine call, the subroutine can be called without an ampersand, like a built-in function. (But there's a catch hidden in those rules, as you'll see in a moment.)

This means that if Perl can see that it's a subroutine call without the ampersand from the syntax alone, that's generally fine. That is, if you've got the parameter list in parentheses, it's got to be a function† call:

```perl
my @cards = shuffle(@deck_of_cards);   # No & necessary on &shuffle
```

If Perl's internal compiler has seen the subroutine definition, that's generally okay, too; in that case, you can omit the parentheses around the argument list:

```perl
sub division {
  $_[0] / $_[1];                # Divide first param by second
}

my $quotient = division 355, 113;  # Uses &division
```

---

* You noticed that we used the string equality test, eq, instead of the numeric equality test, = =, didn't you?

† In this case, the function is the subroutine &shuffle. But it may be a built-in function as you'll see in a moment.

This works because of the rule that parentheses may always be omitted except when doing so would change the meaning of the code.

But don't put that subroutine declaration after the invocation, or the compiler won't know what the attempted invocation of division is all about. The compiler has to see the definition before the invocation to use the subroutine call as if it were a built-in.

That's not the catch, though. The catch is this: if the subroutine has the same name as a Perl built-in, you must use the ampersand to call it. With an ampersand, you're sure to call the subroutine; without it, you can get the subroutine only if there's no built-in with the same name:

```
sub chomp {
  print "Munch, munch!\n";
}

&chomp;  # That ampersand is not optional!
```

Without the ampersand, we'd be calling the built-in chomp, even though we've defined the subroutine &chomp. So, the real rule to use is this one: until you know the names of all of Perl's built-in functions, always use the ampersand on function calls. That means that you will use it for your first hundred programs or so. But when you see someone else has omitted the ampersand in their own code, it's not necessarily a mistake; perhaps they know that Perl has no built-in with that name.[*] When programmers plan to call their subroutines as if they were calling Perl's built-ins, often when writing *modules*, they often use *prototypes* to tell Perl about the parameters to expect. Making modules is an advanced topic though; when you're ready for that, see Perl's documentation (in particular, the *perlmod* and *perlsub* documents) for more information about subroutine prototypes and making modules.

Non-Scalar Return Values

A scalar isn't the only kind of return value a subroutine may have. If you call your subroutine in a list context,[†] it can return a list of values.

Suppose you wanted to get a range of numbers (as from the range operator, ..) except that you want to be able to count down as well as up. The range operator only counts upward, but that's easily fixed:

```
sub list_from_fred_to_barney {
  if ($fred < $barney) {
```

---

[*] Then again, maybe it is a mistake; you can search the *perlfunc* and *perlop* manpages for that name to see if it's the same as a built-in. And Perl will usually be able to warn you about this when you have warnings turned on.

[†] You can detect if a subroutine is being evaluated in a scalar or list context using the wantarray function, which lets you easily write subroutines with specific list or scalar context values.

```
     # Count upwards from $fred to $barney
     $fred..$barney;
   } else {
     # Count downwards from $fred to $barney
     reverse $barney..$fred;
   }
}
$fred = 11;
$barney = 6;
@c = &list_from_fred_to_barney; # @c gets (11, 10, 9, 8, 7, 6)
```

In this case, the range operator gives us the list from 6 to 11, and reverse reverses the list, so it goes from $fred (11) to $barney (6) just as we wanted.

The least you can return is nothing at all. A return with no arguments will return undef in a scalar context or an empty list in a list context. This can be useful for an error return from a subroutine, signalling to the caller that a more meaningful return value is unavailable.

Exercises

See Appendix A for answers to the following exercises:

1. [12] Write a subroutine, called &total, which returns the total of a list of numbers. Hint: The subroutine should not perform any I/O; it should process its parameters and return a value to its caller. Try it out in this sample program, which exercises the subroutine to see that it works. The first group of numbers should add up to 25.

   ```
   my @fred = qw{ 1 3 5 7 9 };
   my $fred_total = &total(@fred);
   print "The total of \@fred is $fred_total.\n";
   print "Enter some numbers on separate lines: ";
   my $user_total = &total(<STDIN>);
   print "The total of those numbers is $user_total.\n";
   ```

2. [5] Using the subroutine from the previous problem, make a program to calculate the sum of the numbers from 1 to 1,000.

3. [18] Extra credit exercise: Write a subroutine, called &above_average, which takes a list of numbers and returns the ones which are above the average (mean). (Hint: Make another subroutine that calculates the average by dividing the total by the number of items.) Try your subroutine in this test program.

   ```
   my @fred = &above_average(1..10);
   print "\@fred is @fred\n";
   print "(Should be 6 7 8 9 10)\n";
   my @barney = &above_average(100, 1..10);
   print "\@barney is @barney\n";
   print "(Should be just 100)\n";
   ```

CHAPTER 5

Input and Output

We've seen how to do some input/output (I/O) to make some of the earlier exercises possible. Now we'll learn more about those operations by covering the 80% of the I/O you'll need for most programs. If you're familiar with the workings of standard input, output, and error streams, you're ahead of the game. If not, we'll get you caught up by the end of this chapter. For now, think of "standard input" as being "the keyboard" and "standard output" as being "the display screen."

Input from Standard Input

Reading from the standard input stream is easy. We've been doing it with the `<STDIN>` operator.* Evaluating this operator in a scalar context gives you the next line of input:

```
$line = <STDIN>;            # read the next line
chomp($line);               # and chomp it

chomp($line = <STDIN>);     # same thing, more idiomatically
```

Since the line-input operator will return undef when you reach end-of-file, this is handy for dropping out of loops:

```
while (defined($line = <STDIN>)) {
  print "I saw $line";
}
```

There's a lot going on in that first line: we're reading the input into a variable, checking that it's defined, and if it is (meaning that we haven't reached the end of the input), we're running the body of the while loop. So, inside the body of the loop,

---

* What we're calling the line-input operator here, `<STDIN>` is actually a line-input operator (represented by the angle brackets) around a *filehandle*. You'll learn about filehandles later in this chapter.

we'll see each line, one after another, in $line.* This is something you'll want to do fairly often, so naturally Perl has a shortcut for it. The shortcut looks like this:

```
while (<STDIN>) {
  print "I saw $_";
}
```

Now, to make this shortcut, Larry chose some useless syntax. That is, this is saying, "Read a line of input, and see if it's true. (Normally it is.) And if it is true, enter the while loop, but *throw away that line of input!*" Larry knew that it was a useless thing to do; nobody should ever need to do that in a real Perl program. So, Larry took this useless syntax and made it useful.

What this is *actually saying* is that Perl should do the same thing as we saw in our earlier loop: it tells Perl to read the input into a variable, and (as long as the result was defined, so we haven't reached end-of-file) then enter the while loop. However, instead of storing the input into $line, Perl will use its favorite default variable, $_, as if you had written this:

```
while (defined($_ = <STDIN>)) {
  print "I saw $_";
}
```

Now, before we go any further, we must be clear about something: this shortcut workparticular, as a statement all on its own) it won't read a line into $_ by default. It works *only* if there's nothing but the line-input operator in the conditional of a while loop.† If you put anything else into the conditional expression, this shortcut won't apply.

Otherwise, there's no other connection between the line-input operator (<STDIN>) and Perl's favorite default variable ($_). In this case, the input is being stored in that variable.

On the other hand, evaluating the line-input operator in a list context gives you all of the (remaining) lines of input as a list, and each element of the list is one line:

```
foreach (<STDIN>) {
  print "I saw $_";
}
```

Once again, there's no connection between the line-input operator and Perl's favorite default variable. In this case, though, the default control variable for foreach is $_. So this loop places each line of input in $_, one after the other.

---

* You probably noticed that we never chomped that input. In this kind of a loop, you can't put chomp into the conditional expression, so it's often the first item in the loop body when it's needed. We'll see examples of that in the next section.

† Well, okay, the conditional of a for loop is just a while conditional in disguise, so it works there, too.

That may sound familiar and for good reason: that's the same behavior as the while loop, isn't it?

The difference is under the hood. In the while loop, Perl reads a line of input, puts it into a variable, and runs the body of the loop. Then, it goes back to find another line of input. But in the foreach loop, the line-input operator is being used in a list context since foreach needs a list to iterate through. So, it has to read all of the input before the loop can start running. That difference will become apparent when the input is coming from your 400MB web server log file. It's generally best to use code like the while loop's shortcut whenever possible, since it processes input one line at a time.

Input from the Diamond Operator

Another way to read input is with the diamond* operator: <>. This is useful for making programs that work like standard Unix† utilities, with respect to the invocation arguments (which we'll see in a moment). If you want to make a Perl program that can be used like the utilities *cat*, *sed*, *awk*, *sort*, *grep*, *lpr*, and many others, the diamond operator will be your friend. If you want to make anything else, the diamond operator probably won't help.

The *invocation arguments* to a program are normally a number of "words" on the command line after the name of the program.‡ In this case, they give the names of the files your program will process in sequence:

```
$ ./my_program fred barney betty
```

That command means to run the command my_program (which will be found in the current directory), and that it should process file *fred*, followed by file *barney*, followed by file *betty*.

If you give no invocation arguments, the program should process the standard input stream. As a special case, if you give a hyphen as one of the arguments, that means standard input as well.§ If the invocation arguments had been fred- betty, that

---

* The diamond operator was named by Larry's daughter, Heidi, when Randal went over to Larry's house one day to show off the new training materials he'd been writing, and complained that there was no spoken name for "that thing." Larry didn't have a name for it, either. Heidi (8 years old at the time) quickly chimed in, "That's a diamond, Daddy." So the name stuck. Thanks, Heidi!

† But not just on Unix systems. Many other systems have adopted this way of using invocation arguments.

‡ Whenever a program is started, it has a list of zero or more invocation arguments, supplied by whatever program is starting it. Often this is the shell, which makes up the list depending on what you type on the command line. But we'll see later that you can invoke a program with pretty much any strings as the invocation arguments. Because they often come from the shell's command line, they are sometimes called "command-line arguments" as well.

§ Here's a possibly unfamiliar Unix fact: most of those standard utilities, like *cat* and *sed*, use this same convention, where a hyphen stands for the standard input stream.

---

would have meant that the program should process file *fred*, followed by the standard input stream, followed by file *betty*.

The benefit of making your programs work like this is that you may choose where the program gets its input at runtime; for example, you won't have to rewrite the program to use it in a pipeline (which we'll discuss more later). Larry put this feature into Perl because he wanted to make it easy for you to write your own programs that work like standard Unix utilities, even on non-Unix machines. Actually, he did it so he could make his *own* programs work like standard Unix utilities. Since some vendors' utilities don't work like others', Larry could make his own utilities, deploy them on a number of machines, and know that they'd all have the same behavior. Of course, this meant porting Perl to every machine he could find.

The diamond operator is a special kind of line-input operator. Instead of getting the input from the keyboard, it comes from the user's choice of input:[*]

```
while (defined($line = <>)) {
  chomp($line);
  print "It was $line that I saw!\n";
}
```

If we run this program with the invocation arguments fred, barney, and betty, it will say something like this: "It was [a line from file *fred*] that I saw!", "It was [another line from file *fred*] that I saw!", until it reaches the end of file fred. Then, it will automatically go on to file *barney*, printing out one line after another, and then on through file *betty*. There's no break when we go from one file to another; when you use the diamond, it's as if the input files have been merged into one big file.[†] The diamond will return undef (and we'll drop out of the while loop) at the end of all of the input.

Since this is a special kind of line-input operator, we may use the same shortcut we saw earlier to read the input into $_ by default:

```
while (<>) {
  chomp;
  print "It was $_ that I saw!\n";
}
```

This works like the loop above but with less typing. You may have noticed we're using the default for chomp; without an argument, chomp will work on $_. Every little bit of saved typing helps.

Since the diamond operator is generally used to process all of the input, it's typically a mistake to use it in more than one place in your program. If you find yourself putting two diamonds into the same program, especially using the second diamond

---

[*] Which may or may not include getting input from the keyboard.

[†] If it matters to you, or even if it doesn't, the current file's name is kept in Perl's special variable $ARGV. This name may be "-" instead of a real filename if the input is coming from the standard input stream.

inside the while loop that is reading from the first one, it's almost certainly not going to do what you want.* In our experience, when beginners put a second diamond into a program, they meant to use $_ instead. Remember, the diamond operator *reads* the input, but the input itself is generally found in $_ (by default).

If the diamond operator can't open one of the files and read from it, it'll print an allegedly helpful diagnostic message, such as:

```
can't open wimla: No such file or directory
```

The diamond operator will go to the next file automatically, much like what you'd expect from *cat* or another standard utility.

The Invocation Arguments

Technically, the diamond operator isn't looking at the invocation arguments—it works from the @ARGV array. This array is a special array preset by the Perl interpreter as the list of the invocation arguments. In other words, this is like any other array, (except for its funny, all caps name), but when your program starts, @ARGV is already stuffed full of the list of invocation arguments.†

You can use @ARGV like any other array; you can shift items off of it or use foreach to iterate over it. You could even check to see if any arguments start with a hyphen, so you could process them as invocation options (like Perl does with its own -w option).‡

The diamond operator looks in @ARGV to determine what filenames it should use. If it finds an empty list, it uses the standard input stream; otherwise, it uses the list of files that it finds. This means that after your program starts and before you start using the diamond, you've got a chance to tinker with @ARGV. For example, here we can process three specific files regardless of what the user chose on the command line:

```
@ARGV = qw# larry moe curly #;   # force these three files to be read
while (<>) {
  chomp;
  print "It was $_ that I saw in some stooge-like file!\n";
}
```

---

* If you re-initialize @ARGV before using the second diamond, then you're on solid ground. We'll see @ARGV in the next section.

† C programmers may be wondering about argc(there isn't one in Perl), and what happened to the program's own name (that's found in Perl's special variable $0, not @ARGV). Depending upon how you've invoked your program, there may be a little more happening than we say here. See the perlrun manpage for the full details.

‡ If you need more than one or two such options, you should almost certainly use a module to process them in a standard way. See the documentation for the Getopt::Long and Getopt::Std modules, which are part of the standard distribution.

Output to Standard Output

The print operator takes a list of values and sends each item (as a string, of course) to standard output in turn, one after another. It doesn't add any extra characters before, after, or in between the items.* If you want spaces between items and a newline at the end, you have to say so:

```
$name = "Larry Wall";
print "Hello there, $name, did you know that 3+4 is ", 3+4, "?\n";
```

Of course, that means printing an array and interpolating an array are different:

```
print @array;      # print a list of items
print "@array";    # print a string (containing an interpolated array)
```

The first print statement will print a list of items, one after another, with no spaces in between. The second one will print one item, which is the string you get by interpolating @array into the empty string—that is, it prints the contents of @array, separated by spaces.† If @array holds qw/ fred barney betty /,‡ the first one will print fredbarneybetty, and the second will print fred barney betty separated by spaces.

But before you decide to use the second form all the time, imagine that @array is a list of unchomped lines of input. That is, imagine that each of its strings has a trailing newline character. Now, the first print statement prints fred, barney, and betty on three separate lines. But the second one prints this:

```
fred
 barney
 betty
```

Do you see where the spaces come from? Perl is interpolating an array, so it puts spaces between the elements. We get the first element of the array (fred and a newline character), a space, the next element of the array (barney and a newline character), a space, and the last element of the array (betty and a newline character). The result is that the lines seem to have become indented except for the first one. Every week or two, a message appears on the newsgroup *comp.lang.perl.misc* with a subject line like this:

> Perl indents everything after the first line

Without reading the message, we know the program used double quotes around an array containing unchomped strings. When asked, "Did you perhaps put an array of unchomped strings inside double quotes?", the answer is always yes.

---

* Well, it doesn't add anything extra by default, but this default (like so many others in Perl) may be changed. Changing these defaults will likely confuse your maintenance programmer, so avoid doing so except in small, quick-and-dirty programs or (rarely) in a small section of a normal program. See the perlvar manpage to learn about changing the defaults.

† Yes, the spaces are another default. See the perlvar manpage again.

‡ You know that we mean a three-element list here, right? This is just Perl notation.

Generally, if your strings contain newlines, you'll simply want to print them:

```
print @array;
```

But if they don't contain newlines, you'll generally want to add one at the end:

```
print "@array\n";
```

If you're using the quote marks, you'll generally be adding the \n at the end of the string anyway; this should help you to remember which is which.

It's normal for your program's output to be *buffered*. Instead of sending out every little bit of output immediately, it'll be saved until there's enough to bother with. If (for example) you're going to save the output to disk, it would be (relatively) slow and inefficient to spin the disk every time you add one or two characters to the file. Generally, then, the output will go into a buffer that is *flushed* (that is, actually written to disk or wherever) only when the buffer gets full or when the output is otherwise finished (such as at the end of runtime). Usually, that's what you want.

But if you (or a program) are waiting impatiently for the output, you may wish to take that performance hit and flush the output buffer each time you print. See the Perl manpages for more information on controlling buffering.

Since print is looking for a list of strings to print, its arguments are evaluated in list context. Since the diamond operator (as a special kind of line-input operator) will return a list of lines in a list context, these can work well together:

```
print <>;          # source code for 'cat'

print sort <>;     # source code for 'sort'
```

To be fair, the standard Unix commands cat and sort do have some additional functionality that these replacements lack, but you can't beat them for the price! You can now reimplement all of your standard Unix utilities in Perl and painlessly port them to any machine that has Perl whether that machine is running Unix or not. And you can be certain that the programs on every different type of machine will have the same behavior.*

What might not be obvious is that print has optional parentheses, which can sometimes cause confusion. Remember the rule that parentheses in Perl may be omitted except when doing so would change the meaning of a statement. Here are two ways to print the same thing:

```
print("Hello, world!\n");
print "Hello, world!\n";
```

---

* In fact, the Perl Power Tools (PPT) project, whose goal is to implement all of the classic Unix utilities in Perl, completed nearly all the utilities (and most of the games) but got bogged down when they got to reimplementing the shell. The PPT project has been useful because it has made these standard utilities available on many non-Unix machines.

So far, so good. Another rule in Perl is that if the invocation of print *looks* like a function call, then it *is* a function call. It's a simple rule, but what does it mean for something to look like a function call?

In a function call, there's a function name immediately[*] followed by parentheses around the function's arguments, like this:

```
print (2+3);
```

That looks like a function call, so it is a function call. It prints 5, but then it returns a value like any other function. The return value of print is a true or false value, indicating the success of the print. It nearly always succeeds unless you get some I/O error, so the $result in the following statement will normally be 1:

```
$result = print("hello world!\n");
```

But what if you used the result in some other way? Suppose you decide to multiply the return value times four:

```
print (2+3)*4;   # Oops!
```

When Perl sees this line of code, it prints 5 as you asked. Then it takes the return value from print, which is 1, and multiplies that times 4. Then, it throws away the product, wondering why you didn't tell it to do something else with it. At this point, someone looking over your shoulder says, "Hey, Perl can't do math! That should have printed 20, rather than 5!"

This is the problem with the optional parentheses; sometimes, we humans forget where the parentheses belong. When there are no parentheses, print is a list operator, printing all of the items in the following list, which is what you'd expect. But when the first thing after print is a open parenthesis, print is a function call, and it will print only what's found inside the parentheses. Since that line had parentheses, it's the same to Perl as if you'd said this:

```
( print(2+3) ) * 4;   # Oops!
```

Fortunately, Perl can almost always help you with this if you ask for warnings. So use -w, or use warnings, at least during program development and debugging.

This rule—If it looks like a function call, it is a function call—applies to all list functions[†] in Perl, not just to print, but you're most likely to notice it with print. If print (or another function name) is followed by an open parenthesis, ensure the corresponding closed parenthesis comes after *all* of the arguments to that function.

---

[*] We say "immediately" here because Perl won't permit a newline character between the function name and the open parenthesis in this kind of function call. If there is a newline there, Perl will see your code as making a list operator, rather than a function call. This is the kind of technical detail that we mention for completeness. If you're terminally curious, see the full story in the manpages.

[†] Functions that take zero or one arguments don't suffer from this problem.

Formatted Output with printf

You may wish to have a little more control with your output than print provides. In fact, you may be accustomed to the formatted output of C's printf function. Fear not—Perl provides a comparable operation with the same name.

The printf operator takes a format string followed by a list of things to print. The format* string is a fill-in-the-blanks template showing the desired form of the output:

```
printf "Hello, %s; your password expires in %d days!\n",
    $user, $days_to_die;
```

The format string holds a number of so-called *conversions*; each conversion begins with a percent sign (%) and ends with a letter. (As we'll see in a moment, there may be significant extra characters between these two symbols.) There should be the same number of items in the following list as there are conversions; if these don't match up, it won't work correctly. The example above has two items and two conversions, so the output might look something like this:

```
Hello, merlyn; your password expires in 3 days!
```

There are many possible printf conversions, so we'll take time here to describe the most common ones. Of course, the full details are available in the perlfunc manpage.

To print a number, generally use %g,† which automatically chooses floating-point, integer, or even exponential notation as needed:

```
printf "%g %g %g\n", 5/2, 51/17, 51 ** 17;  # 2.5 3 1.0683e+29
```

The %d format means a decimal‡ integer, truncated as needed:

```
printf "in %d days!\n", 17.85;  # in 17 days!
```

This is truncated, not rounded; we'll see how to round off a number in a moment.

In Perl, printf is most often used for columnar data since most formats accept a field width. If the data won't fit, the field will generally be expanded as needed:

```
printf "%6d\n", 42;  # output like ....42 (the . symbol stands for a space)
printf "%2d\n", 2e3 + 1.95;  # 2001
```

The %s conversion means a string, so it effectively interpolates the given value as a string but with a given field width:

```
printf "%10s\n", "wilma";  # looks like .....wilma
```

---

* Here, we're using "format" in the generic sense. Perl has a report-generating feature called "formats" that we won't even be mentioning (except in this footnote) until Appendix B, and then only to say that we really aren't going to talk about them. So, you're on your own there. Just wanted to keep you from getting lost.

† "General" numeric conversion. Or maybe a "Good conversion for this number" or "Guess what I want the output to look like."

‡ There's also %x for hexadecimal and %o for octal, if you need those. But we say "decimal" here as a memory aid: %d for Decimal integer.

A negative field width is left-justified (in any of these conversions):

```
printf "%-15s\n", "flintstone";  # looks like flintstone.....
```

The %f conversion (floating-point) rounds off its output as needed and lets you request a certain number of digits after the decimal point:

```
printf "%12f\n", 6 * 7 + 2/3;    # looks like ...42.666667
printf "%12.3f\n", 6 * 7 + 2/3;  # looks like ......42.667
printf "%12.0f\n", 6 * 7 + 2/3;  # looks like ..........43
```

To print a real percent sign, use %%, which is special in that it uses no element from the list:*

```
printf "Monthly interest rate: %.2f%%\n",
  5.25/12;  # the value looks like "0.44%"
```

Arrays and printf

Generally, you won't use an array as an argument to printf. That's because an array may hold any number of items, and a given format string will work with only a certain fixed number of items: if there are three conversions in the format, there will have to be exactly three items.

But there's no reason you can't whip up a format string on the fly since it may be any expression. This can be tricky to get right, so it may be handy (especially when debugging) to store the format into a variable:

```
my @items = qw( wilma dino pebbles );
my $format = "The items are:\n" . ("%10s\n" x @items);
## print "the format is >>$format<<\n"; # for debugging
printf $format, @items;
```

This uses the x operator (which we learned about in Chapter 2) to replicate the given string a number of times given by @items (which is being used in a scalar context). In this case, that's 3 since there are three items, so the resulting format string is the same as if we had written it as "The items are:\n%10s\n%10s\n%10s\n." And the output prints each item on its own line, right-justified in a ten-character column, under a heading line. Pretty cool, huh? But not cool enough, because you can even combine these:

```
printf "The items are:\n".("%10s\n" x @items), @items;
```

Here we have @items being used once in a scalar context to get its length and once in a list context to get its contents. Context is important.

---

* Maybe you thought you could put a backslash in front of the percent sign. Nice try, but no. The reason that won't work is that the format is an expression, and the expression "\%" means the one-character string '%'. Even if we had gotten a backslash into the format string, printf wouldn't know what to do with it. Besides, C programmers are used to printf working like this.

Filehandles

A filehandle is the name in a Perl program for an I/O connection between your Perl process and the outside world. That is, it's the name of a *connection* and not necessarily the name of a file.

Filehandles are named like other Perl identifiers (letters, digits, and underscores, but they can't start with a digit); since they don't have any prefix character, they might be confused with present or future reserved words, or with labels, which we will cover in Chapter 10. Once again, as with labels, the recommendation from Larry is that you use all uppercase letters in the name of your filehandle. It will stand out better and will guarantee your program won't fail when a future (lowercase) reserved word is introduced.

Perl uses six special filehandle names for its own purposes: STDIN, STDOUT, STDERR, DATA, ARGV, and ARGVOUT.* Though you may choose any filehandle name you'd like, you shouldn't choose one of those six unless you intend to use that one's special properties.†

Maybe you've recognized some of those names. When your program starts, STDIN is the filehandle naming the connection between the Perl process and wherever the program should get its input, known as the *standard input stream*. This is generally the user's keyboard unless the user asked for something else to be the source of input, such as a file or the output of another program through a pipe.‡ STDOUT is the *standard output stream*. By default, this one goes to the user's display screen, but the user may send the output to a file or to another program, as we'll see shortly. These standard streams come to us from the Unix standard I/O library, but they work in much the same way on most modern operating systems.§ The general idea is that your program should blindly read from STDIN and blindly write to STDOUT, trusting in the user (or generally whichever program is starting your program) to have set those up. In that way, the user can type a command like this one at the shell prompt:

```
$ ./your_program <dino >wilma
```

---

* Some people hate typing in all caps, even for a moment, and they will try spelling these in lowercase, like stdin. Perl may let you get away with that, but not always. The details of when these work and when they fail are beyond the scope of this book. The important thing is that programs that rely on this kindness will one day break, so it is best to avoid lowercase here.

† In some cases, you could (re)use these names without a problem. But your maintenance programmer may think that you're using the name for its built-in features and may be confused.

‡ The defaults we speak of in this chapter for the three main I/O streams are what the Unix shells do by default. But it's not just shells that launch programs, of course. We'll see in Chapter 14 what happens when you launch another program from Perl.

§ If you're not familiar with how your non-Unix system provides standard input and output, see the perlport manpage and the documentation for that system's equivalent to the Unix shell (the program that runs programs based upon your keyboard input).

That command tells the shell that the program's input should be read from the file *dino*, and the output should go to the file *wilma*. As long as the program blindly reads its input from STDIN, processes it (in whatever way we need), and blindly writes its output to STDOUT, this will work just fine.

And at no extra charge, the program will work in a *pipeline*. This is another concept from Unix, which lets us write command lines like this one:

```
$ cat fred barney | sort | ./your_program | grep something | lpr
```

Now, if you're unfamiliar with these Unix commands, that's okay. This line says that the cat command should print out all of the lines of file *fred* followed by all of the lines of file *barney*. That output should be the input of the sort command, which sorts those lines and passes them on to your_program. After it has done its processing, your_program will send the data on to grep, which discards certain lines in the data, sending the others on to the lpr command, which should print everything that it gets on a printer. Whew!

Pipelines like that are common in Unix and many other systems today because they let you build powerful, complex commands out of simple, standard building blocks. Each building block does one thing well, and it's your job to use them together in the right way.

There's one more standard I/O stream. If (in the previous example) your_program had to emit any warnings or other diagnostic messages, those shouldn't go down the pipeline. The grep command is set to discard anything that it hasn't specifically been told to look for, so it will most likely discard the warnings. Even if it did keep the warnings, you probably don't want to pass them downstream to the other programs in the pipeline. That's why there's the *standard error stream*: STDERR. Even if the standard output is going to another program or file, the errors will go to wherever the user desires. By default, the errors will generally go to the user's display screen,* but the user may send the errors to a file with a shell command like this one:

```
$ netstat | ./your_program 2>/tmp/my_errors
```

Opening a Filehandle

You've seen that Perl provides three filehandles—STDIN, STDOUT, and STDERR—which are automatically open to files or devices established by the program's parent process (probably the shell). When you need other filehandles, use the open operator to

---

* Generally, errors aren't buffered. That means that if the standard error and standard output streams are going to the same place (such as the monitor), the errors may appear earlier than the normal output. For example, if your program prints a line of ordinary text and tries to divide by zero, the output may show the message about dividing by zero first, and the ordinary text second.

tell Perl to ask the operating system to open the connection between your program and the outside world. Here are some examples:

```
open CONFIG, "dino";
open CONFIG, "<dino";
open BEDROCK, ">fred";
open LOG, ">>logfile";
```

The first one opens a filehandle called CONFIG to a file called *dino*. That is, the (existing) file *dino* will be opened and whatever it holds will come into our program through the filehandle named CONFIG. This is similar to the way that data from a file could come in through STDIN if the command line had a shell redirection like <dino. The second example uses the same sequence; it does the same as the first, but the less-than sign explicitly says "use this filename for input," even though that's the default.*

Though you don't have to use the less-than sign to open a file for input, we include that because, as you can see in the third example, a greater-than sign means to create a new file for output. This opens the filehandle BEDROCK for output to the new file *fred*. Just as when the greater-than sign is used in shell redirection, we're sending the output to a *new* file called *fred*. If a file has that name, we'll wipe it out and replace it with this new one.

The fourth example shows how two greater-than signs may be used (again, as the shell does) to open a file for appending. That is, if the file exists, we will add new data at the end. If it doesn't exist, it will be created in much the same way as if we had used one greater-than sign. This is handy for log files; your program could write a few lines to the end of a log file each time it's run. That's why the fourth example names the filehandle LOG and the file *logfile*.

You can use any scalar expression in place of the filename specifier, though typically you'll want to be explicit about the direction specification:

```
my $selected_output = "my_output";
open LOG, "> $selected_output";
```

Note the space after the greater-than sign. Perl ignores this,† but it keeps unexpected things from happening if $selected_output were ">passwd", for example, which would make an append instead of a write.

---

* This may be important for security reasons. As we'll see in a moment (and in further detail in Chapter 14), a number of magical characters may be used in filenames. If $name holds a user-chosen filename, opening $name will allow any of these magical characters to come into play. This could be a convenience to the user, or it could be a security hole. But opening "< $name" is much safer since it explicitly says to open the given name for input. Still, this doesn't prevent all possible mischief. For more information on different ways of opening files, especially when security may be a concern, see the perlopentut manpage.

† Yes, this means that if your filename were to have leading whitespace, Perl would ignore that, too. See perlfunc and perlopentut if you're worried about this.

In modern versions of Perl (starting with Perl 5.6), you can use a "three-argument" open:

```
open CONFIG, "<", "dino";
open BEDROCK, ">", $file_name;
open LOG, ">>", &logfile_name( );
```

The advantage here is that Perl never confuses the mode (the second argument) with some part of the filename (the third argument), which has nice advantages for security.* However, if you need your Perl to be backward compatible to older Perl versions (such as when you are contributing to the CPAN), avoid these forms or mark your Perl sources as being compatible only with newer Perls.†

We'll see how to use these filehandles later in this chapter.

Bad Filehandles

Perl can't open a file all by itself. Like any other programming language, Perl merely asks the operating system to open a file. Of course, the operating system may refuse because of permission settings, an incorrect filename, or other reasons.

If you try to read from a bad filehandle (that is, a filehandle that isn't properly open), you'll see an immediate end-of-file. (With the I/O methods we'll see in this chapter, end-of-file will be indicated by undef in a scalar context or an empty list in a list context.) If you try to write to a bad filehandle, the data is silently discarded.

Fortunately, these dire consequences are avoidable. First of all, if we ask for warnings with -w or the warnings pragma, Perl will generally be able to tell us with a warning when it sees that we're using a bad filehandle. But even without that, open always tells us if it succeeded or failed by returning true for success or false for failure. You could write code like this:

```
my $success = open LOG, ">>logfile";  # capture the return value
if ( ! $success) {
  # The open failed
  ...
}
```

You *could* do it like that, but there's another way that we'll see in the next section.

---

* The disadvantage for security is that, presumably, you're letting a possibly malicious user inject possibly malicious characters into the delicate workings of your innocent program. Once you learn about regular expressions (starting in Chapter 7), you'll be able to use those to enforce some sanity checks on user input. And if your program has possibly malicious users, read up on Perl's helpful security features in the Alpaca book, in the perlsec manpage, or both.

† Via use 5.6, for example.

Closing a Filehandle

When you are finished with a filehandle, you may close it with the close operator like this:

```
close BEDROCK;
```

Closing a filehandle tells Perl to inform the operating system that we're all done with the given data stream, so any last output data should be written to disk in case someone is waiting for it.* Perl will automatically close a filehandle if you reopen it (that is, if you reuse the filehandle name in a new open) or if you exit the program.†

Because of this, many Perl programs don't bother with close. But it's there if you want to be tidy, with one close for every open. In general, it's best to close each filehandle soon after you're done with it, though the end of the program often arrives soon enough.‡

Fatal Errors with die

Let's step aside for a moment. We need some stuff that isn't directly related to (or limited to) I/O but is more about getting out of a program earlier than normal.

When a fatal error happens inside Perl (for example, if you divide by zero, use an invalid regular expression, or call a subroutine that hasn't been declared), your program stops with an error message telling why.§ This functionality is available to us with the die function, so we can make our own fatal errors.

The die function prints out the message you give it (to the standard error stream, where such messages should go) and ensures that your program exits with a nonzero exit status.

You may not know it, but every program that runs on Unix (and many other modern operating systems) has an exit status, telling if it was successful. Programs that

---

* If you know much about I/O systems, you'll know there's more to the story. Generally, when a filehandle is closed, here's what happens. If there's input remaining in a file, it's ignored. If there's input remaining in a pipeline, the writing program may get a signal that the pipeline is closed. If there's output going to a file or pipeline, the buffer is flushed (that is, pending output is sent on its way). If the filehandle had a lock, the lock is released. See your system's I/O documentation for further details.

† Any exit from the program will close all filehandles, but if Perl breaks, pending output buffers won't get flushed. That is to say, if you accidentally crash your program by dividing by zero, for example, Perl will still run and ensure that data you've written will get output. But if Perl can't run (because you ran out of memory or caught an unexpected signal), the last few pieces of output may not be written to disk. Usually, this isn't a big issue.

‡ Closing a filehandle will flush any output buffers and release any locks on the file. Since someone else may be waiting for those things, a long-running program should close each filehandle as soon as possible. But many of our programs will take only one or two seconds to run to completion, so this may not matter. Closing a filehandle also releases possibly limited resources, so it's more than being tidy.

§ Well, it does this by default, but errors may be trapped with an eval block, as we'll see in Chapter 16.

---

run other programs (like the *make* utility program) look at that exit status to see that everything happened correctly. The exit status is a single byte, so it can't say much; traditionally, it is zero for success and a nonzero value for failure. Perhaps one means a syntax error in the command arguments, two means that something went wrong during processing, and three means the configuration file couldn't be found; the details differ from one command to the next. But zero always means that everything worked. When the exit status shows failure, a program like *make* knows not to go on to the next step.

We could rewrite the previous example, perhaps with something like this:

```
if ( ! open LOG, ">>logfile") {
    die "Cannot create logfile: $!";
}
```

If the open fails, die will terminate the program and tell you it cannot create the logfile. But what's that $! in the message? That's the human-readable complaint from the system. In general, when the system refuses to do something we've requested (like opening a file), $! will give you a reason (perhaps "permission denied" or "file not found," in this case). This is the string that you may have obtained with perror in C or a similar language. This human-readable complaint message will be available in Perl's special variable $!.* It's a good idea to include $! in the message when it could help the user to figure out what he or she did wrong. But if you use die to indicate an error that is not the failure of a system request, don't include $! since it will generally hold an unrelated message left over from something Perl did internally. It will hold a useful value only immediately after a *failed* system request. A successful request won't leave anything useful there.

There's one more thing that die will do for you: it will automatically append the Perl program name and line number† to the end of the message, so you can easily identify which die in your program is responsible for the untimely exit. The error message from the previous code might look like this if $! contained the message permission denied:

```
Cannot create logfile: permission denied at your_program line 1234.
```

That's helpful because we always seem to want more information in our error messages than we included the first time around. If you don't want the line number and

---

* On some non-Unix operating systems, $! may say something like error number 7, which leaves it up to the user to look that one up in the documentation. On Windows and VMS, the variable $^E may have additional diagnostic information.

† If the error happened while reading from a file, the error message will include the "chunk number" (usually the line number) from the file and the name of the filehandle as well since those are often useful in tracking down a bug.

file revealed, make sure that the dying words have a newline on the end. That is, another way you could use die is with a trailing newline on the message:

```
if (@ARGV < 2) {
    die "Not enough arguments\n";
}
```

If there aren't at least two command-line arguments, that program will say so and quit. It won't include the program name and line number since the line number is of no use to the user; this is the user's error after all. As a rule of thumb, put the newline on messages that indicate a usage error and leave it off when the error might be something you want to track down during debugging.*

You should always check the return value of open since the rest of the program is relying upon its success.

Warning Messages with warn

Just as die can indicate a fatal error that acts like one of Perl's built-in errors (like dividing by zero), you can use the warn function to cause a warning that acts like one of Perl's built-in warnings (like using an undef value as if it were defined when warnings are enabled).

The warn function works as die does, except for that last step because it doesn't quit the program. But it adds the program name and line number if needed, and it prints the message to standard error as die would.†

And having talked about death and dire warnings, we now return you to your regularly scheduled I/O instructional material. Read on.

Using Filehandles

Once a filehandle is open for reading, you can read lines from it the same way you can read from standard input with STDIN. So, for example, to read lines from the Unix password file:

```
if ( ! open PASSWD, "/etc/passwd") {
    die "How did you get logged in? ($!)";
}
```

---

* The program's name is in Perl's special variable $0, so you may wish to include that in the string: "$0:Not enough arguments\n". This is useful if the program may be used in a pipeline or shell script, for example, where it's not obvious which command is complaining. $0 can be changed during the execution of the program, however. You might want to look into the special __FILE__ and __LINE__ tokens (or the caller function) to get the information that is being omitted by adding the newline, so you can print it in your own choice of format.

† Warnings can't be trapped with an eval block, like fatal errors can. But see the documentation for the __WARN__ pseudo-signal (in the perlvar manpage) if you need to trap a warning.

```
while (<PASSWD>) {
  chomp;
  ...
}
```

In this example, the die message uses parentheses around $!. Those are literal parentheses around the message in the output. (Sometimes, a punctuation mark is just a punctuation mark.) As you can see, what we've been calling the "line-input operator" is two components; the angle brackets (the *real* line-input operator) are around an input filehandle.

A filehandle open for writing or appending may be used with print or printf, appearing immediately after the keyword but before the list of arguments:

```
print LOG "Captain's log, stardate 3.14159\n";  # output goes to LOG
printf STDERR "%d percent complete.\n", $done/$total * 100;
```

Did you notice that there's no comma between the filehandle and the items to be printed?* This looks especially weird if you use parentheses. Either of these forms is correct:

```
printf (STDERR "%d percent complete.\n", $done/$total * 100);
printf STDERR ("%d percent complete.\n", $done/$total * 100);
```

Changing the Default Output Filehandle

By default, if you don't give a filehandle to print (or to printf as everything we say here about one applies equally well to the other), the output will go to STDOUT. But that default may be changed with the select operator. Here we'll send some output lines to BEDROCK:

```
select BEDROCK;
print "I hope Mr. Slate doesn't find out about this.\n";
print "Wilma!\n";
```

Once you've selected a filehandle as the default for output, it will stay that way. But it's generally a bad idea to confuse the rest of the program, so set it back to STDOUT when you're done.† Also by default, the output to each filehandle is buffered. Setting the special $| variable to 1 will set the selected filehandle (the one selected at the time the variable is modified) to flush the buffer after each output operation. If you want

---

* If you got straight A's in freshman English or Linguistics, then when we say this is called "indirect object syntax," you may say "Ah, of course! I see why there's no comma after the filehandle name—it's an indirect object!" We didn't get straight A's; we don't understand why there's no comma, but we omit it because Larry told us to do that.

† In the unlikely case that STDOUT might not be the selected filehandle, you could save and restore the filehandle using the technique shown in the documentation for select in the *perlfunc* manpage. And as long as we're sending you to that manpage, we may as well tell you that there are *two* built-in functions in Perl named select, and both covered in the *perlfunc* manpage. The other select has four arguments, so it's sometimes called "four-argument select".

to ensure the logfile gets its entries immediately, in case you might be reading the log to monitor progress of your long-running program, you could use something like this:

```
select LOG;
$| = 1;  # don't keep LOG entries sitting in the buffer
select STDOUT;
# ...time passes, babies learn to walk, tectonic plates shift, and then...
print LOG "This gets written to the LOG at once!\n";
```

Reopening a Standard Filehandle

We mentioned earlier that if you were to reopen a filehandle (that is, if you were to open a filehandle FRED when you've got an open filehandle named FRED), the old one would be closed for you automatically. And we said that you shouldn't reuse one of the six standard filehandle names unless you intended to get its special features. And we also said that the messages from die and warn, along with Perl's internally generated complaints, go automatically to STDERR. If you put those three pieces of information together, you will have an idea about how you could send error messages to a file rather than to your program's standard error stream:*

```
# Send errors to my private error log
if ( ! open STDERR, ">>/home/barney/.error_log") {
  die "Can't open error log for append: $!";
}
```

After reopening STDERR, any error messages from Perl will go into the new file. What happens if the die is executed—where will *that* message go if the new file couldn't be opened to accept the messages?

The answer is that if one of the three system filehandles—STDIN, STDOUT, or STDERR— fails to reopen, Perl kindly restores the original one.† That is, Perl closes the original one (of those three) only when it sees that opening the new connection is successful. Thus, this technique could be used to redirect any (or all) of those three system filehandles from inside your program,‡ almost as if the program had been run with that I/O redirection from the shell in the first place.

---

* Don't do this without a reason. It's nearly always better to let the user set up redirection when launching your program rather than have redirection hardcoded. But this is handy in cases where your program is being run automatically by another program (say, by a web server or a scheduling utility like cron or at). Another reason might be that your program is going to start another process (probably with system or exec, which we'll see in Chapter 14), and you need that process to have different I/O connections.

† At least, this is true if you haven't changed Perl's special $^F variable, which tells Perl that only those three are special like this. But you'd never change that.

‡ But don't open STDIN for output or the others for input. Just thinking about that makes our heads hurt.

Exercises

See Appendix A for answers to the following exercises:

1. [7] Write a program that acts like *cat* but reverses the order of the output lines. (Some systems have a utility like this named *tac*.) If you run yours as `./tac fred barney betty`, the output should be all of file *betty* from the last line to the first, then *barney* and then *fred*, also from the last line to the first. (Be sure to use the `./` in your program's invocation if you call it *tac* so you don't get the system's utility instead!)

2. [8] Write a program that asks the user to enter a list of strings on separate lines, printing each string in a right-justified 20-character column. To be certain that the output is in the proper columns, print a "ruler line" of digits as well. (This is a debugging aid.) Make sure that you're not using a 19-character column by mistake. For example, entering `hello`, `good-bye` should give output something like this:

    ```
    12345678901234567890123456789012345678901234567890123456789012345678901234567890
                   hello
                good-bye
    ```

3. [8] Modify the previous program to let the user choose the column width, so entering `30`, `hello`, `good-bye` (on separate lines) would put the strings at the 30th column. (Hint: See the section in Chapter 2 about controlling variable interpolation.) For extra credit, make the ruler line longer when the selected width is larger.

## CHAPTER 6

Hashes

In this chapter, you will see a feature that makes Perl one of the world's great programming languages—*hashes*.* Though hashes are a powerful and useful feature, you may have used other powerful languages for years without ever hearing of hashes. But you'll use hashes in nearly every Perl program you'll write from now on; they're that important.

What Is a Hash?

A hash is a data structure like an array, in that it can hold any number of values and retrieve these values at will. However, instead of indexing the values by *number*, as we did with arrays, we'll look up the values by *name*. That is, the *indices* (here, we'll call them *keys*) aren't numbers but are arbitrary unique strings (see Figure 6-1).

The keys are *strings*, first of all, so instead of getting element number 3 from an array, we'll be accessing the hash element named `wilma`.

These keys are arbitrary strings—you can use any string expression for a hash key. And they are unique strings; as there's only one array element numbered 3, there's only one hash element named `wilma`.

Another way to think of a hash is that it's like a barrel of data (see Figure 6-2), where each piece of data has a tag attached. You can reach into the barrel and pull out any tag and see what piece of data is attached. But there's no "first" item in the barrel; it's just a jumble. In an array, we'd start with element 0 and then element 1, element 2, and so on. But in a hash, there's no fixed order, no first element. It's just a collection of key/value pairs.

---

* In the olden days, we called these "associative arrays." In about 1995, the Perl community decided this was too many letters to type and too many syllables to say, so we changed the name to "hashes."

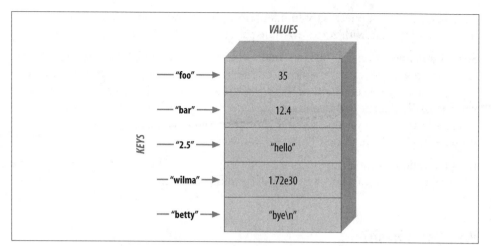

Figure 6-1. Hash keys and values

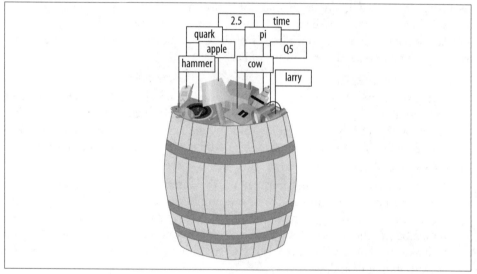

Figure 6-2. A hash as a barrel of data

The keys and values are both arbitrary scalars, but the keys are always converted to strings. So, if you used the numeric expression 50/20 as the key,* it would be turned into the three-character string "2.5", which is one of the keys shown in the diagram above.

---

* That's a numeric expression, not the five-character string "50/20". If we used that five-character string as a hash key, it would stay the same five-character string.

As usual, Perl's no-unnecessary-limits philosophy applies: a hash may be of any size, from an empty hash with zero key/value pairs, up to whatever fills up your memory.

Some implementations of hashes (such as in the original *awk* language, from where Larry borrowed the idea) slow down as the hashes get larger. This is not the case in Perl—it has a good, efficient, scalable algorithm.* So, if a hash has only three key/value pairs, it's quick to "reach into the barrel" and pull out any one of those. If the hash has 3 million key/value pairs, it should be about as quick to pull out any one of those. A big hash is nothing to fear.

Keys are unique, though the values can be duplicated. The values of a hash may be all numbers, strings, undef values, or a mixture,† but the keys are arbitrary, unique strings.

Why Use a Hash?

When you first hear about hashes, especially if you've lived a long and productive life as a programmer using languages that don't have hashes, you may wonder why anyone would want one of these strange beasts. Well, the general idea is that you'll have one set of data "related to" another set of data. For example, here are some hashes you might find in typical applications of Perl:

Given name, family name
> The given name (first name) is the key, and the family name is the value. This requires unique given names; if two people were named randal, this wouldn't work. With this hash, you can look up anyone's given name, and find the corresponding family name. If you use the key tom, you get the value phoenix.

Hostname, IP address
> You may know that each computer on the Internet has a hostname (such as *www.stonehenge.com*) and an IP address number (such as 123.45.67.89) because machines like working with the numbers, but we humans have an easier time remembering the names. The hostnames are unique strings, so they can be used to make this hash. With this hash, you could look up a hostname and find the corresponding IP address.

IP address, hostname
> Or you could go in the opposite direction. We generally think of the IP address as a number, but it's also a unique string, so it's suitable for use as a hash key. In this hash, we can use the IP address to look up the corresponding hostname. This is not the same hash as the previous example: hashes are a one-way street, running from key to value; there's no way to look up a value in a hash and find

---

* Technically, Perl rebuilds the hash table as needed for larger hashes. The term "hashes" comes from the fact that a hash table is used for implementing them.

† Or, in fact, any scalar values, including scalar types other than the ones we'll see in this book.

the corresponding key. So, these two are a pair of hashes, one for storing IP addresses, one for hostnames. It's easy enough to create one of these given the other, though, as we'll see below.

Word, count of number of times that word appears

This is a common use of a hash. It's so common, in fact, that it just might turn up in the exercises at the end of the chapter.

The idea here is that you want to know how often each word appears in a given document. Perhaps you're building an index to a number of documents, so when a user searches for fred, you'll know that a certain document mentions fred five times, another mentions fred seven times, and another doesn't mention fred at all. The index shows which documents the user is likely to want. As the index-making program reads through a given document, each time it sees a mention of fred, it adds one to the value filed under the key of fred. That is, if we had seen fred twice already in this document, the value would be 2, but now we'll increment it to 3. If we had never seen fred before, we'd change the value from undef (the implicit, default value) to 1.

Username, number of disk blocks they are using [wasting]

System administrators like this one. The usernames on a given system are unique strings, so they can be used as keys in a hash to look up information about that user.

Driver's license number, name

There may be many people named John Smith, but we hope each one has a different driver's license number. That number makes for a unique key, and the person's name is the value.

Another way to think of a hash is as a simple database, in which one piece of data may be filed under each key. If your task description includes phrases like "finding duplicates," "unique," "cross-reference," or "lookup table," it's likely that a hash will be useful in the implementation.

Hash Element Access

To access an element of a hash, use syntax that looks like this:

```
$hash{$some_key}
```

This is similar to what we used for array access, but here we use curly braces instead of square brackets around the subscript (key).* That key expression is now a string, rather than a number:

```
$family_name{"fred"} = "flintstone";
$family_name{"barney"} = "rubble";
```

---

* Here's a peek into the mind of Larry Wall: Larry says that we use curly braces instead of square brackets because we're doing something fancier than ordinary array access, so we should use fancier punctuation.

Figure 6-3 shows how the resulting hash keys are assigned.

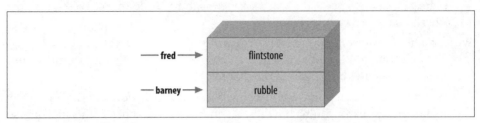

Figure 6-3. Assigned hash keys

This lets us use code like this:

```
foreach $person (qw< barney fred >) {
  print "I've heard of $person $family_name{$person}.\n";
}
```

The name of the hash is like any other Perl identifier (letters, digits, and underscores, but it can't start with a digit). And it's from a separate namespace; that is, there's no connection between the hash element $family_name{"fred"} and a subroutine &family_name, for example. Of course, there's no reason to confuse everyone by giving everything the same name. But Perl won't mind if you have a scalar called $family_name and array elements like $family_name[5]. We humans will have to do as Perl does; we'll have to look to see what punctuation appears before and after the identifier to see what it means. When there is a dollar sign in front of the name and curly braces afterward, it's a hash element that's being accessed.

When choosing the name of a hash, it's often nice to think of the word "for" between the name of the hash and the key. As in, "the family_name for fred is flintstone." So, the hash is named family_name, and the relationship between the keys and their values becomes clear.

The hash key may be any expression and not just the literal strings and scalar variables that we're showing here:

```
$foo = "bar";
print $family_name{ $foo . "ney" };  # prints "rubble"
```

When you store something into an existing hash element, it overwrites the previous value:

```
$family_name{"fred"} = "astaire";  # gives new value to existing element
$bedrock = $family_name{"fred"};   # gets "astaire"; old value is lost
```

That's analogous to what happens with arrays and scalars; if you store something new into $pebbles[17] or $dino, the old value is replaced. If you store something new into $family_name{"fred"}, the old value is replaced as well.

Hash elements spring into existence by assignment:

```
$family_name{"wilma"} = "flintstone";              # adds a new key (and value)
$family_name{"betty"} .= $family_name{"barney"};  # creates the element if needed
```

That's like what happens with arrays and scalars; if you didn't have $pebbles[17] or $dino before, you will have it after you assign to it. If you didn't have $family_name{"betty"} before, you do now.

Accessing outside the hash gives undef:

```
$granite = $family_name{"larry"};   # No larry here: undef
```

This is like what happens with arrays and scalars; if there's nothing yet stored in $pebbles[17] or $dino, accessing them will yield undef. If there's nothing yet stored in $family_name{"larry"}, accessing it will yield undef.

The Hash as a Whole

To refer to the entire hash, use the percent sign ("%") as a prefix. The hash we've been using for the last few pages is actually called %family_name.

For convenience, a hash may be converted into a list and back again. Assigning to a hash (in this case, the one from Figure 6-1) is a list-context assignment, where the list is made of key/value pairs:*

```
%some_hash = ("foo", 35, "bar", 12.4, 2.5, "hello",
      "wilma", 1.72e30, "betty", "bye\n");
```

The value of the hash (in a list context) is a list of key/value pairs:

```
@any_array = %some_hash;
```

We call this *unwinding* the hash—turning it back into a list of key/value pairs. The pairs won't necessarily be in the same order as the original list:

```
print "@any_array\n";
  # might give something like this:
  # betty bye (and a newline) wilma 1.72e+30 foo 35 2.5 hello bar 12.4
```

The order is jumbled because Perl keeps the key/value pairs in an order that's convenient for Perl so it can look up any item quickly. You use a hash when you don't care what order the items are in or when you have an easy way to put them into the order you want.

Though the order of the key/value pairs is jumbled, each key "sticks" with its corresponding value in the resulting list. So, though we don't know where the key foo will appear in the list, we know that its value, 35, will be right after it.

Hash Assignment

It's rare to do so, but a hash may be copied using this syntax:

```
%new_hash = %old_hash;
```

---

* Though any list expression may be used, it must have an even number of elements because the hash is made of key/value *pairs*. An odd element will likely do something unreliable, though it's a warnable offense.

This is more work for Perl than meets the eye. Unlike what happens in languages like Pascal or C, where such an operation would copy a block of memory, Perl's data structures are more complex. So, that line of code tells Perl to unwind the %old_hash into a list of key/value pairs and assign those to %new_hash, building it up one key/value pair at a time.

Transforming the hash in some way is more common. For example, we could make an inverse hash:

```
%inverse_hash = reverse %any_hash;
```

This takes %any_hash and unwinds it into a list of key/value pairs, making a list like (*key*, *value*, *key*, *value*, *key*, *value*,...). Then, reverse turns that list end-for-end, making a list like (*value*, *key*, *value*, *key*, *value*, *key*,...). The keys are where the values used to be, and the values are where the keys used to be. When that's stored into %inverse_hash, we'll be able to look up a string that was a value in %any_hash, because it's now a key of %inverse_hash. And the value we'll find is one that was one of the keys from %any_hash. This gives us a way to look up a "value" (now a key), and find a "key" (now a value).

You might guess (or determine from scientific principles if you're clever) that this will work properly only if the values in the original hash are unique; otherwise, we'd have duplicate keys in the new hash, and keys are always unique. Here's the rule that Perl uses: the last one in wins. That is, the later items in the list overwrite any earlier ones. We don't know what order the key/value pairs will have in this list, so there's no telling which ones will win. You'd use this technique only if you know there are no duplicates among the original values.* But that's the case for the IP address and hostname examples given earlier:

```
%ip_address = reverse %host_name;
```

We can look up a hostname or IP address with equal ease to find the corresponding IP address or hostname.

The Big Arrow

When assigning a list to a hash, sometimes it's not obvious which elements are keys and which are values. For example, in this assignment (which we saw earlier), we have to count through the list, saying, "key, value, key, value..." to determine whether 2.5 is a key or a value:

```
%some_hash = ("foo", 35, "bar", 12.4, 2.5, "hello",
    "wilma", 1.72e30, "betty", "bye\n");
```

---

* Or if you don't care that there are duplicates. For example, we could invert the %family_name hash (in which the keys are people's given names and values are their family names) to make it easy to determine if anyone has a given family name in the group. Thus, in the inverted hash, if there's no key of slate, we'll know that there's no one with that name in the original hash.

Wouldn't it be nice if Perl gave us a way to pair up keys and values in that kind of a list so we could easily see see which ones were which? Larry thought so, too, which is why he invented the big arrow, (=>).* To Perl, it's just a different way to "spell" a comma, so it's also sometimes called the "fat comma." In the Perl grammar, any time that you need a comma (,), you can use the big arrow instead; it's all the same to Perl.† Here's another way to set up the hash of last names:

```
my %last_name = (   # a hash may be a lexical variable
    "fred"   => "flintstone",
    "dino"   => undef,
    "barney" => "rubble",
    "betty"  => "rubble",
);
```

Here, it's easy (or perhaps at least easier) to see whose name pairs with which value even if we end up putting many pairs on one line. And notice the extra comma at the end of the list. As we saw earlier, this is harmless but convenient; if we need to add additional people to this hash, we'll simply make sure that each line has a key/value pair and a trailing comma. Perl will see that there is a comma between each item and the next, and one extra (harmless) comma at the end of the list.

Hash Functions

Some useful functions can work on an entire hash simultaneously.

The keys and values Functions

The keys function yields a list of all the keys in a hash, and the values function gives the corresponding values. If there are no elements to the hash, then either function returns an empty list:

```
my %hash = ("a" => 1, "b" => 2, "c" => 3);
my @k = keys %hash;
my @v = values %hash;
```

So, @k will contain "a", "b", and "c", and @v will contain 1, 2, and 3 in some order. Remember, Perl doesn't maintain the order of elements in a hash. But, whatever order the keys are in, the values will be in the corresponding order: if "b" is last in the keys, 2 will be last in the values; if "c" is the first key, 3 will be the first value. That's true as long as you don't modify the hash between the request for the keys and the

---

* Yes, there's also a *little* arrow, (->). It's used with references, which are an advanced topic. See the `perlreftut` and `perlref` manpage when you're ready for that.

† Well, there's one technical difference: any bareword (a sequence of nothing but letters, digits, and underscores not starting with a digit but optionally prefixed with plus or minus) to the left of the big arrow is implicitly quoted. So you can omit the quote marks on a bareword to the left of the big arrow. You may also omit the quote marks if there's nothing but a bareword as a key inside the curly braces of a hash.

one for the values. If you add elements to the hash, Perl reserves the right to rearrange it as needed to keep the access quick.* In a scalar context, these functions give the number of elements (key/value pairs) in the hash. They do this efficiently without having to visit each element of the hash:

```
my $count = keys %hash;  # gets 3, meaning three key/value pairs
```

Once in a while, you'll see that someone has used a hash as a Boolean (true/false) expression like this:

```
if (%hash) {
  print "That was a true value!\n";
}
```

That will be true if (and only if) the hash has at least one key/value pair.† So, it's saying, "if the hash is not empty…." This is a rare construct, as such things go.

The each Function

If you wish to iterate over (that is, examine every element of) an entire hash, one of the usual ways is to use the each function, which returns a key/value pair as a two-element list.‡ On each evaluation of this function for the same hash, the next successive key/value pair is returned, until all the elements have been accessed. When there are no more pairs, each returns an empty list.

In practice, the only way to use each is in a while loop like this:

```
while ( ($key, $value) = each %hash ) {
  print "$key => $value\n";
}
```

There's a lot going on here. First, each %hash returns a key/value pair from the hash, as a two-element list; let's say that the key is "c" and the value is 3, so the list is ("c", 3). That list is assigned to the list ($key, $value), so $key becomes "c" and $value becomes 3.

But that list assignment is happening in the conditional expression of the while loop, which is a scalar context. (Specifically, it's a Boolean context looking for a true/false value, and a Boolean context is a particular kind of scalar context.) The value of a list assignment in a scalar context is the number of elements in the source list, 2, in this case. Since 2 is a true value, we enter the body of the loop and print the message c => 3.

---

* If you started adding elements to the hash between keys and values, your list of values (or keys, whichever you did second) would have additional items, which would be tough to match up with the first list. No normal programmer would do that.

† The result is an internal debugging string useful to the people who maintain Perl. It looks something like "4/16," but the value is guaranteed to be true when the hash is non-empty and false when it's empty, so the rest of us can still use it for that.

‡ Another way to iterate over an entire hash is to use foreach on a list of keys from the hash; we'll see that by the end of this section.

The next time through the loop, each %hash gives a new key/value pair. Say it's ("a", 1) this time. (It knows to return a different pair than previously because it keeps track of where it is; in technical jargon, there's an iterator stored in with each hash.*) Those two items are stored into ($key, $value). Since the number of elements in the source list was again 2, a true value, the while condition is true, and the loop body runs again, telling us a => 1.

We go one more time through the loop, and by now we know what to expect, so it's no surprise to see b => 2 appear in the output.

But we knew it couldn't go on forever. The next time Perl evaluates each %hash, no more key/value pairs are available, so each has to return an empty list.† The empty list is assigned to ($key, $value), so $key gets undef, and $value also gets undef.

But that hardly matters because the whole thing is being evaluated in the conditional expression of the while loop. The value of a list assignment in a scalar context is the number of elements in the source list; in this case, that's 0. Since 0 is a false value, the while loop is done, and execution continues with the rest of the program.

Of course, each returns the key/value pairs in a jumbled order. (It's the same order as keys and values would give, which is the "natural" order of the hash.) If you need to go through the hash in order, sort the keys, perhaps something like this:

```
foreach $key (sort keys %hash) {
  $value = $hash{$key};
  print "$key => $value\n";
  # Or, we could have avoided the extra $value variable:
  #  print "$key => $hash{$key}\n";
}
```

We'll see more about sorting hashes in Chapter 13.

Typical Use of a Hash

At this point, a concrete example might help.

The Bedrock library uses a Perl program in which a hash tracks how many books each person has checked out:

```
$books{"fred"} = 3;
$books{"wilma"} = 1;
```

---

* Since each hash has its own private iterator, loops using each may be nested as long as they are iterating over different hashes. As long as we're in a footnote, we may as well tell you that you may reset the iterator of a hash by using the keys or values function on the hash. The iterator is also automatically reset if a new list is stored into the entire hash or if each has iterated through all of the items to the "end" of the hash. On the other hand, adding new key/value pairs to the hash while iterating over it is generally a bad idea since that won't necessarily reset the iterator. That's likely to confuse you, your maintenance programmer, and each as well.

† It's being used in list context, so it can't return undef to signal failure; that would be the one-element list (undef) instead of the empty (zero-element) list ( ).

It's easy to see if an element of the hash is true or false; do this:

```
if ($books{$someone}) {
  print "$someone has at least one book checked out.\n";
}
```

But there are some elements of the hash that are false:

```
$books{"barney"} = 0;      # no books currently checked out
$books{"pebbles"} = undef; # no books EVER checked out - a new library card
```

Since Pebbles has never checked out any books, her entry has the value of undef, rather than 0.

There's a key in the hash for everyone who has a library card. For each key (or library patron), the value is the number of books checked out or undef if that person's library card has never been used.

The exists Function

To see if a key exists in the hash, (whether someone has a library card), use the exists function, which returns a true value if the given key exists in the hash, whether the corresponding value is true or false:

```
if (exists $books{"dino"}) {
  print "Hey, there's a library card for dino!\n";
}
```

That is to say, exists $books{"dino"} will return a true value if (and only if) dino is found in the list of keys from keys %books.

The delete Function

The delete function removes the given key (and its corresponding value) from the hash. (If there's no such key, its work is done; there's no warning or error in that case.)

```
my $person = "betty";
delete $books{$person};  # Revoke the library card for $person
```

This is not the same as storing undef into that hash element. Checking exists($books{"betty"}) will give opposite results in these two cases. After a delete, the key can't exist in the hash; after storing undef, the key *must* exist.

In the example, delete versus storing undef is the difference between taking away Betty's library card versus giving her a card that has never been used.

Hash Element Interpolation

You can interpolate a single hash element into a double-quoted string:

```
foreach $person (sort keys %books) {           # each patron, in order
  if ($books{$person}) {
```

```
    print "$person has $books{$person} items\n";   # fred has 3 items
  }
}
```

But there's no support for entire hash interpolation; "%books" is nothing more than the literal six characters of %books.* You've seen all of the magical characters that need backslashing in double quotes $ and @ introduce a variable that Perl will try to interpolate, ", since that's the quoting character that would otherwise end the double-quoted string and \, the backslash. Any other characters in a double-quoted string are nonmagical and should stand for themselves.†

Exercises

See Appendix A for answers to the following exercises:

1. [7] Write a program that will ask the user for a given name and report the corresponding family name. Use the names of people you know, or (if you spend so much time on the computer that you don't know any people) use Table 6-1.

Table 6-1. Sample data

Input	Output
fred	flintstone
barney	rubble
wilma	flintstone

2. [15] Write a program that reads a series of words (with one word per line)‡ until end-of-input, then print a summary of how many times each word was seen. (Hint: remember that when an undefined value is used as if it were a number, Perl automatically converts it to 0. It may help to look back at the earlier exercise that kept a running total.) If the input words were fred, barney, fred, dino, wilma, fred (all on separate lines), the output should tell us that fred was seen 3 times. For extra credit, sort the summary words in ASCII order in the output.

---

* Well, it couldn't be anything else. If we tried to print out the entire hash as a series of key/value pairs, that would be nearly useless. And, as you saw in the last chapter, the percent sign is frequently used in printf format strings. Giving it another meaning here would be terribly inconvenient.

† Beware of the apostrophe ('), left square bracket ([), left curly brace ({), the small arrow (->), or double-colon (::) following a variable name in a double-quoted string, as they could perhaps mean something you didn't intend.

‡ It has to be one word per line because we still haven't shown you how to extract individual words from a line of input.

## CHAPTER 7

In the World of Regular Expressions

Perl has many features that set it apart from other languages. Of all those features, one of the most important is its strong support for regular expressions. These allow fast, flexible, and reliable string handling.

But that power comes at a price. Regular expressions are tiny programs in their own special language, built inside Perl. (Yes, you're about to learn another programming language.* Fortunately, it's a simple one.) In this chapter, you'll visit the world of regular expressions, where (mostly) you can forget about the world of Perl. In the next chapter, we'll show you where this world fits into Perl's world.

Regular expressions aren't merely part of Perl; they're also found in *sed* and *awk*, *procmail*, *grep*, most programmers' text editors like *vi* and *emacs*, and in more esoteric places. If you've seen some of these, you're ahead of the game. Keep watching, and you'll see many more tools that use or support regular expressions, such as search engines on the Web (often written in Perl), email clients, and others. The bad news is that everybody's regular expressions have slightly different syntax, so you may need to learn to include or omit an occasional backslash.

What Are Regular Expressions?

A *regular expression*, often called a *pattern* in Perl, is a template that matches or doesn't match a given string.† An infinite number of possible text strings exist, and a given pattern divides that infinite set into two groups: the ones that match and the ones that don't. There's never any kinda-sorta-almost-up-to-here wishy-washy matching: either it matches or it doesn't.

---

* Some might argue that regular expressions are not a complete programming language. We won't argue.

† Purists would ask for a more rigorous definition. But then again, purists say that Perl's patterns aren't really regular expressions. If you're serious about regular expressions, we recommend the book *Mastering Regular Expressions* by Jeffrey Friedl (O'Reilly).

A pattern may match one possible string, two or three, a dozen, a hundred, or an infinite number. It may match all strings except for one, except for some, or except for an infinite number.* We've referred to regular expressions as being little programs in their own simple programming language. It's a simple language because the programs have one task: to look at a string and say "it matches" or "it doesn't match".† That's all they do.

One of the places you're likely to have seen regular expressions is in the Unix grep command, which prints out text lines matching a given pattern. For example, if you wanted to see which lines in a given file mention flint and, somewhere later on the same line, stone, you might do something like this with the Unix grep command:

```
$ grep 'flint.*stone' chapter*.txt
chapter3.txt:a piece of flint, a stone which may be used to start a fire by striking
chapter3.txt:found obsidian, flint, granite, and small stones of basaltic rock, which
chapter9.txt:a flintlock rifle in poor condition. The sandstone mantle held several
```

Don't confuse regular expressions with shell filename-matching patterns, called *globs*. A typical glob is what you use when you type *.pm to the Unix shell to match all filenames that end in .pm. The previous example uses a glob of chapter*.txt. (You may have noticed that you had to quote the pattern to prevent the shell from treating it like a glob.) Though globs use many of the same characters you use in regular expressions, those characters are used in different ways.‡ You'll visit globs in Chapter 12.

Using Simple Patterns

To match a pattern (regular expression) against the contents of $_, put the pattern between a pair of forward slashes (/) as we do here:

```
$_ = "yabba dabba doo";
if (/abba/) {
  print "It matched!\n";
}
```

The expression /abba/ looks for that four-letter string in $_; if it finds it, it returns a true value. In this case, it's found more than once, but that doesn't make any difference. If it's found at all, it's a match; if it's not in there at all, it fails.

---

* As you'll see, you could have a pattern that always matches or that never does. In rare cases, even these may be useful, but generally they're mistakes.

† The programs also pass back some information that Perl can use later. One such piece of information is the "regular expressions memories" that you'll learn about a little later.

‡ Globs are also (alas) sometimes called patterns. What's worse is that some bad Unix books for beginners (and possibly written by beginners) have taken to calling globs "regular expressions," which they certainly are not. This confuses many folks at the start of their work with Unix.

Because the pattern match is generally being used to return a true or false value, it is almost always found in the conditional expression of if or while.

All of the usual backslash escapes that you can put into double-quoted strings are available in patterns, so you could use the pattern /coke\tsprite/ to match the eleven characters of coke, a tab, and sprite.

About Metacharacters

If patterns matched only literal strings, they wouldn't be very useful. That's why a number of special characters, called *metacharacters*, have special meanings in regular expressions.

For example, the dot (.) is a wildcard character—it matches any single character except a newline (which is represented by "\n"). So, the pattern /bet.y/ would match betty. It would also match betsy, bet=y, bet.y, or any other string that has bet, followed by any one character (except a newline), followed by y. It wouldn't match bety or betsey since those don't have one character between the t and the y. The dot always matches exactly one character.

If you wanted to match a period in the string, you could use the dot. But that would match any possible character (except a newline), which might be more than you wanted. If you want the dot to match a period, you can backslash it. That rule goes for all of Perl's regular expression metacharacters: a backslash in front of any metacharacter makes it nonspecial. So, the pattern /3\.14159/ doesn't have a wildcard character.

The backslash is our second metacharacter. If you mean a real backslash, use a pair of them—a rule that applies everywhere else in Perl.

Simple Quantifiers

It often happens that you'll need to repeat something in a pattern. The star (*) means to match the preceding item zero or more times. So, /fred\t*barney/ matches any number of tab characters between fred and barney. It matches "fred\tbarney" with one tab, "fred\t\tbarney" with two tabs, "fred\t\t\tbarney" with three tabs, or "fredbarney" with nothing in between at all. That's because the star means "zero or more"—so you could have hundreds of tab characters in between but nothing other than tabs. Think of the star as saying, "That previous thing, any number of times, even zero times" (because * is the "times" operator in multiplication).

What if you wanted to allow something besides tab characters? The dot matches any character,* so .* will match any character, any number of times. That means that the /fred.*barney/ pattern matches "any old junk" between fred and barney. Any line that mentions fred and (somewhere later) barney will match that pattern. We often call .* the "any old junk" pattern because it can match any old junk in your strings.

The star is formally called a *quantifier*, meaning that it specifies a quantity of the preceding item. It's not the only quantifier; the plus (+) is another. The plus means to match the preceding item one or more times: /fred +barney/ matches if fred and barney are separated by spaces and only spaces. (The space is not a metacharacter.) This won't match fredbarney since the plus means there must be one or more spaces between the two names, so at least one space is required. Think of the plus as saying, "That last thing, *plus* (optionally) more of the same thing."

There's a third quantifier like the star and plus, which is more limited. It's the question mark (?), which means that the preceding item is optional in that it may occur once or not at all. Like the other two quantifiers, the question mark means that the preceding item appears a certain number of times. In this case, the item may match one time (if it's there) or zero times (if it's not). There aren't any other possibilities. So, /bamm-?bamm/ matches either spelling: bamm-bamm or bammbamm. This is easy to remember since it's saying, "That last thing, maybe? Or maybe not?"

All three of these quantifiers must follow something since they tell how many times the previous item may repeat.

Grouping in Patterns

Parentheses are also metacharacters. As in mathematics, parentheses (( )) may be used for grouping. As an example, the pattern /fred+/ matches strings like freddddddddd, but strings like that don't show up often in real life. But the pattern /(fred)+/ matches strings like fredfredfred, which is more likely to be what you wanted. What about the pattern /(fred)*/? That matches strings like hello, world.†

Alternatives

The vertical bar (|), often pronounced "or" in this usage, means that the left or right side may match. That is, if the part of the pattern on the left of the bar fails, the part

---

* Except newline. But we're going to stop reminding you of that so often because you know it by now. Most of the time it doesn't matter because your strings will most often not have newlines. Don't forget this detail because someday a newline will sneak into your string and you'll need to remember that the dot doesn't match newline.

† The star means to match zero or more repetitions of fred. When you're willing to settle for zero, it's hard to be disappointed. That pattern will match any string, even the empty string.

on the right gets a chance to match. So, /fred|barney|betty/ will match any string that mentions fred, or barney, or betty.

Now you can make patterns like /fred(|\t)+barney/, which matches if fred and barney are separated by spaces, tabs, or a mixture of the two. The plus means to repeat one or more times; each time it repeats, the (|\t) has the chance to match a space or a tab.[*] There must be at least one of those characters between the two names.

If you wanted the characters between fred and barney to all be the same, you could rewrite that pattern as /fred(+|\t+)barney/. In this case, the separators must be all spaces or all tabs.

The pattern /fred (and|or) barney/ matches any string containing either of the two possible strings: fred and barney, or fred or barney.[†] You could match the same two strings with the pattern /fred and barney|fred or barney/, but that would be too much typing. It would probably also be less efficient, depending upon what optimizations are built into the regular expression engine.

Character Classes

A *character class*, a list of possible characters inside square brackets ([ ]), matches any single character from within the class. It matches one character, but that character may be any of the ones listed.

For example, the character class [abcwxyz] may match any one of those seven characters. For convenience, you may specify a range of characters with a hyphen (-), so that class may also be written as [a-cw-z]. That didn't save much typing, but it's more common to make a character class like [a-zA-Z] to match any one letter out of that set of 52.[‡] You may use the same character shortcuts as in any double-quoted string to define a character, so the class [\000-\177] matches any seven-bit ASCII character.[§] Of course, a character class will be just part of a full pattern and will never stand on its own in Perl. For example, you might see code that says something like this:

```
$_ = "The HAL-9000 requires authorization to continue.";
if (/HAL-[0-9]+/) {
    print "The string mentions some model of HAL computer.\n";
}
```

---

[*] This particular match would normally be done more efficiently with a character class, as you'll see later in this chapter.

[†] The words and and or are not operators in regular expressions! They are shown here in a fixed-width typeface because they're part of the strings.

[‡] Notice that those 52 don't include letters such as Å, É, Î, Ø, and Ü. But when Unicode processing is available, that particular character range is noticed and enhanced to do the right thing automatically.

[§] At least, if you use ASCII and not EBCDIC.

Sometimes, it's easier to specify the omitted characters rather than the ones within the character class. A caret ("^") at the start of the character class negates it. That is, [^def] will match any single character except one of those three. And [^n\-z] matches any character except for n, hyphen, or z. (The hyphen is backslashed because it's special inside a character class. But the first hyphen in /HAL-[0-9]+/ doesn't need a backslash because hyphens aren't special outside a character class.)

Character Class Shortcuts

Some character classes appear so frequently that they have shortcuts. For example, the character class for any digit, [0-9], may be abbreviated as \d. Thus, the pattern from the example about HAL could be written /HAL-\d+/ instead.

The shortcut \w is a so-called "word" character: [A-Za-z0-9_]. If your "words" are made up of ordinary letters, digits, and underscores, you'll be happy with this. The rest of us have words made up of ordinary letters, hyphens, and apostrophes,[*] so we wish we could change this definition of "word".[†] So use this one only when you want ordinary letters, digits, and underscores.

Of course, \w doesn't match a "word" but matches a single "word" character. To match an entire word the plus modifier is handy. A pattern such as /fred \w+ barney/ will match fred and a space, a "word," and then a space and barney. That is, it'll match if there's one word[‡] between fred and barney, set off by single spaces.

As you may have noticed in that previous example, it might be handy to be able to match spaces more flexibly. The \s shortcut is good for whitespace. It's the same as [\f\t\n\r], which is a class containing the five whitespace characters: form-feed, tab, newline, carriage return, and the space character. These characters move the printing position around and don't use any ink. Like the other shortcuts you've seen, \s matches a single character from the class, so it's usual to use either \s* for any amount of whitespace (including none at all), or \s+ for one or more whitespace characters. (In fact, it's rare to see \s without one of those quantifiers.) Since all of those whitespace characters look about the same, you can treat them all in the same way with this shortcut.

---

[*] At least, in usual English you do. In other languages, you may have different components of words. Locales recognize these differences to a limited but useful extent. See the perllocale manpage.

[†] When looking at ASCII-encoded English text, you have the problem that the single quote and the apostrophe are the same character, so it's not possible in isolation to tell whether cats' is a word with an apostrophe or a word at the end of a quotation. This is probably one reason that computers haven't been able to take over the world yet.

[‡] We're going to stop saying "word" in quotes so much; you know by now that these letter-digit-underscore words are the ones we mean.

Negating the Shortcuts

Sometimes you may want the opposite of one of these three shortcuts. That is, you may want [^\d], [^\w], or [^\s], meaning a nondigit character, a nonword character, or a nonwhitespace character. That's easy enough to accomplish by using their uppercase counterparts: \D, \W, or \S. These match any character that their counterpart would not match.

Any of these shortcuts will work in place of a character class (standing on their own in a pattern) or inside the square brackets of a larger character class. That means that you could use /[\dA-Fa-f]+/ to match hexadecimal (base 16) numbers, which use letters ABCDEF (or the same letters in lowercase) as additional digits.

Another compound character class is [\d\D], which means any digit or any non-digit, which means any character at all. This is a common way to match any character, even a newline as opposed to ., which matches any character except a newline. The totally useless [^\d\D] matches anything that's not either a digit or a non-digit. Right—nothing!

Exercises

See Appendix A for answers to the following exercises:

Remember, it's normal to be surprised by some of the things that regular expressions do. That's one reason the exercises in this chapter are more important than the others. Expect the unexpected.

1. [10] Make a program that prints each line of its input that mentions fred. (It shouldn't do anything for other lines of input.) Does it match if your input string is Fred, frederick, or Alfred? Make a small text file with a few lines mentioning "fred flintstone" and his friends. Then use that file as input to this program and the ones later in this section.

2. [6] Modify the previous program to allow Fred to match as well. Does it match now if your input string is Fred, frederick, or Alfred? (Add lines with these names to the text file.)

3. [6] Make a program that prints each line of its input that contains a period (.), ignoring other lines of input. Try it on the small text file from the previous exercise: Does it notice Mr. Slate?

4. [8] Make a program that prints each line with a word that is capitalized but not ALL capitalized. Does it match Fred but neither fred nor FRED?

5. [8] Extra credit exercise: Write a program that prints out any input line that mentions *both* wilma and fred.

## CHAPTER 8

Matching with Regular Expressions

In the previous chapter, you visited the world of regular expressions. Now you'll see how that world fits into the world of Perl.

Matches with m//

We've been writing patterns in pairs of forward slashes, like /fred/. This is a short-cut for the m// (pattern match) operator. As you saw with the qw// operator, you may choose any pair of delimiters to quote the contents. So, you could write that same expression as m(fred), m<fred>, m{fred}, or m[fred] using those paired delimiters, or as m,fred,, m!fred!, m^fred^, or many other ways using nonpaired delimiters. *

The shortcut is that if you choose the forward slash as the delimiter, you may omit the initial m. Since Perl folks love to avoid typing extra characters, you'll see most pattern matches written using slashes, as in /fred/.

Choose a delimiter that doesn't appear in your pattern.† If you wanted to make a pattern to match the beginning of an ordinary web URL, you might write /http:\/\// to match the initial "http://". But that'll be easier to read, write, maintain, and debug if you use a better choice of delimiter: m%http://%.‡ It's common to use curly braces as the delimiter. If you use a programmer's text editor, it probably has the

---

* Nonpaired delimiters are the ones that don't have a different "left" and "right" variety; the same punctuation mark is used for both ends.

† If you're using paired delimiters, generally you shouldn't have to worry about using the delimiter inside the pattern since that delimiter generally will be paired inside your pattern. That is, m(fred(.*)barney) and m{\w{2,}} and m[wilma[\n \t]+betty] are all fine even though the pattern contains the quoting character, since each "left" has a corresponding "right." But the angle brackets (< and >) aren't regular expression metacharacters, so they may not be paired. If the pattern were m{(\d+)\s*>=?\s*(\d+)}, quoting it with angle brackets would mean having to backslash the greater-than sign so that it wouldn't prematurely end the pattern.

‡ Remember, the forward slash is not a metacharacter, so you don't need to escape it when it's not the delimiter.

ability to jump from an opening curly brace to the corresponding closing one, which can be handy in maintaining code.

Option Modifiers

Several option modifier letters, sometimes called *flags*, may be appended as a group right after the ending delimiter of a regular expression to change its behavior from the default.

Case-Insensitive Matching with /i

To make a case-insensitive pattern match, so you can match FRED as easily as fred or Fred, use the /i modifier:

```
print "Would you like to play a game? ";
chomp($_ = <STDIN>);
if (/yes/i) {  # case-insensitive match
  print "In that case, I recommend that you go bowling.\n";
}
```

Matching Any Character with /s

By default, the dot (.) doesn't match newline, and this makes sense for most "look within a single line" patterns. If you have newlines in your strings and want the dot to be able to match them, the /s modifier will do the job. It changes every dot* in the pattern to act as the character class [\d\D] does, which is to match any character, even if it is a newline. You have to have a string with newlines for this to make a difference:

```
$_ = "I saw Barney\ndown at the bowling alley\nwith Fred\nlast night.\n";
if (/Barney.*Fred/s) {
  print "That string mentions Fred after Barney!\n";
}
```

Without the /s modifier, that match would fail since the two names aren't on the same line.

Adding Whitespace with /x

The /x modifier allows you to add arbitrary whitespace to a pattern to make it easier to read.

```
/-?\d+\.?\d*/          # what is this doing?
/ -? \d+ \.? \d* /x    # a little better
```

---

* If you wish to change some of them, but not all, you'll probably want to replace those few with [\d\D].

Since /x allows whitespace inside the pattern, a literal space or tab character within the pattern is ignored. You could use a backslashed space or \t (among many other ways) to match these, but using \s (or \s* or \s+) is more common when you want to match whitespace anyway.

In Perl, comments may be included as part of the whitespace, so with /x, we can put comments into that pattern to tell what it's doing:

```
/
   -?       # an optional minus sign
   \d+      # one or more digits before the decimal point
   \.?      # an optional decimal point
   \d*      # some optional digits after the decimal point
/x           # end of pattern
```

Since the pound sign indicates the start of a comment, use \# or [#] in the rare case that you need to match a pound sign. And be careful not to include the closing delimiter inside the comments, or that will prematurely terminate the pattern.

Combining Option Modifiers

If you have more than one option modifier to use on the same pattern, they may be used one after the other. Their order isn't significant:

```
if (/barney.*fred/is) {  # both /i and /s
  print "That string mentions Fred after Barney!\n";
}
```

For a more expanded version with comments:

```
if (m{
  barney # the little guy
  .*       # anything in between
  fred    # the loud guy
}six) {  # all three of /s and /i and /x
  print "That string mentions Fred after Barney!\n";
}
```

Note the shift to curly braces here for the delimiters as well, allowing programmer-style editors to easily bounce from the beginning to the ending of the regular expression.

Other Options

Many other option modifiers are available. We'll cover those as we get to them, or you can read about them in the perlop manpage and in the descriptions of m// and the other regular expression operators that you'll see later in this chapter.

Anchors

By default, if a pattern doesn't match at the start of the string, it can "float" on down the string trying to match somewhere else. But a number of anchors may be used to hold the pattern at a particular point in a string.

The caret* anchor (^) marks the beginning of the string, and the dollar sign ($) marks the end.† So, the pattern /^fred/ will match fred only at the start of the string; it wouldn't match manfred mann. And /rock$/ will match rock only at the end of the string; it wouldn't match knute rockne.

Sometimes, you'll want to use both of these anchors to ensure that the pattern matches an entire string. A common example is /^\s*$/, which matches a blank line. But this "blank" line may include some whitespace characters, like tabs and spaces, which are invisible. Any line that matches this pattern looks like any other one on paper, so this pattern treats all blank lines equally. Without the anchors, it would match nonblank lines as well.

Word Anchors

Anchors aren't just at the ends of the string. The word-boundary anchor, \b, matches at either end of a word.‡ So you can use /\bfred\b/ to match the word fred but not frederick, alfred, or manfred mann. This is similar to the feature often called "match whole words only" in a word processor's search command.

Alas, these aren't words as you and I are likely to think of them; they're those \w-type words made up of ordinary letters, digits, and underscores. The \b anchor matches at the start or end of a group of \w characters.

In Figure 8-1, a gray underline is under each "word," and the arrows show the corresponding places where \b could match. There are always an even number of word boundaries in a given string since there's an end-of-word for every start-of-word.

The "words" are sequences of letters, digits, and underscores. A word in this sense is what's matched by /\w+/. There are five words in that sentence: That, s, a, word, and

---

* Yes, you've seen the caret used in another way in patterns. As the first character of a character class, it negates the class. But outside of a character class, it's a metacharacter in a different way, being the start-of-string anchor. There are only so many characters, so you have to use some of them twice.

† Actually, it matches either the end of the string or at a newline at the end of the string. That's so you can match the end of the string whether it has a trailing newline or not. Most folks don't worry about this distinction much, but once in a while it's important to remember that /^fred$/ will match "fred" or "fred\n" with equal ease.

‡ Some regular expression implementations have one anchor for start-of-word and another for end-of-word, but Perl uses \b for both.

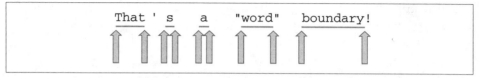

Figure 8-1. Word-boundary matches with \b

boundary.* The quote marks around word don't change the word boundaries; these words are made of \w characters.

Each arrow points to the beginning or the end of one of the gray underlines since the word-boundary anchor \b matches only at the beginning or the end of a group of word characters.

The word-boundary anchor is useful to ensure we don't accidentally find cat in delicatessen, dog in boondoggle, or fish in selfishness. Sometimes, you'll want one word-boundary anchor, as when using /\bhunt/ to match words like hunt or hunting or hunter, but not shunt, or when using /stone\b/ to match words like sandstone or flintstone but not capstones.

The nonword-boundary anchor is \B; it matches at any point where \b would not match. So, the pattern /\bsearch\B/ will match searches, searching, and searched but not search or researching.

The Binding Operator, =~

Matching against $_ is merely the default; the *binding operator* (=~) tells Perl to match the pattern on the right against the string on the left, instead of matching against $_.[†] For example:

```
my $some_other = "I dream of betty rubble.";
if ($some_other =~ /\brub/) {
  print "Aye, there's the rub.\n";
}
```

The first time you see it, the binding operator looks like some kind of assignment operator, but it's not. It is saying, "This pattern match that would attach to $_ by default—make it work with this string on the left instead." If there's no binding operator, the expression is using $_ by default.

In the (somewhat unusual) example below, $likes_perl is set to a Boolean value according to what the user typed at the prompt. This is a little on the quick-and-dirty side because the line of input itself is discarded. This code reads the line of input,

---

* You can see why we wish we could change the definition of "word"; That's should be one word, not two words with an apostrophe in between. Even in text that may be mostly ordinary English, it's normal to find a soupçon of other characters spicing things up.

† The binding operator is used with some other operations besides the pattern match, as you'll see later.

tests that string against the pattern, and discards the line of input.* It doesn't use or change $_ at all.

```
print "Do you like Perl? ";
my $likes_perl = (<STDIN> =~ /\byes\b/i);
... # Time passes...
if ($likes_perl) {
  print "You said earlier that you like Perl, so...\n";
  ...
}
```

Because the binding operator has fairly high precedence, the parentheses around the pattern-test expression aren't required, so the following line does the same thing as the one above—it stores the result of the test (and not the line of input) into the variable:

```
my $likes_perl = <STDIN> =~ /\byes\b/i;
```

Interpolating into Patterns

The regular expression is double-quote interpolated as if it were a double-quoted string. This allows us to write a quick *grep*-like program like this:

```
#!/usr/bin/perl -w
my $what = "larry";

while (<>) {
  if (/^($what)/) {  # pattern is anchored at beginning of string
    print "We saw $what in beginning of $_";
  }
}
```

The pattern will be built up out of whatever's in $what when we run the pattern match. In this case, it's the same as if we had written /^(larry)/, looking for larry at the start of each line.

We didn't have to get the value of $what from a literal string and could have gotten it from the command-line arguments in @ARGV:

```
my $what = shift @ARGV;
```

If the first command-line argument is fred|barney, the pattern becomes /^(fred|barney)/, looking for fred or barney at the start of each line.† The parentheses (which weren't necessary when searching for larry) have become important because without them we'd be matching fred at the start or barney anywhere in the string.

---

* The line of input is not automatically stored into $_ unless the line-input operator (<STDIN>) is alone in the conditional expression of a while loop.

† The astute reader will know that you can't generally type fred|barney as an argument at the command line because the vertical bar is a shell metacharacter. See the documentation to your shell to learn about how to quote command-line arguments.

With that line changed to get the pattern from @ARGV, this program resembles the Unix grep command. But we have to watch out for metacharacters in the string. If $what contains 'fred(barney', the pattern will look like /^(fred(barney)/. You know that can't work—it'll crash your program with an invalid regular expression error. With some advanced techniques,* you can trap this kind of error (or prevent the magic of the metacharacters in the first place) so it won't crash your program. But for now, just know that if you give your users the power of regular expressions, they'll need the responsibility to use them correctly.

The Match Variables

So far, when we've put parentheses into patterns, they've been used only for their ability to group parts of a pattern together. But parentheses also trigger the regular expression engine's memory. The memory holds the part of the string matched by the part of the pattern inside parentheses. If there are more than one pair of parentheses, there will be more than one memory. Each regular expression memory holds part of the original *string*, not part of the pattern.

Since these variables hold strings, they are scalar variables; in Perl, they have names like $1 and $2. There are as many of these variables as there are pairs of memory parentheses in the pattern. As you'd expect, $4 means the string matched by the fourth set of parentheses. †

These match variables are a big part of the power of regular expressions because they let us pull out the parts of a string:

```
$_ = "Hello there, neighbor";
if (/\s(\w+),/) {                # memorize the word between space and comma
  print "the word was $1\n";     # the word was there
}
```

Or you could use more than one memory at once:

```
$_ = "Hello there, neighbor";
if (/(\S+) (\S+), (\S+)/) {
  print "words were $1 $2 $3\n";
}
```

That tells us that the words were Hello there neighbor. Notice that there's no comma in the output. Because the comma is outside of the memory parentheses in

---

* In this case, you would use an eval block to trap the error, or you would quote the interpolated text using quotemeta (or its \Q equivalent form) so it's no longer treated as a regular expression.

† This is the same string that the backreference \4 would refer to during the pattern match. But these aren't two different names for the same thing; \4 refers back to the memory during the pattern while it is trying to match, and $4 refers to the memory of a completed pattern match. For more information on backreferences, see the perlre manpage.

the pattern, there is no comma in memory two. Using this technique, we can choose what we want in the memories, as well as what we want to leave out.

You could have an empty match variable[*] if that part of the pattern might be empty. That is, a match variable may contain the empty string:

```
my $dino = "I fear that I'll be extinct after 1000 years.";
if ($dino =~ /(\d*) years/) {
  print "That said '$1' years.\n";  # 1000
}

$dino = "I fear that I'll be extinct after a few million years.";
if ($dino =~ /(\d*) years/) {
  print "That said '$1' years.\n";  # empty string
}
```

The Persistence of Memory

These match variables generally stay around until the next successful pattern match.[†] That is, an unsuccessful match leaves the previous memories intact, but a successful one resets them all. This correctly implies that you shouldn't use these match variables unless the match succeeded; otherwise, you could be seeing a memory from some previous pattern. The following (bad) example is supposed to print a word matched from $wilma. But if the match fails, it's using whatever leftover string happens to be found in $1:

```
$wilma =~ /(\w+)/;  # BAD! Untested match result
print "Wilma's word was $1... or was it?\n";
```

This is another reason a pattern match is almost always found in the conditional expression of an if or while:

```
if ($wilma =~ /(\w+)/) {
  print "Wilma's word was $1.\n";
} else {
  print "Wilma doesn't have a word.\n";
}
```

Since these memories don't stay around forever, you shouldn't use a match variable like $1 more than a few lines after its pattern match. If your maintenance programmer adds a new regular expression between your regular expression and your use of $1, you'll be getting the value of $1 for the second match, rather than the first. For

---

[*] As opposed to an undefined one. If you have three or fewer sets of parentheses in the pattern, $4 will be undef.

[†] The scoping rule is more complex (see the documentation if you need it), but as long as you don't expect the match variables to be untouched many lines after a pattern match, you shouldn't have problems.

this reason, if you need a memory for more than a few lines, copy it into an ordinary variable. Doing this helps make the code more readable at the same time:

```
if ($wilma =~ /(\w+)/) {
  my $wilma_word = $1;
  ...
}
```

Later, in Chapter 9, you'll see how to get the memory value *directly* into the variable at the same time as the pattern match happens, without having to use $1 explicitly.

The Automatic Match Variables

There are three more match variables that you get free,[*] whether the pattern has memory parentheses or not. That's the good news; the bad news is that these variables have weird names.

Larry probably would have been happy enough to call these by slightly less weird names, like perhaps $gazoo or $ozmodiar. But those are names you might want to use in your own code. To keep ordinary Perl programmers from having to memorize the names of all of Perl's special variables before choosing their first variable names in their first programs,[†] Larry has given strange names to many of Perl's built-in variables, names that break the rules. In this case, the names are punctuation marks: $&, $`, and $'. They're strange, ugly, and weird, but those are their names.[‡] The part of the string that matched the pattern is automatically stored in $&:

```
if ("Hello there, neighbor" =~ /\s(\w+),/) {
  print "That actually matched '$&'.\n";
}
```

The part that matched was " there," (with a space, a word, and a comma). Memory one, in $1, has the five-letter word there, but $& has the entire matched section.

Whatever came before the matched section is in $`, and whatever was after it is in $'. Another way to say that is that $` holds whatever the regular expression engine had to skip over before it found the match, and $' has the remainder of the string that the pattern never got to. If you glue these three strings together in order, you'll always get back the original string:

```
if ("Hello there, neighbor" =~ /\s(\w+),/) {
  print "That was ($`)($&)($').\n";
}
```

---

[*] Yeah, right. There's no such thing as a free match. These are "free" only in the sense that they don't require match parentheses. Don't worry; we'll mention their real cost a little later.

[†] You should still avoid a few classical variable names like $ARGV, but these few are in all-caps. All of Perl's built-in variables are documented in the perlvar manpage.

[‡] If you can't stand these names, check out the English module, which attempts to give all of Perl's strangest variables nearly normal names. But the use of this module has never really caught on; instead, Perl programmers have grown to love the punctuation-mark variable names, strange as they are.

The message shows the string as (Hello)(there,)(neighbor), showing the three automatic match variables in action. Any or all of these three automatic match variables may be empty like the numbered match variables. And they have the same scope as the numbered match variables. Generally, that means they'll stay around until the next successful pattern match.

Now, we said earlier that these three are "free." Well, freedom has its price. In this case, the price is that once you use any one of these automatic match variables anywhere in your entire program, other regular expressions will run a little more slowly*. Now, this isn't a giant slowdown, but it's enough of a worry that many Perl programmers will never use these automatic match variables.† Instead, they'll use a workaround. For example, if the only one you need is $&, put parentheses around the whole pattern and use $1 instead. (You may need to renumber the pattern's memories.)

Match variables (the automatic ones and the numbered ones) are most often used in substitutions, which you'll see in the next chapter.

General Quantifiers

A *quantifier* in a pattern means to repeat the preceding item a certain number of times. You've seen three quantifiers: *, +, and ?. But if none of those three suits your needs, use a comma-separated pair of numbers inside curly braces ({ }) to specify how few and how many repetitions are allowed.

The pattern /a{5,15}/ will match from five to fifteen repetitions of the letter a. If the a appears three times, that's too few, so it won't match. If it appears five times, it's a match. If it appears ten times, that's still a match. If it appears twenty times, the first fifteen will match since that's the upper limit.

If you omit the second number (but include the comma), there's no upper limit to the number of times the item will match. So, /(fred){3,}/ will match if there are three or more instances of fred in a row (with no extra characters, like spaces, allowed between each fred and the next). There's no upper limit, so that would match 88 instances of fred, if you had a string with that many.

If you omit the comma as well as the upper bound, the number given is an exact count: /\w{8}/ will match exactly eight word characters (occurring as part of a larger

---

* For every block entry and exit, which is practically everywhere

† Most of these folks haven't benchmarked their programs to see if their workarounds save time; it's as though these variables were poisonous or something. But we can't blame them for not benchmarking; many programs that could benefit from these three variables take up only a few minutes of CPU time in a week, so benchmarking and optimizing would be a waste of time. But in that case, why fear a possible extra millisecond? By the way, the Perl developers are working on this problem, but there will probably be no solution before Perl 6.

string, perhaps). And /,{5}chameleon/ matches "comma comma comma comma comma chameleon." By George, that is nice.

The three quantifier characters that you saw earlier are common shortcuts. The star is the same as the quantifier {0,}, meaning zero or more. The plus is the same as {1,}, meaning one or more. And the question mark could be written as {0,1}. In practice, it's unusual to need any curly-brace quantifiers since the three shortcut characters are nearly always the only ones needed.

Precedence

With all of these metacharacters in regular expressions, you may feel you can't keep track of the players without a scorecard. That's the precedence chart, which shows us which parts of the pattern stick together the most tightly. Unlike the precedence chart for operators, the regular expression precedence chart is simple, with only four levels. As a bonus, this section will review all of the metacharacters that Perl uses in patterns.

1. At the top of the precedence chart are the parentheses, (( )), used for grouping and memory. Anything in parentheses will stick together more tightly than anything else.

2. The second level is the quantifiers. These are the repeat operators—star (*), plus (+), and question mark (?)—as well as the quantifiers made with curly braces, like {5,15}, {3,}, and {5}. These always stick to the item they're following.

3. The third level of the precedence chart holds anchors and sequence. The anchors are the caret (^) start-of-string anchor, the dollar-sign ($) end-of-string anchor, the (\b) word-boundary anchor, and the (\B) nonword-boundary anchor. Sequence (putting one item after another) is actually an operator, even though it doesn't use a metacharacter. That means that letters in a word will stick together just as tightly as the anchors stick to the letters.

4. The lowest level of precedence is the vertical bar (|) of alternation. Since this is at the bottom of the chart, it effectively cuts the pattern into pieces. It's at the bottom of the chart because we want the letters in the words in /fred|barney/ to stick together more tightly than the alternation. If alternation were higher priority than sequence, that pattern would mean to match fre, followed by a choice of d or b and by arney. So, alternation is at the bottom of the chart, and the letters within the names stick together.

Besides the precedence chart, there are the so-called *atoms* that make up the most basic pieces of the pattern. These are the individual characters, character classes, and backreferences.

Examples of Precedence

When you need to decipher a complex regular expression, you'll need to do as Perl does and use the precedence chart to see what's going on.

For example, /^fred|barney$/ is probably not what the programmer intended. That's because the vertical bar of alternation is low precedence; it cuts the pattern in two. That pattern matches either fred at the beginning of the string or barney at the end. It's much more likely that the programmer wanted /^(fred|barney)$/, which will match if the whole line has nothing but fred or nothing but barney.* And what will /(wilma|pebbles?)/ match? The question mark applies to the previous character,† so that will match wilma, pebbles, or pebble, perhaps as part of a larger string (since there are no anchors).

The pattern /^(\w+)\s+(\w+)$/ matches lines that have a "word," some required whitespace, and another "word," with nothing else before or after. That might be used to match lines like fred flintstone, for example. The parentheses around the words aren't needed for grouping, so they may be intended to save those substrings into the regular expression memories.

When you're trying to understand a complex pattern, it may be helpful to add parentheses to clarify the precedence. That's okay, but remember that grouping parentheses are also automatically memory parentheses; you may need to change the numbering of other memories when you add the parentheses.‡

And There's More

Though we've covered all of the regular expression features that most people are likely to need for everyday programming, there are more features. A few are covered in the Alpaca book. Also check the perlre, perlrequick, and perlretut manpages for more information about what patterns in Perl can do.§

A Pattern Test Program

When in the course of Perl events it becomes necessary for a programmer to write a regular expression, it may be difficult to tell what the pattern will do. It's normal to find that a pattern matches more than you expected, or less. Or it may match earlier in the string than you expected, or later, or not at all.

---

* And, perhaps, a newline at the end of the string, as we mentioned earlier in connection with the $ anchor.

† Because a quantifier sticks to the letter s more tightly than the s sticks to the other letters in pebbles.

‡ But look in the perlre manpage for information about nonmemory parentheses, which are used for grouping without memory.

§ And check out YAPE::Regexp::Explain in CPAN as a regular-expression-to-English translator.

This program is useful to test out a pattern on some strings and see what it matches and where:

```
#!/usr/bin/perl
while (<>) {                         # take one input line at a time
  chomp;
  if (/YOUR_PATTERN_GOES_HERE/) {
    print "Matched: |$`<$&>$'|\n";   # the special match vars
  } else {
    print "No match: |$_|\n";
  }
}
```

This pattern test program is written for programmers and not end users to use, you can tell because it doesn't have any prompts or usage information. It will take any number of input lines and check each one against the pattern that you'll put in place of the string saying YOUR_PATTERN_GOES_HERE. For each line that matches, it uses the three special match variables ($`, $&, and $') to make a picture of where the match happened. What you'll see is this: if the pattern is /match/ and the input is beforematchafter, the output will say "|before<match>after|", using angle brackets to show you what part of the string was matched by your pattern. If your pattern matches something you didn't expect, you'll see it right away.

Exercises

See Appendix A for answers to the following exercises.

Several of these exercises ask you to use the test program from this chapter. You could manually type this program, taking great care to get all of the odd punctuation marks correct.[*] But you'll probably find it faster and easier to download the program and some other goodies from the O'Reilly web-site, as we mentioned in the Preface. You'll find this program under the name *pattern_test*.[†]

1. [8] Using the pattern test program, make a pattern to match the string match. Try the program with the input string beforematchafter. Does the output show the three parts of the match in the right order?

2. [7] Using the pattern test program, make a pattern that matches if any word (in the \w sense of word) ends with the letter a. Does it match wilma but not barney? Does it match Mrs. Wilma Flintstone? What about wilma&fred? Try it on the sample text file from the previous chapter's exercises (and add these test strings if they weren't already in there).

---

[*] If you *do* type it up on your own, remember that the backtick character (`) is not the same as the apostrophe ('). On most full-sized computer keyboards these days (in the U.S., at least), the backtick is found on a key immediately to the left of the 1 key.

[†] Don't be surprised if the program you download is a slightly different version than what we have in the book.

3. [5] Modify the program from the previous exercise so the word ending with the letter a is captured into memory $1. Update the code to display that variable's contents in single quotes, something like $1 contains 'Wilma'.

4. [5] Extra credit exercise: Modify the program from the previous exercise so that immediately following the word ending in a it will capture up to five characters (if there are that many characters) in a separate memory variable. Update the code to display both memory variables. For example, if the input string says I saw Wilma yesterday, the up to five characters are ˌyest. If the input is I, Wilma!, the extra memory should have one character. Does your pattern still match just plain wilma?

5. [5] Write a new program (not the test program) that prints out any input line ending with whitespace (other than a newline). Put a marker character at the end of the output line so as to make the whitespace visible.

## CHAPTER 9

Processing Text with Regular Expressions

You can use regular expresssions to change text, too. So far, we've only shown you how to match a pattern. Now, we'll show you how to use patterns to locate the parts of strings that you want to change.

Substitutions with s///

If you think of the m// pattern match as being like your word processor's "search" feature, the "search and replace" feature would be Perl's s/// substitution operator. This replaces whichever part of a variable[*] matches a pattern with a replacement string:

```
$_ = "He's out bowling with Barney tonight.";
s/Barney/Fred/;  # Replace Barney with Fred
print "$_\n";
```

If the match fails, nothing happens, and the variable is untouched:

```
# Continuing from above; $_ has "He's out bowling with Fred tonight."
s/Wilma/Betty/;  # Replace Wilma with Betty (fails)
```

The pattern and the replacement string could be more complex. Here, the replacement string uses the first memory variable, $1, which is set by the pattern match:

```
s/with (\w+)/against $1's team/;
print "$_\n";  # says "He's out bowling against Fred's team tonight."
```

Here are some other possible substitutions. (These are here only as samples; in the real world, it would not be typical to do so many unrelated substitutions in a row.)

```
$_ = "green scaly dinosaur";
s/(\w+) (\w+)/$2, $1/;  # Now it's "scaly, green dinosaur"
s/^/huge, /;            # Now it's "huge, scaly, green dinosaur"
```

---

[*] Unlike m//, which can match against any string expression, s/// is modifying data that must be contained in what's known as an *lvalue*. This is nearly always a variable, though it could be anything that could be used on the left side of an assignment operator.

```
s/,.*een//;            # Empty replacement: Now it's "huge dinosaur"
s/green/red/;          # Failed match: still "huge dinosaur"
s/\w+$/($`!)$&/;       # Now it's "huge (huge !)dinosaur"
s/\s+(!\W+)/$1 /;      # Now it's "huge (huge!) dinosaur"
s/huge/gigantic/;      # Now it's "gigantic (huge!) dinosaur"
```

There's a useful Boolean value from s///. It's true if a substitution was successful; otherwise it's false:

```
$_ = "fred flintstone";
if (s/fred/wilma/) {
  print "Successfully replaced fred with wilma!\n";
}
```

Global Replacements with /g

As you may have noticed in a previous example, s/// will make only one replacement even if others are possible. Of course, that's just the default. The /g modifier tells s/// to make all possible nonoverlapping* replacements:

```
$_ = "home, sweet home!";
s/home/cave/g;
print "$_\n";  # "cave, sweet cave!"
```

A fairly common use of a global replacement is to collapse whitespace—that is, to turn any arbitrary whitespace into a single space:

```
$_ = "Input  data\t may have    extra whitespace.";
s/\s+/ /g;  # Now it says "Input data may have extra whitespace."
```

Once we show collapsing whitespace, everyone wants to know about stripping leading and trailing whitespace. That's easy enough, in two steps:

```
s/^\s+//;  # Replace leading whitespace with nothing
s/\s+$//;  # Replace trailing whitespace with nothing
```

We could do that in one step with an alternation and the /g flag, but that turns out to be a bit slower, at least when we wrote this. The regular expression engine is always being tuned, but to learn more about that, you can get *Mastering Regular Expressions* (O'Reilly) and find out what makes regular expressions fast (or slow).

```
s/^\s+|\s+$//g;  # Strip leading, trailing whitespace
```

Different Delimiters

As we did with m// and qw//, we can change the delimiters for s///. But the substitution uses three delimiter characters, so things are a little different.

---

* It's nonoverlapping because each new match starts looking just beyond the latest replacement.

With ordinary (non-paired) characters, which don't have a left and right variety, use three of them as we did with the forward slash. Here, we've chosen the pound sign[*] as the delimiter:

```
s#^https://#http://#;
```

But if you use paired characters, which have a left and right variety, you have to use two pairs: one to hold the pattern and one to hold the replacement string. In this case, the delimiters don't have to be the same kind around the string as they are around the pattern. In fact, the delimiters of the string could even be non-paired. These are all the same:

```
s{fred}{barney};
s[fred](barney);
s<fred>#barney#;
```

Option Modifiers

In addition to the /g modifier,[†] substitutions may use the /i, /x, and /s modifiers that you saw in ordinary pattern matching. The order of modifiers isn't significant.

```
s#wilma#Wilma#gi;  # replace every WiLmA or WILMA with Wilma
s{__END__.*}{}s;   # chop off the end marker and all following lines
```

The Binding Operator

As you saw with m//, we can choose a different target for s/// by using the binding operator:

```
$file_name =~ s#^.*/##s;  # In $file_name, remove any Unix-style path
```

Case Shifting

It often happens in a substitution that you'll want to ensure that a replacement word is properly capitalized (or not, as the case may be). That's easy to accomplish with Perl, by using some backslash escapes. The \U escape forces what follows to all uppercase:

```
$_ = "I saw Barney with Fred.";
s/(fred|barney)/\U$1/gi;  # $_ is now "I saw BARNEY with FRED."
```

Similarly, the \L escape forces lowercase:

```
s/(fred|barney)/\L$1/gi;  # $_ is now "I saw barney with fred."
```

---

[*] With apologies to our British friends, to whom the pound sign is something else. Though the pound sign is generally the start of a comment in Perl, it won't start a comment when the parser knows to expect a delimiter—in this case, immediately after the s that starts the substitution.

[†] We still speak of the modifiers with names like "/i" even if the delimiter is something other than a slash.

By default, these affect the rest of the (replacement) string. You can turn off case shifting with \E:

```
s/(\w+) with (\w+)/\U$2\E with $1/i;  # $_ is now "I saw FRED with barney."
```

When written in lowercase (\l and \u), they affect only the next character:

```
s/(fred|barney)/\u$1/ig;  # $_ is now "I saw FRED with Barney."
```

You can even stack them up. Using \u with \L means "all lower case, but capitalize the first letter":[*]

```
s/(fred|barney)/\u\L$1/ig;  # $_ is now "I saw Fred with Barney."
```

As it happens, though we're covering case shifting in relation to substitutions, these escape sequences are available in any double-quotish string:

```
print "Hello, \L\u$name\E, would you like to play a game?\n";
```

The split Operator

Another operator that uses regular expressions is split, which breaks up a string according to a pattern. This is useful for tab-separated, colon-separated, whitespace-separated, or *anything*-separated data.[†] Anywhere you can specify the separator with a regular expression (generally, it's a simple regular expression), you can use split. It looks like this:

```
@fields - split /separator/, $string;
```

The split operator[‡] drags the pattern through a string and returns a list of fields (substrings) that were separated by the separators. Whenever the pattern matches, that's the end of one field and the start of the next. So, anything that matches the pattern will never show up in the returned fields. Here's a typical split pattern, splitting on colons:

```
@fields = split /:/, "abc:def:g:h";  # gives ("abc", "def", "g", "h")
```

You could even have an empty field if there were two delimiters together:

```
@fields = split /:/, "abc:def::g:h";  # gives ("abc", "def", "", "g", "h")
```

---

[*] The \L and \u may appear together in either order. Larry realized that people would sometimes get those two backward, so he made Perl figure out that you want the first letter capitalized and the rest lowercase. Larry is a pretty nice guy.

[†] Except "comma-separated values," normally called CSV files. Those are a pain to do with split; you're better off getting the Text::CSV module from CPAN.

[‡] It's an operator, though it acts a lot like a function, and everyone generally calls it a function. But the technical details of the difference are beyond the scope of this book.

Here's a rule that seems odd at first, but it rarely causes problems: leading empty fields are always returned, but trailing empty fields are discarded:[*]

```
@fields = split /:/, ":::a:b:c:::";  # gives ("", "", "", "a", "b", "c")
```

It's common to split on whitespace using /\s+/ as the pattern. Under that pattern, all whitespace runs are equivalent to a single space:

```
my $some_input = "This  is a \t        test.\n";
my @args = split /\s+/, $some_input;  # ("This", "is", "a", "test.")
```

The default for split is to break up $_ on whitespace:

```
my @fields = split;  # like split /\s+/, $_;
```

This is almost the same as using /\s+/ as the pattern except, in this special case, a leading empty field is suppressed. So, if the line starts with whitespace, you won't see an empty field at the start of the list. (If you'd like to get the same behavior when splitting another string on whitespace, use a single space in place of the pattern: split ' ', $other_string. Using a space instead of the pattern is a special kind of split.)

Generally, the patterns used for split are as simple as the ones you see here. But if the pattern becomes more complex, avoid using memory parentheses in the pattern. See the perlfunc manpage for more information.[†]

The join Function

The join function doesn't use patterns but performs the opposite function of split: split breaks up a string into a number of pieces, and join glues together a bunch of pieces to make a single string. The join function looks like this:

```
my $result = join $glue, @pieces;
```

The first argument to join is the glue, which may be any string. The remaining arguments are a list of pieces. join puts the glue string between the pieces and returns the resulting string:

```
my $x = join ":", 4, 6, 8, 10, 12;  # $x is "4:6:8:10:12"
```

In that example, we had five items, so there are only four colons or four pieces of glue. The glue shows up only between the pieces, never before or after them. So, there will be one fewer piece of glue than the number of items in the list.

---

[*] This is merely the default. It's this way for efficiency. If you worry about losing trailing empty fields, use -1 as a third argument to split and they'll be kept. See the perlfunc manpage.

[†] You might want to check out the nonmemory grouping-only parentheses notation as well in the perlre manpage.

This means there may be no glue at all if the list doesn't have at least two elements:

```
my $y = join "foo", "bar";       # gives just "bar", since no fooglue is needed
my @empty;                       # empty array
my $empty = join "baz", @empty;  # no items, so it's an empty string
```

Using $x from above, we can break up a string and put it back together with a different delimiter:

```
my @values = split /:/, $x;  # @values is (4, 6, 8, 10, 12)
my $z = join "-", @values;   # $z is "4-6-8-10-12"
```

Though split and join work well together, don't forget that the first argument to join is always a string, not a pattern.

m// in List Context

When you use split, the pattern specifies the separator: the part that isn't the useful data. Sometimes it's easier to specify what you want to keep.

When a pattern match (m//) is used in a list context, the return value is a list of the memory variables created in the match or an empty list if the match failed:

```
$_ = "Hello there, neighbor!";
my($first, $second, $third) = /(\S+) (\S+), (\S+)/;
print "$second is my $third\n";
```

This makes it easy to give the match variables easy-to-use names, and these names may persist past the next pattern match. (Because there's no =~ in that code, the pattern matches against $_ by default.)

The /g modifier you first saw on s/// also works with m//, which lets it match at more than one place in a string. In this case, a pattern with a pair of parentheses will return a memory from each time it matches:

```
my $text = "Fred dropped a 5 ton granite block on Mr. Slate";
my @words = ($text =~ /([a-z]+)/ig);
print "Result: @words\n";
# Result: Fred dropped a ton granite block on Mr Slate
```

This is like using split inside out. Instead of specifying what we want to remove, we specify what we want to keep.

If there are more than one pair of parentheses, each match may return more than one string. Let's say we have a string we want to read into a hash, like this:

```
my $data = "Barney Rubble Fred Flintstone Wilma Flintstone";
my %last_name = ($data =~ /(\w+)\s+(\w+)/g);
```

Each time the pattern matches, it returns a pair of memories. Those pairs of values become the key/value pairs in the newly created hash.

More Powerful Regular Expressions

After reading (almost) three chapters about regular expressions, you know they're a powerful feature in the core of Perl. The Perl developers have added more features, and you'll see some of the most important ones in this section. At the same time, you'll see a little more about the internal operation of the regular expression engine.

Non-Greedy Quantifiers

The four quantifiers you've already seen (in Chapters 7 and 8) are all *greedy*. That means they match as much as they can, reluctantly giving some back if that's necessary to allow the overall pattern to succeed. Here's an example: Suppose you're using the pattern /fred.+barney/ on the string fred and barney went bowling last night. We know that the regular expression will match that string, but let's see how it goes about it.* First, the subpattern fred matches the identical literal string. The next part of the pattern is the .+, which matches any character except newline, at least one time. But the plus quantifier is greedy; it prefers to match as much as possible. So, it immediately matches all of the rest of the string, including the word night. (This may surprise you, but the story isn't over yet.)

Now the subpattern barney would like to match, but it can't because we're at the end of the string. Since the .+ could be successful even if it matched one fewer character, it reluctantly gives back the letter t at the end of the string. (It's greedy, but it wants the whole pattern to succeed more than it wants to match everything all by itself.)

The subpattern barney tries again to match, and still can't. So, the .+ gives back the letter h and lets it try again. One character after another, the .+ gives back what it matched until it gives up all of the letters of barney. Finally, the subpattern barney can match, and the overall match succeeds.

Regular expression engines do a lot of backtracking like that, trying every different way of fitting the pattern to the string until one of them succeeds or until none of them has.† As this example shows, that can involve a lot of backtracking, as the quantifier gobbles up too much of the string and the regular expression engine forces it to return some of it.

For each greedy quantifier, a non-greedy alternative is available. Instead of the plus (+), we can use the non-greedy quantifier +?, which matches one or more times (as

---

* The regular expression engine makes a few optimizations that make the true story different than we tell it here, and those optimizations change from one release of Perl to the next. You shouldn't be able to tell from the functionality that it's not doing as we say. If you want to know how it works, you should read the latest source code. Be sure to submit patches for any bugs you find.

† Some regular expression engines try every different way, continuing on after they find one that fits. But Perl's regular expression engine is primarily interested in whether the pattern can match, so finding even one match means that the engine's work is done. Again, see Jeffrey Friedl's *Mastering Regular Expressions* (O'Reilly).

the plus does), except that it prefers to match as few times as possible, rather than as many as possible. Let's see how that new quantifier works when the pattern is rewritten as /fred.+?barney/.

Once again, fred matches right at the start. This time, the next part of the pattern is .+?, which prefers to match no more than one character, so it matches the space after fred. The next subpattern is barney, but that won't match here (since the string at the current position begins with and barney...). The .+? reluctantly matches the a and lets the rest of the pattern try again. Again, barney can't match, so the .+? accepts the letter n and so on. Once the .+? has matched five characters, barney can match, and the pattern is a success.

There was still some backtracking, but since the engine only had to go back and try again a few times, it should be a big improvement in speed. Well, it's an improvement if you generally find barney near fred. If your data often had fred near the start of the string and barney only at the end, the greedy quantifier might be a faster choice. In the end, the speed of the regular expression depends upon the data.

Non-greedy quantifiers aren't just about efficiency. Though they'll always match (or fail to match) the same strings as their greedy counterparts, they may match different amounts of the strings. For example, suppose you had some HTML-like* text and you want to remove all of the tags <BOLD> and </BOLD>, leaving their contents intact. Here's the text:

```
I'm talking about the cartoon with Fred and <BOLD>Wilma</BOLD>!
```

And here's a substitution to remove those tags. But what's wrong with it?

```
s#<BOLD>(.*)</BOLD>#$1#g;
```

The problem is that the star is greedy.† What if the text had said this instead?

```
I thought you said Fred and <BOLD>Velma</BOLD>, not <BOLD>Wilma</BOLD>
```

In that case, the pattern would match from the first <BOLD> to the last </BOLD>, leaving intact the ones in the middle of the line. Oops! Instead, we want a non-greedy quantifier. The non-greedy form of star is *?, so the substitution now looks like this:

```
s#<BOLD>(.*?)</BOLD>#$1#g;
```

And it does the right thing.

Since the non-greedy form of the plus was +? and the non-greedy form of the star was *?, you've probably realized the other two quantifiers look similar. The non-greedy

---

* Once again, we aren't using real HTML because you can't correctly parse HTML with simple regular expressions. If you need to work with HTML or a similar markup language, use a module that's made to handle the complexities.

† There's another possible problem: we should have used the /s modifier as well since the end tag may be on a different line than the start tag. It's a good thing that this is just an example; if we were writing something like this for real, we would have taken our own advice and used a well-written module.

form of any curly-brace quantifier looks the same, but with a question mark after the closing brace, like {5,10}? or {8,}?.* Even the question-mark quantifier has a non-greedy form: ??. That matches once or not at all, but it prefers not to match anything.

Matching Multiline Text

Classic regular expressions were used to match single lines of text. Since Perl can work with strings of any length, Perl's patterns can match multiple lines of text as easily as single lines. Of course, you have to include an expression that holds more than one line of text. Here's a string that's four lines long:

```
$_ = "I'm much better\nthan Barney is\nat bowling,\nWilma.\n";
```

The anchors ^ and $ are normally anchors for the start and end of the whole string (see Chapter 8). But the /m regular expression option lets them match at internal newlines as well (think m for multiple lines). This makes them anchors for the start and end of each line, rather than the whole string. So, this pattern can match:

```
print "Found 'wilma' at start of line\n" if /^wilma\b/im;
```

Similarly, you could do a substitution on each line in a multiline string. Here, we read an entire file into one variable,† then add the file's name as a prefix at the start of each line:

```
open FILE, $filename
  or die "Can't open '$filename': $!";
my $lines = join '', <FILE>;
$lines =~ s/^/$filename: /gm;
```

Updating Many Files

The most common way of programmatically updating a text file is by writing a new file that looks similar to the old one, but making whatever changes we need as we go along. As you'll see, this technique gives nearly the same result as updating the file, but it has some beneficial side effects as well.

In this example, we've got hundreds of files with a similar format. One of them is *fred03.dat*, and it's full of lines like these:

```
Program name: granite
Author: Gilbert Bates
Company: RockSoft
Department: R&D
Phone: +1 503 555-0095
Date: Tues March 9, 2004
```

---

* In theory, there's a non-greedy quantifier form that specifies an exact number, like {3}?. Since that says to match exactly three of the preceding items, it has no flexibility to be greedy or non-greedy.

† Hope it's a small one. The file, that is, not the variable.

```
Version: 2.1
Size: 21k
Status: Final beta
```

We need to fix this file so that it has some different information. Here's roughly what this one should look like when we're done:

```
Program name: granite
Author: Randal L. Schwartz
Company: RockSoft
Department: R&D
Date: June 12, 2008 6:38 pm
Version: 2.1
Size: 21k
Status: Final beta
```

In short, we need to make three changes. The name of the Author should be changed, the Date should be updated to today's date, and the Phone should be removed completely. We have to make these changes in hundreds of similar files as well.

Perl supports a way of in-place editing of files with help from the diamond operator (<>). Here's a program to do what we want, though it may not be obvious how it works at first. This program's only new feature is the special variable $^I; ignore that for now, and we'll come back to it:

```
#!/usr/bin/perl -w

use strict;

chomp(my $date = `date`);
$^I = ".bak";

while (<>) {
  s/^Author:.*/Author: Randal L. Schwartz/;
  s/^Phone:.*\n//;
  s/^Date:.*/Date: $date/;
  print;
}
```

Since we need today's date, the program starts by using the system date command. A better way to get the date (in a slightly different format) would be to use Perl's own localtime function in a scalar context:

```
my $date = localtime;
```

The next line sets $^I but keep ignoring that for the moment.

The list of files for the diamond operator here are coming from the command line. The main loop reads, updates, and prints one line at a time. (With what you know so far, that means all of the files' newly modified contents will be dumped to your terminal, scrolling furiously past your eyes, without the files being changed at all. But stick with us.) The second substitution can replace the entire line containing the phone number with an empty string, leaving not even a newline. When that's printed, nothing comes out, and it's as if the Phone never existed. Most input lines won't match any of the three patterns, and those will be unchanged in the output.

This result is close to what we want, except that we haven't shown you how the updated information gets back out on to the disk. The answer is in the variable $^I. By default it's undef, and everything is normal. But when it's set to some string, it makes the diamond operator (<>) more magical than usual.

We know about much of the diamond's magic: it will automatically open and close a series of files for you or read from the standard-input stream if there aren't any file-names given. But when there's a string in $^I, that string is used as a backup file-name's extension. Let's see that in action.

Let's say it's time for the diamond to open our file *fred03.dat*. It opens it like before but renames it, calling it *fred03.dat.bak*.* We have the same file open, but it has a different name on the disk. Next, the diamond creates a new file and gives it the name *fred03.dat*. That's okay because we weren't using that name anymore. Now the diamond selects the new file as the default for output, so anything we print will go into that file.† The while loop will read a line from the old file, update that, and print it out to the new file. This program can update hundreds of files in a few seconds on a typical machine. Pretty powerful, huh?

Once the program has finished, what does the user see? The user says, "Ah, I see what happened. Perl edited my file *fred03.dat*, making the changes I needed, and saved a copy of the original in the backup file *fred03.dat.bak* just to be helpful." But we know the truth: Perl didn't really edit any file. It made a modified copy, said "Abracadabra!" and switched the files around while we were watching sparks come out of the magic wand. Tricky.

Some folks use a tilde (~) as the value for $^I since that resembles what *emacs* does for backup files. Another possible value for $^I is the empty string. This enables in-place editing but doesn't save the original data in a backup file. Since a small typo in your pattern could wipe out all of the old data, only use the empty string if you want to find out how good your backup tapes are. It's easy enough to delete the backup files when you're done. When something goes wrong and you need to rename the backup files to their original names, you'll be glad you know how to use Perl to do that. (See the multiple-file rename example in Chapter 13.)

---

* Some of the details of this procedure will vary on non-Unix systems, but the end result should be nearly the same. See the release notes for your port of Perl.

† The diamond also tries to duplicate the original file's permission and ownership settings as much as possible; for example, if the old one was world-readable, the new one should be, as well.

In-Place Editing from the Command Line

A program like the example from the previous section is fairly easy to write. But Larry decided it wasn't easy enough.

Imagine you need to update hundreds of files with the misspelling Randall instead of the one-l name Randal. You could write a program like the one in the previous section. Or you could do it all with a one-line program on the command line:

```
$ perl -p -i.bak -w -e 's/Randall/Randal/g' fred*.dat
```

Perl has a whole slew of command-line options that can be used to build a complete program in a few keystrokes.[*] Let's see what these few do.

Starting the command with perl does something like putting #!/usr/bin/perl at the top of a file does: it says to use the program *perl* to process what follows.

The -p option tells Perl to write a program for you. It's not much of a program, though; it looks something like this:[†]

```
while (<>) {
    print;
}
```

If you want less, you could use -n instead; that leaves out the automatic print statement, so you can print only what you wish. (Fans of *awk* will recognize -p and -n.) Again, it's not much of a program, but it's pretty good for the price of a few keystrokes.

The next option is -i.bak, which sets $^I to ".bak" before the program starts. If you don't want a backup file, you can use -i alone with no extension. If you don't want a spare parachute, you can leave the airplane with just one.

We've seen -w before: it turns on warnings.

The -e option says "executable code follows." That means the s/Randall/Randal/g string is treated as Perl code. Since we've got a while loop (from the -p option), this code is put inside the loop before the print. For technical reasons, the last semicolon in the -e code is optional. If you have more than one -e and so more than one chunk of code, only the semicolon at the end of the last one may safely be omitted.

The last command-line parameter is fred*.dat, which says that @ARGV should hold the list of filenames that match that filename pattern. Put the pieces all together, and it's as if we had written a program like this, and put it to work on all of those fred*.dat files:

```
#!/usr/bin/perl -w
```

---

[*] See the perlrun manpage for the complete list.

[†] The print occurs in a continue block. See the perlsyn and perlrun manpages for more information.

```
$^I = ".bak";

while (<>) {
  s/Randall/Randal/g;
  print;
}
```

Compare this program to the one we used in the previous section. It's pretty similar. These command-line options are pretty handy, aren't they?

Non-Capturing Parentheses

So far, you've seen parentheses that capture parts of a matched string and store them in the memory variables, but what if you just want to use the parentheses to group things? Consider a regular expression where we want to make part of it optional but only capture another part of it. In this example, we want "bronto" to be optional, but to make it optional, we have to group that sequence of characters with parentheses. Later, the pattern uses an alternation to get "steak" or "burger," and captures the one it finds.

```
if (/(bronto)?saurus (steak|burger)/)
        {
        print "Fred wants a $2\n";
        }
```

Even if "bronto" is absent, its part of the pattern goes into $1. Perl counts the order of the opening parentheses to decide what the memory variables will be. The part we want to remember ends up in $2. In more complicated patterns, this situation can become confusing.

Fortunately, Perl's regular expressions have a way to use parentheses to group things but not trigger the memory variables. We call these *non-capturing parentheses*, and we write them with a special sequence. We add a question mark and a colon after the opening parenthesis, (?:),* and that tells Perl we only use these parentheses for grouping.

We change our regular expression to use non-capturing parentheses around "bronto," and the part that we want to remember appears in $1.

```
if (/(?:bronto)?saurus (steak|burger)/)
        {
        print "Fred wants a $1\n";
        }
```

Later, when we change our regular expression, perhaps to include a possible barbecue version of the brontosaurus burger, we can make the added "BBQ" (with a

---

* This is the fourth type of ? you've seen in regular expressions: a literal question mark (escaped), the 0 or 1 quantifier, the non-greedy modifier, and now the start of an extended pattern.

space) optional and non-capturing so the part we want to remember still shows up in $1. Otherwise, we'd potentially have to shift all of our memory variable names every time we add grouping parentheses to our regular expression.

```
if (/(?:bronto)?saurus (?:BBQ )?(steak|burger)/)
    {
    print "Fred wants a $1\n";
    }
```

Perl's regular expressions have several other special parentheses sequences that do fancy and complicated things such as look-ahead, look-behind, embedded comments, or even run code right in the middle of a pattern. You'll have to check out the perlre manpage for the details.

Exercises

See Appendix A for answers to the following exercises:

1. [7] Make a pattern that will match three consecutive copies of whatever is currently contained in $what. That is, if $what is fred, your pattern should match fredfredfred. If $what is fred|barney, your pattern should match fredfredbarney, barneyfredfred, barneybarneybarney, or many other variations. (Hint: You should set $what at the top of the pattern test program with a statement like my $what = 'fred|barney';.)

2. [12] Write a program that makes a modified copy of a text file. In the copy, every string Fred (case insensitive) should be replaced with Larry. (So, "Manfred Mann" should become "ManLarry Mann".) The input filename should be given on the command line (don't ask the user), and the output file name should be the corresponding file name ending with .out.

3. [8] Modify the previous program to change every Fred to Wilma and every Wilma to Fred. Now input like fred&wilma should look like Wilma&Fred in the output.

4. [10] Extra credit exercise: Write a program to add a copyright line to all of your exercise answers so far, by placing a line such as:

```
## Copyright (C) 20XX by Yours Truly
```

Place it in the file immediately after the "shebang" line. You should edit the files "in place" and keep a backup. Presume that the program will be invoked with the filenames to edit on the command line.

5. [15] Extra extra credit exercise: Modify the previous program so it doesn't edit the files that contain the copyright line. Hint: You might need to know that the name of the file being read by the diamond operator is in $ARGV.

## CHAPTER 10

More Control Structures

In this chapter, you'll see some alternative ways to write Perl code. For the most part, these techniques don't make the language more powerful, but they make it easier or more convenient to get the job done. You don't have to use these techniques in your own code, but don't skip this chapter. You're certain to see these control structures in other people's code, sooner or later. In fact, you'll see these things in use by the time you finish reading this book.

The unless Control Structure

In an if control structure, the block of code is executed only when the conditional expression is true. If you want to execute a block of code only when the conditional is false, change if to unless:

```
unless ($fred =~ /^[A-Z_]\w*$/i) {
    print "The value of \$fred doesn't look like a Perl identifier name.\n";
}
```

Using unless says to run the block of code *unless* this condition is true. It's like using an if test with the opposite condition. Another way to say it is that it's like having the else clause on its own. Whenever you see an unless you don't understand, you can rewrite it (in your head or in reality) as an if test:

```
if ($fred =~ /^[A-Z_]\w*$/i) {
    # Do nothing
} else {
    print "The value of \$fred doesn't look like a Perl identifier name.\n";
}
```

It's no more or less efficient, and it should compile to the same internal byte codes. Another way to rewrite it would be to negate the conditional expression by using the negation operator (!):

```
if ( ! ($fred =~ /^[A-Z_]\w*$/i) ) {
    print "The value of \$fred doesn't look like a Perl identifier name.\n";
}
```

You should pick the way of writing code that makes the most sense to you since that will probably make the most sense to your maintenance programmer. If it makes the most sense to write if with a negation, do that. More often, you'll likely find it natural to use unless.

The else Clause with unless

You can have an else clause with an unless. Though this syntax is supported, it can be confusing:

```
unless ($mon =~ /^Feb/) {
  print "This month has at least thirty days.\n";
} else {
  print "Do you see what's going on here?\n";
}
```

Some people may wish to use this, especially when the first clause is short (perhaps only one line) and the second is several lines of code. But we'd make this one a negated if or maybe swap the clauses to make a normal if:

```
if ($mon =~ /^Feb/) {
  print "Do you see what's going on here?\n";
} else {
  print "This month has at least thirty days.\n";
}
```

Remember you're always writing code for two readers: the computer that will run the code and the human being who has to keep the code working. If the human can't understand what you've written, pretty soon the computer won't be doing the right thing either.

The until Control Structure

Sometimes, you'll want to reverse the condition of a while loop. To do that, use until:

```
until ($j > $i) {
  $j *= 2;
}
```

This loop runs until the conditional expression returns true. It's really just a while loop in disguise, except it repeats as long as the conditional is false, rather than true. The conditional expression is evaluated before the first iteration, so this is a zero-or-more-times loop, just like the while loop.* As with if and unless, you could rewrite

---

* Pascal programmers, take note: in Pascal, the repeat-until always runs at least one iteration, but an until loop in Perl may not run at all if the conditional expression is true before the loop starts.

any until loop to become a while loop by negating the condition. But generally, you'll find it simple and natural to use until from time to time.

Expression Modifiers

For a more compact notation, an expression may be followed by a modifier that controls it. For example, the if modifier works in a way analogous to an if block:

```
print "$n is a negative number.\n" if $n < 0;
```

That gives the same result as if we had used this code, except that we saved some typing by leaving out the parentheses and curly braces:*

```
if ($n < 0) {
  print "$n is a negative number.\n";
}
```

Perl folks generally like to avoid typing. The shorter form reads like in English: print this message if $n is less than zero.

The conditional expression is still evaluated first, even though it's written at the end. This is backward from the usual left-to-right ordering. In understanding Perl code, you'll have to do as Perl's internal compiler does, and read to the end of the statement before you can tell what it's doing.

There are other modifiers as well:

```
&error("Invalid input") unless &valid($input);
$i *= 2 until $i > $j;
print " ", ($n += 2) while $n < 10;
&greet($_) foreach @person;
```

These work as you would expect (we hope). Each one could be rewritten in a similar way to rewriting the if-modifier example earlier. Here is one:

```
while ($n < 10) {
  print " ", ($n += 2);
}
```

The expression in parentheses inside the print argument list is noteworthy because it adds two to $n, storing the result back into $n. Then, it returns that new value, which will be printed.

These shorter forms read almost like a natural language: call the &greet subroutine for each @person in the list. Double $i until it's larger than $j.† One of the common uses of these modifiers is in a statement like this one:

```
print "fred is '$fred', barney is '$barney'\n"        if $I_am_curious;
```

---

* We also left out the line breaks. But we should mention that the curly-brace form does create a new scope. In the rare case that you need the full details, check the documentation.

† Well, it helps us to think of them like that.

By writing the code "in reverse," you can put the important part of the statement at the beginning. The point of that statement is to monitor some variables; the point is not to check if you're curious.* Some people prefer to write the whole statement on one line, perhaps with some tab characters before the if, to move it over toward the right margin as we showed in the previous example. Others put the if modifier indented on a new line:

```
print "fred is '$fred', barney is '$barney'\n"
    if $I_am_curious;
```

Though you can rewrite any of these expressions with modifiers as a block (the "old-fashioned" way), the converse isn't necessarily true. Only a single expression is allowed on either side of the modifier. You can't write *something* if *something* while *something* until *something* unless *something* foreach *something*, which would be too confusing anyway. And you can't put multiple statements on the left of the modifier. If you need more than one expression on each side, write the code the old-fashioned way, with the parentheses and curly braces.

As we mentioned in relation to the if modifier, the control expression (on the right) is evaluated first as it would be in the old-fashioned form.

With the foreach modifier, there's no way to choose a different control variable—it's always $_. Usually, that's no problem, but if you want to use a different variable, you'll need to rewrite it as a traditional foreach loop.

The Naked Block Control Structure

The so-called "naked" block is one without a keyword or condition. That is, suppose you start with a while loop, which looks something like this:

```
while (condition) {
    body;
    body;
    body;
}
```

Remove the while keyword and the conditional expression, and you'll have a naked block:

```
{
    body;
    body;
    body;
}
```

---

* We made up the name $I_am_curious; it's not a built-in Perl variable. Generally, folks who use this technique will call their variable $TRACING or use a constant declared with the constant pragma.

The naked block is like a `while` or `foreach` loop, except that it doesn't loop; it executes the body of the loop once, and it's done. It's an un-loop!

You'll see other uses for the naked block, but one of its features is providing a scope for temporary lexical variables:

```
{
    print "Please enter a number: ";
    chomp(my $n = <STDIN>);
    my $root = sqrt $n;  # calculate the square root
    print "The square root of $n is $root.\n";
}
```

In this block, `$n` and `$root` are temporary variables scoped to the block. As a general guideline, all variables should be declared in the smallest scope available. If you need a variable for a few lines of code, you can put those lines into a naked block and declare the variable inside that block. If you need the value of `$n` or `$root` later, you will need to declare them in a larger scope.

You may have noticed the `sqrt` function in that code and wondered about it; yes, we haven't shown this function before. Perl has many built-in functions beyond the scope of this book. When you're ready, check the `perlfunc` manpage to learn about more of them.

The elsif Clause

Every so often, you may need to check a number of conditional expressions, one after another, to see which one of them is true. This can be done with the `if` control structure's `elsif` clause, as in this example:

```
if ( ! defined $dino) {
  print "The value is undef.\n";
} elsif ($dino =~ /^-?\d+\.?$/) {
  print "The value is an integer.\n";
} elsif ($dino =~ /^-?\d*\.\d+$/) {
  print "The value is a _simple_ floating-point number.\n";
} elsif ($dino eq '') {
  print "The value is the empty string.\n";
} else {
  print "The value is the string '$dino'.\n";
}
```

Perl will test the conditional expressions one after another. When one succeeds, the corresponding block of code is executed, the whole control structure is done,[*] and the execution goes on to the rest of the program. If none has succeeded, the `else` block at the end is executed. (The `else` clause is optional, though in this case it's often a good idea to include it.)

---

[*] There's no "fall-through" to the next block as in the "switch" structure of languages such as C.

There's no limit to the number of elsif clauses, but Perl has to evaluate the first 99 tests before it can get to the hundredth. If you'll have more than half a dozen elsifs, you should consider whether there's a more efficient way to write it. The Perl FAQ (see the perlfaq manpage) has a number of suggestions for emulating the "case" or "switch" statements of other languages.

You may have noticed by this point that the keyword is spelled elsif, with one e. If you write it as "elseif," with a second e, Perl will tell you that it is the incorrect spelling. Why? Because Larry says so.[*]

Autoincrement and Autodecrement

You'll often want a scalar variable to count up or down by one. Since these are frequent constructs, there are shortcuts for them like nearly everything else we do frequently.

The autoincrement operator (++) adds one to a scalar variable as the same operator in C and similar languages:

```
my $bedrock = 42;
$bedrock++;  # add one to $bedrock; it's now 43
```

Like other ways of adding one to a variable, the scalar will be created if necessary:

```
my @people = qw{ fred barney fred wilma dino barney fred pebbles };
my %count;                        # new empty hash
$count{$_}++ foreach @people;  # creates new keys and values as needed
```

The first time through that foreach loop, $count{$_} is incremented. That's $count{"fred"}, which goes from undef (since it didn't previously exist in the hash) up to 1. The next time through the loop, $count{"barney"} becomes 1; after that, $count{"fred"} becomes 2. Each time through the loop, one element in %count is incremented and possibly created as well. After that loop is done, $count{"fred"} is 3. This provides a quick and easy way to see which items are in a list and how many times each one appears.

Similarly, the autodecrement operator (--) subtracts one from a scalar variable:

```
$bedrock--;  # subtract one from $bedrock; it's 42 again
```

---

[*] In fact, he resists any suggestion that it even be permitted as a valid alternative spelling: "If you want to spell it with a second e, it's simple. Step 1: Make up your own language. Step 2: Make it popular." When you make your own programming language, you can spell the keywords any way you'd like. We hope you will decide that yours shouldn't be the first to have an "elseunless."

The Value of Autoincrement

You can fetch the value of a variable and change that value at the same time. Put the ++ operator in front of the variable name to increment the variable first and then fetch its value. This is a *preincrement*:

```
my $m = 5;
my $n = ++$m;   # increment $m to 6, and put that value into $n
```

Or put the -- operator in front to decrement the variable first and fetch its value. This is a *predecrement*:

```
my $c = --$m;   # decrement $m to 5, and put that value into $c
```

Here's the tricky part. Put the variable name first to fetch the value first, and then do the increment or decrement. This is called a *postincrement* or *postdecrement*:

```
my $d = $m++;   # $d gets the old value (5), then increment $m to 6
my $e = $m--;   # $e gets the old value (6), then decrement $m to 5
```

It's tricky because we're doing two things at once. We're fetching the value, and we're changing it in the same expression. If the operator is first, we increment (or decrement) and then use the new value. If the variable is first, we return its (old) value first, and then do the increment or decrement. Another way to say it is that these operators return a value, but they also have the side effect of modifying the variable's value.

If you write these in an expression of their own,[*] not using the value but only the side effect, there's no difference[†] if you put the operator before or after the variable:

```
$bedrock++;   # adds one to $bedrock
++$bedrock;   # just the same; adds one to $bedrock
```

A common use of these operators is in connection with a hash to identify when an item has been seen before:

```
my @people = qw{ fred barney bamm-bamm wilma dino barney betty pebbles };
my %seen;

foreach (@people) {
  print "I've seen you somewhere before, $_!\n"
    if $seen{$_}++;
}
```

When barney shows up for the first time, the value of $seen{$_}++ is false since it's the value of $seen{$_}, which is $seen{"barney"} and is undef. But that expression

---

[*] That is, in a void context.

[†] Programmers who get inside the implementations of languages may expect that postincrement and postdecrement would be less efficient than their counterparts, but Perl's not like that. Perl automatically optimizes the post- forms when they're used in a void context.

has the side effect of incrementing $seen{"barney"}. When barney shows up again, $seen{"barney"} is now a true value, so the message is printed.

The for Control Structure

Perl's for control structure is like the common for control structure you may have seen in other languages such as C. It looks like this:

```
for (initialization; test; increment) {
  body;
  body;
}
```

To Perl, this loop is a while loop in disguise, something like this:*

```
initialization;
while (test) {
  body;
  body;
  increment;
}
```

The most common use of the for loop, by far, is for making computed iterations:

```
for ($i = 1; $i <= 10; $i++) {  # count from 1 to 10
  print "I can count to $i!\n";
}
```

When you've seen these before, you'll know what the first line is saying before you read the comment. Before the loop starts, the control variable, $i, is set to 1. Then, the loop is a while loop in disguise, looping while $i is less than or equal to 10. Between each iteration and the next is the increment, which here is a literal increment, adding one to the control variable, which is $i.

The first time through this loop, $i is 1. Since that's less than or equal to 10, we see the message. Though the increment is written at the top of the loop, it logically happens at the bottom of the loop after printing the message. So, $i becomes 2, which is less than or equal to 10; we print the message again, and $i is incremented to 3, which is less than or equal to 10, and so on.

Eventually, we print the message that our program can count to 9; $i is incremented to 10, which is less than or *equal* to 10. We run the loop one last time and print that our program can count to 10. Finally, $i is incremented for the last time, to 11, which is not less than or equal to 10. Control drops out of the loop, and we're on to the rest of the program.

---

* The increment happens in a continue block, which is beyond the scope of this book. See the perlsyn manpage for the truth.

All three parts are together at the top of the loop, so it's easy for an experienced programmer to read that first line and say, "Ah, it's a loop that counts $i from 1 to 10."

After the loop is done, the control variable has a value "after" the loop. In this case, the control variable has gone all the way to 11.* This loop is versatile, since you can make it count in all sorts of ways. For example, we can count down from 10 to 1:

```
for ($i = 10; $i >= 1; $i--) {
  print "I can count down to $i\n";
}
```

And this loop counts from -150 to 1000 by threes:†

```
for ($i = -150; $i <= 1000; $i += 3) {
  print "$i\n";
}
```

You could make any of the three control parts (initialization, test, or increment) empty if you wish, but you still need the two semicolons. In this unusual example, the test is a substitution, and the increment is empty:

```
for ($_ = "bedrock"; s/(.)//; ) {  # loops while the s/// is successful
  print "One character is: $1\n";
}
```

The test expression (in the implied while loop) is the substitution, which will return a true value if it succeeded. In this case, the first time through the loop, the substitution will remove the b from bedrock. Each iteration will remove another letter. When the string is empty, the substitution will fail, and the loop is done.

If the test expression (the one between the two semicolons) is empty, it's automatically true, making an infinite loop. But don't make an infinite loop like this until you see how to break out of such a loop, which we'll discuss later in this chapter:

```
for (;;) {
  print "It's an infinite loop!\n";
}
```

A more Perl-like way to write an intentional infinite loop, when you want one,‡ is with while:

```
while (1) {
  print "It's another infinite loop!\n";
}
```

Though C programmers are familiar with the first way, even a beginning Perl programmer should recognize that 1 is always true, so the second is generally a better

---

* Obligatory *This is Spinal Tap* outdated pop-culture reference.

† It never gets to 1000 exactly. The last iteration uses 999 since each value of $i is a multiple of three.

‡ If you somehow made an infinite loop that's gotten away from you, see whether Ctrl-C will halt it. It's possible that you'll get a lot of output after typing Ctrl-C, depending upon your system's I/O and other factors. Hey, we warned you.

way to write an intentional infinite loop. Perl is smart enough to recognize a constant expression like that and optimize it away, so there's no difference in efficiency.

The Secret Connection Between foreach and for

It turns out that inside the Perl parser the keyword foreach is equivalent to the keyword for. That is, any time Perl sees one of them, it's the same as if you had typed the other. Perl can tell which you meant by looking inside the parentheses. If you've got the two semicolons, it's a computed for loop (like we've just been talking about). If you don't have the semicolons, it's a foreach loop:

```
for (1..10) {  # Really a foreach loop from 1 to 10
  print "I can count to $_!\n";
}
```

That's a foreach loop, but it's written for. Except for that one example, we'll spell out foreach wherever it appears throughout this book. In the real world, do you think that Perl folks will type those extra four letters?* Excepting only beginners' code, it's always written for, and you'll have to do as Perl does and look for the semicolons to tell which kind of loop it is.

In Perl, the true foreach loop is almost always a better choice. In the foreach loop (written for) in that previous example, it's easy to see at a glance that the loop will go from 1 to 10. But do you see what's wrong with this computed loop that's trying to do the same thing? Don't peek at the answer in the footnote until you think you've found what's wrong:†

```
for ($i = 1; $i < 10; $i++) {  # Oops! Something is wrong here!
  print "I can count to $_!\n";
}
```

Loop Controls

Perl is one of the "structured" programming languages. In particular, there's one entrance to any block of code, which is at the top of that block. But there are times when you may need more control or versatility than what we've shown so far. For example, you may need to make a loop like a while loop but that always runs at least once. Or maybe you need to occasionally exit a block of code early. Perl has

---

* If you think that, you haven't been paying attention. Among programmers, especially Perl programmers, laziness is one of the classic virtues. If you don't believe us, ask someone at the next Perl Mongers' meeting.

† There are two and one-half bugs. First, the conditional uses a less-than sign, so the loop will run nine times instead of ten. It's easy to get a "fencepost" bug with this kind of loop, like what happened when the rancher needed enough fenceposts to make a 30-meter-long fence with a post every three meters. (The answer is not ten fenceposts.) Second, the control variable is $i, but the loop body is using $_. And second and a half, it's a lot more work to read, write, maintain, and debug this type of loop, which is why we say that the true foreach is generally a better choice in Perl.

---

three loop-control operators you can use in loop blocks to make the loop do all sorts of tricks.

The last Operator

The last operator immediately ends the execution of the loop. (If you've used the "break" operator in C or a similar language, it's like that.) It's the "emergency exit" for loop blocks. When you hit last, the loop is done as in this example:

```
# Print all input lines mentioning fred, until the __END__ marker
while (<STDIN>) {
  if (/__END__/) {
    # No more input on or after this marker line
    last;
  } elsif (/fred/) {
    print;
  }
}
## last comes here ##
```

Once an input line has the __END__ marker, that loop is done. The comment line at the end is not required, but we threw it in to clarify what's happening.

The five kinds of loop blocks in Perl are for, foreach, while, until, and the naked block.* The curly braces of an if block or subroutine† don't qualify. In the example above, the last operator applied to the entire loop block.

The last operator will apply to the innermost currently running loop block. To jump out of outer blocks, stay tuned; that's coming up in a little bit.

The next Operator

Sometimes you're not ready for the loop to finish, but you're done with the current iteration. That's what the next operator is good for. It jumps to the inside of the bottom of the current loop block.‡ After next, control continues with the next iteration of the loop (much like the "continue" operator in C or a similar language):

```
# Analyze words in the input file or files
while (<>) {
  foreach (split) {   # break $_ into words, assign each to $_ in turn
```

---

* Yes, you can use last to jump out of a naked block. That's not the same as jumping naked out into your block.

† It's probably a bad idea, but you could use these loop control operators from inside a subroutine to control a loop that is *outside* the subroutine. That is, if a subroutine is called in a loop block and the subroutine executes last when there's no loop block running inside the subroutine, the flow of control will jump to just after the loop block *in the main code*. This ability to use loop control from within a subroutine may go away in a future version of Perl, and no one is likely to miss it.

‡ This is another of our many lies. In truth, next jumps to the start of the (usually omitted) continue block for the loop. See the perlsyn manpage for the full details.

```
            $total++;
            next if /\W/;      # strange words skip the remainder of the loop
            $valid++;
            $count{$_}++;      # count each separate word
            ## next comes here ##
        }
    }

    print "total things = $total, valid words = $valid\n";
    foreach $word (sort keys %count) {
        print "$word was seen $count{$word} times.\n";
    }
```

This one is more complex than most of our examples up to this point, so let's take it step by step. The while loop is reading lines of input from the diamond operator, one after another, into $_; you've seen that before. Each time through that loop, another line of input will be in $_.

Inside that loop, the foreach loop is iterating over the return value split. Do you remember the default for split with no arguments?* That splits $_ on whitespace, in effect breaking $_ into a list of words. Since the foreach loop doesn't mention some other control variable, the control variable will be $_. So, we'll see one word after another in $_.

But didn't we just say that $_ holds one line of input after another? Well, in the outer loop, that's what it is. But inside the foreach loop, it holds one word after another. It's no problem for Perl to reuse $_ for a new purpose; this happens all the time.

Now, inside the foreach loop, we're seeing one word at a time in $_. $total is incremented, so it must be the total number of words. But the next line (which is the point of this example) checks to see if the word has any nonword characters: anything but letters, digits, and underscores. So, if the word is Tom's, if it is full-sized, or if it has an adjoining comma, quote mark, or any other strange character, it will match that pattern and we'll skip the rest of the loop, going on to the next word.

But let's say that it's an ordinary word, like fred. In that case, we count $valid up by one and also $count{$_}, keeping a count for each different word. When we finish the two loops, we've counted every word in every line of input from every file the user wanted us to use.

We're not going to explain the last few lines. By now, we hope you've got stuff like that down.

Like last, next may be used in any of the five kinds of loop blocks: for, foreach, while, until, or the naked block. If loop blocks are nested, next works with the innermost one. You'll see how to change that at the end of this section.

---

* If you don't remember it, don't worry too much. Don't waste any brain cells remembering things that you can look up with perldoc.

The redo Operator

The third member of the loop control triad is redo. It says to go back to the top of the current loop block, without testing any conditional expression or advancing to the next iteration. (If you've used C or a similar language, you've never seen this one before. Those languages don't have this kind of operator.) Here's an example:

```
# Typing test
my @words = qw{ fred barney pebbles dino wilma betty };
my $errors = 0;

foreach (@words) {
  ## redo comes here ##
  print "Type the word '$_': ";
  chomp(my $try = <STDIN>);
  if ($try ne $_) {
    print "Sorry - That's not right.\n\n";
    $errors++;
    redo;  # jump back up to the top of the loop
  }
}
print "You've completed the test, with $errors errors.\n";
```

Like the other two operators, redo will work with any of the five kinds of loop blocks, and it will work with the innermost loop block when they're nested.

The big difference between next and redo is that next will advance to the next iteration, but redo will redo the current iteration. Here's an example program that you can play with to get a feel for how these three operators work:[*]

```
foreach (1..10) {
  print "Iteration number $_.\n\n";
  print "Please choose: last, next, redo, or none of the above? ";
  chomp(my $choice = <STDIN>);
  print "\n";
  last if $choice =~ /last/i;
  next if $choice =~ /next/i;
  redo if $choice =~ /redo/i;
  print "That wasn't any of the choices... onward!\n\n";
}
print "That's all, folks!\n";
```

If you press return without typing anything (try it two or three times), the loop counts along from one number to the next. If you choose last when you get to number four, the loop is done and you won't go on to number five. If you choose next when you're on four, you're on to number five without printing the "onward" message. And if you choose redo when you're on four, you're back to doing number four all over again.

---

[*] If you've downloaded the example files from the O'Reilly web site (see the Preface), you'll find this program called *lnr-example*.

Labeled Blocks

When you need to work with a loop block that's not the innermost one, use a label. Labels in Perl are like other identifiers; they are made of letters, digits, and underscores, but they can't start with a digit. Since they have no prefix character, labels could be confused with the names of built-in function names or with your own subroutines' names. It would be a poor choice to make a label called print or if. Because of that, Larry recommends they be all uppercase. That ensures the label won't conflict with another identifier and makes it easy to spot the label in the code. In any case, labels are rare, only showing up in a small percentage of Perl programs.

To label a loop block, put the label and a colon in front of the loop. Inside the loop, you may use the label after last, next, or redo as needed:

```
LINE: while (<>) {
  foreach (split) {
    last LINE if /__END__/;  # bail out of the LINE loop
    ...
  }
}
```

For readability, it's generally nice to put the label at the left margin even if the current code is at a higher indentation. The label names the entire block; it's not marking a target point in the code.[*] In that previous snippet of sample code, the special __END__ token marks the end of all input. Once that token shows up, the program will ignore any remaining lines (even from other files).

It often makes sense to choose a noun as the name of the loop.[†] That is, the outer loop is processing a line at a time, so we called it LINE. If we had to name the inner loop, we would have called it WORD since it processes a word at a time. That makes it convenient to say things like "(move on to the) next WORD" or "redo (the current) LINE."

Logical Operators

Perl has all of the necessary logical operators needed to work with Boolean (true/false) values. For example, it's often useful to combine logical tests by using the logical AND operator (&&) and the logical OR operator (||):

```
if ($dessert{'cake'} && $dessert{'ice cream'}) {
  # Both are true
  print "Hooray! Cake and ice cream!\n";
} elsif ($dessert{'cake'} || $dessert{'ice cream'}) {
```

---

[*] This isn't goto, after all.

[†] That is, it makes more sense to do that than not to do that. Perl doesn't care if you call your loop labels things like XYZZY or PLUGH. However, unless you were friendly with the Colossal Cave in the '70s, you might not get the reference.

```
    # At least one is true
    print "That's still good...\n";
} else {
    # Neither is true - do nothing (we're sad)
}
```

There may be a shortcut. If the left side of a logical AND operation is false, the whole thing is false since logical AND needs both sides to be true to return true. In that case, there's no reason to check the right side, so it will not be evaluated. Consider what happens in this example if $hour is 3:

```
if ( (9 <= $hour) && ($hour < 17) ) {
    print "Aren't you supposed to be at work...?\n";
}
```

Similarly, if the left side of a logical OR operation is true, the right side will not be evaluated. Consider what happens here if $name is fred:

```
if ( ($name eq 'fred') || ($name eq 'barney') ) {
    print "You're my kind of guy!\n";
}
```

Because of this behavior, these operators are called "short-circuit" logical operators. They take a short circuit to the result whenever they can. In fact, it's fairly common to rely upon this short-circuit behavior. Suppose you need to calculate an average:

```
if ( ($n != 0) && ($total/$n < 5) ) {
    print "The average is below five.\n";
}
```

In that example, the right side will be evaluated only if the left side is true, so we can't accidentally divide by zero and crash the program.

The Value of a Short-Circuit Operator

Unlike what happens in C (and similar languages), the value of a short-circuit logical operator is the last part evaluated and not just a Boolean value. This provides the same result, in that the last part evaluated is true when the whole thing should be true, and it's false when the whole thing should be false.

But it's a more useful return value. Among other things, the logical OR operator is handy for selecting a default value:

```
my $last_name = $last_name{$someone} || '(No last name)';
```

If $someone is not listed in the hash, the left side will be undef, which is false. So, the logical OR will have to look to the right side for the value, making the right side the default.* You'll see other uses for this behavior later.

---

* In this idiom, the default value won't merely replace undef but will replace any false value equally well. That's fine for most names, but zero and the empty string are useful yet false values. This idiom should be used only when you're willing to replace any false value with the expression on the right.

The Ternary Operator, ?:

When Larry was deciding which operators to make available in Perl, he didn't want former C programmers to miss for something that C had and Perl didn't, so he brought over all of C's operators to Perl.* That meant bringing over C's most confusing operator: the ternary ?: operator. While it may be confusing, it can also be quite useful.

The ternary operator is like an if-then-else test, all rolled into one expression. It is called a "ternary" operator because it takes three operands. It looks like this:

```
expression ? if_true_expr : if_false_expr
```

First, the expression is evaluated to see whether it's true or false. If it's true, the second expression is used; otherwise, the third expression is used. Every time, one of the two expressions on the right is evaluated, and the other is ignored. That is, if the first expression is true, the second expression is evaluated, and the third is ignored. If the first expression is false, the second is ignored, and the third is evaluated as the value of the whole thing.

In this example, the result of the subroutine &is_weekend determines which string expression will be assigned to the variable:

```
my $location = &is_weekend($day) ? "home" : "work";
```

And here, we calculate and print out an average—or just a placeholder line of hyphens, if there's no average available:

```
my $average = $n ? ($total/$n) : "-----";
print "Average: $average\n";
```

You could rewrite any use of the ?: operator as an if structure, often less conveniently and concisely:

```
my $average;
if ($n) {
  $average = $total / $n;
} else {
  $average = "-----";
}
print "Average: $average\n";
```

Here's a trick you might see, used to code up a nice multiway branch:

```
my $size =
  ($width < 10) ? "small"  :
  ($width < 20) ? "medium" :
  ($width < 50) ? "large"  :
                  "extra-large"; # default
```

---

* Well, to be sure, he did leave out the ones that have no use in Perl, such as the operator that turns a number into the memory address of a variable. And he added several operators (like the string concatenation operator), which make C folks jealous of Perl.

That is really three nested ?: operators, and it works quite well once you get the hang of it.

You're not obliged to use this operator. Beginners may wish to avoid it. But you'll see it in others' code, and we hope that one day you'll find a good reason to use it in your own programs.

Control Structures Using Partial-Evaluation Operators

These three operators that you've just seen—&&, ||, and ?:—all share a peculiar property: depending on whether the value on the left side is true or false, they may or may not evaluate an expression. Sometimes the expression is evaluated, and sometimes it isn't. For that reason, these are sometimes called *partial-evaluation* operators since they may not evaluate all of the expressions around them. Partial-evaluation operators are automatically control structures.* It's not as if Larry felt a burning need to add more control structures to Perl. But once he had decided to put these partial-evaluation operators into Perl, they automatically became control structures as well. After all, anything that can activate and deactivate a chunk of code is a control structure.

Fortunately, you'll notice this only when the controlled expression has side effects, like altering a variable's value or causing some output. For example, suppose you ran across this line of code:

```
($m < $n) && ($m = $n);
```

Right away, you should notice that the result of the logical AND isn't being assigned anywhere.† Why not?

If $m is less than $n, the left side is true and the right side will be evaluated, thereby doing the assignment. But if $m is not less than $n, the left side will be false, and the right side will be skipped. That line of code will do essentially the same thing as this one, which is easier to understand:

```
if ($m < $n) { $m = $n }
```

Maybe you'll be maintaining a program, and you'll see a line like this one:

```
($m > 10) || print "why is it not greater?\n";
```

If $m is greater than ten, the left side is true, and the logical OR is done. But if it's not, the left side is false, and this will go on to print the message. This could (and probably should) be written in the traditional way, probably with if or unless.

---

* Some of you were wondering why these logical operators are being covered in this chapter, weren't you?

† Though it might be a return value, as the last expression in a subroutine.

If you have a particularly twisted brain, you might learn to read these lines as if they were written in English. For example, check that $m is less than $n, *and if it is*, then do the assignment. Check that $m is more than 10, *or if it's not*, then print the message.

It's generally former C programmers or old-time Perl programmers who most often use these ways of writing control structures. Why do they do it? Some have the mistaken idea that these are more efficient. Some think these tricks make their code cooler. Some are merely copying what they saw someone else do.

In the same way, the ternary operator may be used for control. In this case, we want to assign $x to the smaller of two variables:

```
($m < $n) ? ($m = $x) : ($n = $x);
```

If $m is smaller, it gets $x. Otherwise, $n does.

There is another way to write the logical AND and logical OR operators. You may wish to write them out as words: and and or.* These word-operators have the same behaviors as the ones written with punctuation, but the words are down at the bottom of the precedence chart. Since the words don't stick so tightly to the nearby parts of the expression, they may need fewer parentheses:

```
$m < $n and $m = $n;   # but better written as the corresponding if
```

Then again, you may need more parentheses. Precedence is a bugaboo. Be sure to use parentheses to say what you mean unless you're sure of the precedence. Nevertheless, since the word forms are very low precedence, you can generally understand that they cut the expression into big pieces, doing everything on the left first, and then (if needed) everything on the right.

Though using logical operators as control structures can be confusing, sometimes they're the accepted way to write code. The idiomatic way of opening a file in Perl looks like this:

```
open CHAPTER, $filename
  or die "Can't open '$filename': $!";
```

By using the low-precedence short-circuit or operator, we're telling Perl it should "open this file... or die!" If the open succeeds, returning a true value, the or is complete. But if it fails, the false value causes the or to evaluate the part on the right, which will die with a message.

So, using these operators as control structures is part of idiomatic Perl, Perl as she is spoken. Used properly, they can make your code more powerful; otherwise they can make your code unmaintainable. Don't overuse them.†

---

* There are the low-precedence not (like the logical-negation operator, !) and the rare xor.

† Using these weird forms (anything but or die) more than once per month counts as overuse.

Exercise

See Appendix A for an answer to the following exercise:

1. [25] Make a program that will repeatedly ask the user to guess a secret number from 1 to 100 until the user guesses the secret number. Your program should pick the number at random by using the magical formula int(1 + rand 100).* When the user guesses wrong, the program should respond "Too high" or "Too low." If the user enters the word quit or exit, or if the user enters a blank line, the program should quit. If the user guesses correctly, the program should quit then as well.

* See what the perlfunc manpage says about int and rand if you're curious about these functions.

## CHAPTER 11

File Tests

Earlier, we showed how to open a filehandle for output. Normally, that will create a new file, wiping out any existing file with the same name. Perhaps you want to check that there isn't a file by that name. Perhaps you need to know how old a given file is. Or perhaps you want to go through a list of files to find which ones are larger than a certain number of bytes and not accessed for a certain amount of time. Perl has a complete set of tests you can use to find information about files.

File Test Operators

Before we start a program that creates a new file, let's make sure the file doesn't already exist so that we don't accidentally overwrite a vital spreadsheet data file or that important birthday calendar. For this, we use the -e file test, testing a filename for existence:

```
die "Oops! A file called '$filename' already exists.\n"
  if -e $filename;
```

We didn't include $! in this die message since we're not reporting that the system refused a request in this case. Here's an example of checking if a file is being kept up to date. In this case, we're testing an already opened filehandle instead of a string file name. Let's say that our program's configuration file should be updated every week or two. (Maybe it's checking for computer viruses.) If the file hasn't been modified in the past 28 days, then something is wrong:

```
warn "Config file is looking pretty old!\n"
  if -M CONFIG > 28;
```

The third example is more complex. Let's say disk space is filling up; rather than buy more disks, we've decided to move any large, useless files to the backup tapes. So let's go through our list of files* to see which of them are larger than 100 KB. But even if a file is large, we shouldn't move it to the backup tapes unless it hasn't been accessed in the last 90 days (so we know it's not used too often):†

```perl
my @original_files = qw/ fred barney betty wilma pebbles dino bamm-bamm /;
my @big_old_files;  # The ones we want to put on backup tapes
foreach my $filename (@original_files) {
  push @big_old_files, $filename
    if -s $filename > 100_000 and -A $filename > 90;
}
```

This is the first time that you've seen it, so maybe you noticed that the control variable of the foreach loop is a my variable. That declares it to have the scope of the loop, so this example should work under use strict. Without the my keyword, this would be using the global $filename.

The file tests look like a hyphen and a letter, which is the name of the test, followed by a filename or a filehandle to test. Many of them return a true/false value, but several give something more interesting. See Table 11-1 for the complete list and read the following discussion to learn more about the special cases.

Table 11-1. File tests and their meanings

File test	Meaning
-r	File or directory is readable by this (effective) user or group
-w	File or directory is writable by this (effective) user or group
-x	File or directory is executable by this (effective) user or group
-o	File or directory is owned by this (effective) user
-R	File or directory is readable by this real user or group
-W	File or directory is writable by this real user or group
-X	File or directory is executable by this real user or group
-O	File or directory is owned by this real user
-e	File or directory name exists
-z	File exists and has zero size (always false for directories)
-s	File or directory exists and has nonzero size (the value is the size in bytes)
-f	Entry is a plain file
-d	Entry is a directory
-l	Entry is a symbolic link
-S	Entry is a socket

* It's more likely that, instead of having the list of files in an array as our example shows, you'll read it directly from the filesystem using a glob or directory handle as we will show in Chapter 12. Since you haven't seen that yet, we'll just start with the list and go from there.

† There's a way to make this example more efficient as you'll see by the end of the chapter.

Table 11-1. File tests and their meanings (continued)

File test	Meaning
-p	Entry is a named pipe (a "fifo")
-b	Entry is a block-special file (like a mountable disk)
-c	Entry is a character-special file (like an I/O device)
-u	File or directory is setuid
-g	File or directory is setgid
-k	File or directory has the sticky bit set
-t	The filehandle is a TTY (as reported by the `isatty( )` system function; filenames can't be tested by this test)
-T	File looks like a "text" file
-B	File looks like a "binary" file
-M	Modification age (measured in days)
-A	Access age (measured in days)
-C	Inode-modification age (measured in days)

The tests -r, -w, -x, and -o tell if the given attribute is true for the effective user or group ID,* which essentially refers to the person who is in charge of running the program.† These tests look at the permission bits on the file to see what is permitted. If your system uses Access Control Lists (ACLs), the tests will use those as well. These tests generally tell if the system would *try* to permit something, but it doesn't mean that it really would be possible. For example, -w may be true for a file on a CD-ROM, though you can't write to it, or -x may be true on an empty file, which can't truly be executed.

The -s test does return true if the file is non-empty, but it's a special kind of true. It's the length of the file, measured in bytes, which evaluates as true for a nonzero number.

A Unix filesystem‡ has seven types of items, represented by the seven file tests -f, -d, -l, -S, -p, -b, and -c. Any item should be one of those. If you have a symbolic link pointing to a file, that will report true for -f and -l. So if you want to know whether something is a symbolic link, you should generally test that first. (You'll learn more about symbolic links in Chapter 12.)

---

* The -o and -O tests relate only to the user ID and not to the group ID.

† For advanced students, the corresponding -R, -W, -X, and -O tests use the real user or group ID, which becomes important if your program may be running set-ID. In that case, it's generally the ID of the person who requested running it. See any good book about advanced Unix programming for a discussion of set-ID programs.

‡ This is the case on many non-Unix filesystems but not all of the file tests are meaningful everywhere. For example, you aren't likely to have block special files on your non-Unix system.

The age tests, -M, -A, and -C (yes, they're uppercase) return the number of days since the file was last modified, accessed, or had its inode changed.* (The inode contains all of the information about the file except for its contents. See the stat system call manpage or a good book on Unix internals for details.) This age value is a full floating-point number, so you might get a value of 2.00001 if a file were modified two days and one second ago. These "days" aren't necessarily the same as a human would count. For example, if it's 1:30 A.M. when you check a file modified at about an hour before midnight, the value of -M for this file would be around 0.1, even though it was modified "yesterday."

When checking the age of a file, you might get a negative value like -1.2, which means that the file's last access timestamp is set at about thirty hours in the future. The zero point on this timescale is the moment your program started running,† so that value might mean a long-running program was looking at a file that had just been accessed. Or a timestamp could be set (accidentally or intentionally) to a time in the future.

The tests -T and -B determine if a file is text or binary. But people who know a lot about filesystems know there's no bit (at least in Unix-like operating systems) to indicate that a file is a binary or text file, so how can Perl tell? The answer is that Perl cheats: it opens the file, looks at the first few thousand bytes, and makes an educated guess. If it sees a lot of null bytes, unusual control characters, and bytes with the high bit set, then that looks like a binary file. If there's not much weird stuff, then it looks like text. It sometimes guesses wrong. If a text file has a lot of Swedish or French words (which may have characters represented with the high bit set, as some ISO-8859-something variant, or perhaps even a Unicode version), it may fool Perl into declaring it binary. So it's not perfect, but if you need to separate your source code from compiled files, or HTML files from PNGs, these tests should do the trick.

You'd think that -T and -B would always disagree since a text file isn't a binary and vice versa, but there are two special cases where they're in complete agreement. If the file doesn't exist, or can't be read, both are false since it's neither a text file nor a binary. Alternatively, if the file is empty, it's an empty text file and an empty binary file at the same time, so they're both true.

The -t file test returns true if the given filehandle is a TTY—if it's interactive because it's not a simple file or pipe. When -t STDIN returns true, it generally means that you can interactively ask the user questions. If it's false, your program is probably getting input from a file or pipe, rather than a keyboard.

---

* This information will be somewhat different on non-Unix systems since not all keep track of the same times that Unix does. For example, on some systems, the ctime field (which the -C test looks at) is the file creation time (which Unix doesn't keep track of), rather than the inode change time. See the perlport manpage.

† As recorded in the $^T variable, which you could update (with a statement like $^T = time;) if you needed to get the ages relative to a different starting time.

Don't worry if you don't know what some of the other file tests mean—if you've never heard of them, you won't be needing them. But if you're curious, get a good book about programming for Unix. (On non-Unix systems, these tests all try to give results analogous to what they do on Unix, or give undef for an unavailable feature. Usually, you'll be able to guess what they'll do.)

If you omit the filename or filehandle parameter to a file test (that is, if you have -r or just -s), the default operand is the file named in $_.* So, to test a list of filenames to see which ones are readable, you type the following:

```
foreach (@lots_of_filenames) {
  print "$_ is readable\n" if -r;  # same as -r $_
}
```

But if you omit the parameter, be careful that whatever follows the file test doesn't look like it could be a parameter. For example, if you wanted to find out the size of a file in KB rather than in bytes, you might be tempted to divide the result of -s by 1000 (or 1024), like this:

```
# The filename is in $_
my $size_in_K = -s / 1000;  # Oops!
```

When the Perl parser sees the slash, it doesn't think about division. Since it's looking for the optional operand for -s, it sees what looks like the start of a regular expression in forward slashes. To prevent this confusion, put parentheses around the file test:

```
my $size_in_k = (-s) / 1024;  # Uses $_ by default
```

Explicitly giving a file test a parameter is safer.

The stat and lstat Functions

Though these file tests are fine for testing various attributes regarding a particular file or filehandle, they don't tell the whole story. For example, there's no file test that returns the number of links to a file or the owner's user ID (uid). To get at the remaining information about a file, call the stat function, which returns pretty much everything that the stat Unix system call returns (and more than you want to know).† The operand to stat is a filehandle or an expression that evaluates to a filename. The return value is either the empty list indicating that the stat failed (usually because

---

* The -t file test is an exception since that test isn't useful with filenames (they're never TTYs). By default, it tests STDIN.

† On a non-Unix system, stat and lstat, as well as the file tests, should return "the closest thing available." For example, a system that doesn't have user IDs (that is, a system that has just one "user," in the Unix sense) might return zero for the user and group IDs as if the only user is the system administrator. If stat or lstat fails, it will return an empty list. If the system call underlying a file test fails (or isn't available on the given system), that test will generally return undef. See the perlport manpage for the latest about what to expect on different systems.

the file doesn't exist), or a 13-element list of numbers, most easily described using the following list of scalar variables:

```
my($dev, $ino, $mode, $nlink, $uid, $gid, $rdev,
   $size, $atime, $mtime, $ctime, $blksize, $blocks)
      = stat($filename);
```

The names here refer to the parts of the stat structure, described in detail in the stat(2) manpage. You should look there for the detailed descriptions. Here's a quick summary of the important ones:

$dev and $ino

The device number and inode number of the file. Together, they make up a "license plate" for the file. Even if it has more than one name (hard link), the combination of device and inode numbers will be unique.

$mode

The set of permission bits for the file and some other bits. If you've ever used the Unix command ls -l to get a detailed (long) file listing, you'll see that each line of output starts with something like -rwxr-xr-x. The nine letters and hyphens of file permissions* correspond to the nine least significant bits of $mode, which would give the octal number 0755 in this case. The other bits, beyond the lowest nine, indicate other details about the file. If you need to work with the mode, you'll want to use the bitwise operators covered later in this chapter.

$nlink

The number of (hard) links to the file or directory. This is the number of true names that the item has. This number is always 2 or more for directories and (usually) 1 for files. You'll see more about this when we talk about creating links to files in Chapter 12. In the listing from ls -l, this is the number just after the permission bits string.

$uid and $gid

The numeric user ID and group ID showing the file's ownership.

$size

The size in bytes, as returned by the -s file test.

$atime, $mtime, and $ctime

The three timestamps, but here they're represented in the system's timestamp format: a 32-bit number telling how many seconds have passed since the *Epoch*, which is an arbitrary starting point for measuring system time. On Unix systems and some others, the Epoch is the beginning of 1970 at midnight Universal Time, but the Epoch is different on some machines. There's more information later in this chapter on turning that timestamp number into something useful.

---

* The first character in that string isn't a permission bit. It indicates the type of entry: a hyphen for an ordinary file, d for directory, or l for symbolic link, among others. The ls command determines this from the other bits past the least significant nine.

Invoking stat on the name of a symbolic link returns information on what the symbolic link points at and not information about the symbolic link itself unless the link happens to be pointing at nothing currently accessible. If you need the (mostly useless) information about the symbolic link itself, use lstat rather than stat (which returns the same information in the same order). If the operand isn't a symbolic link, lstat returns the same things that stat would.

Like the file tests, the operand of stat or lstat defaults to $_, meaning the underlying stat system call will be performed on the file named by the scalar variable $_.

The localtime Function

When you have a timestamp number (such as the ones from stat), it will typically look something like 1180630098. That won't help you, unless you need to compare two timestamps by subtracting. You may need to convert it to something human-readable, such as a string like "Thu May 31 09:48:18 2007". Perl can do that with the localtime function in a scalar context:

```
my $timestamp = 1180630098;
my $date = localtime $timestamp;
```

In a list context, localtime returns a list of numbers, several of which may not be what you'd expect:

```
my($sec, $min, $hour, $day, $mon, $year, $wday, $yday, $isdst)
  = localtime $timestamp;
```

The $mon is a month number, ranging from 0 to 11, which is handy as an index into an array of month names. The $year is the number of years since 1900, oddly enough, so add 1900 to get the real year number. The $wday ranges from 0 (for Sunday) through 6 (for Saturday), and the $yday is the day-of-the-year (ranging from 0 for January 1, through 364 or 365 for December 31).

Two related functions are also useful. The gmtime function is the same as localtime, except that it returns the time in Universal Time (what we once called Greenwich Mean Time). If you need the current timestamp number from the system clock, use the time function. Both localtime and gmtime default to using the current time value if you don't supply a parameter:

```
my $now = gmtime;  # Get the current universal timestamp as a string
```

For more information on manipulating date and time information, see the information about some useful modules in Appendix B.

Bitwise Operators

When you need to work with numbers bit by bit, as when working with the mode bits returned by stat, you'll need to use the bitwise operators. These operators perform binary math operations on values. The bitwise-and operator (&) reports which bits are set in the left argument *and* in the right argument. For example, the expression 10 & 12 has the value 8. The bitwise-and needs to have a one-bit in both operands to produce a one-bit in the result. That means that the logical-and operation on ten (which is 1010 in binary) and twelve (which is 1100) gives eight (which is 1000, with a one-bit only where the left operand has a one-bit *and* the right operand also has a one-bit). See Figure 11-1.

$$\begin{array}{r} 1010 \\ \&\ 1100 \\ \hline 1000 \end{array}$$

Figure 11-1. Bitwise-and addition

The different bitwise operators and their meanings are shown in Table 11-2.

Table 11-2. Bitwise operators

Expression	Meaning
10 & 12	Bitwise-and; which bits are true in both operands (this gives 8)
10 | 12	Bitwise-or; which bits are true in one operand or the other (this gives 14)
10 ^ 12	Bitwise-xor; which bits are true in one operand or the other but not both (this gives 6)
6 << 2	Bitwise shift left; shift the left operand the number of bits shown by the right operand, adding zero-bits at the least-significant places (this gives 24)
25 >> 2	Bitwise shift right; shift the left operand the number of bits shown by the right operand, discarding the least-significant bits (this gives 6)
~ 10	Bitwise negation, also called unary bit complement; return the number with the opposite bit for each bit in the operand (this gives 0xFFFFFFF5, but see the text)

So, here's an example of some things you could do with the $mode returned by stat. The results of these bit manipulations could be useful with chmod, which you'll see in Chapter 12:

```
# $mode is the mode value returned from a stat of CONFIG
warn "Hey, the configuration file is world-writable!\n"
  if $mode & 0002;                          # configuration security problem
my $classical_mode = 0777 & $mode;          # mask off extra high-bits
my $u_plus_x = $classical_mode | 0100;      # turn one bit on
my $go_minus_r = $classical_mode & (~ 0044); # turn two bits off
```

Using Bitstrings

All of the bitwise operators can work with bitstrings, as well as with integers. If the operands are integers, the result will be an integer. (The integer will be at least a 32-bit integer but may be larger if your machine supports that. That is, if you have a 64-bit machine, ~10 may give the 64-bit result 0xFFFFFFFFFFFFFFF5, rather than the 32-bit result 0xFFFFFFF5.)

But if any operand of a bitwise operator is a string, Perl will perform the operation on that bitstring. That is, "\xAA" | "\x55" will give the string "\xFF". Note that these values are single-byte strings and the result is a byte with all eight bits set. Bitstrings may be arbitrarily long.

This is one of the few places where Perl distinguishes between strings and numbers. See the perlop manpage for more information on using bitwise operators on strings.

Using the Special Underscore Filehandle

Every time you use stat, lstat, or a file test in a program, Perl has to go out to the system to ask for a stat buffer on the file (that is, the return buffer from the stat system call). That means if you want to know if a file is readable and writable, you'll ask the system twice for the same information, which isn't likely to change in a nonhostile environment.

This looks like a waste of time,* and can be avoided. Doing a file test, stat, or lstat on the special _ filehandle (the operand being a single underscore) tells Perl to use whatever happens to be lounging around in memory from the previous file test, stat, or lstat function, rather than going out to the operating system again. Sometimes this is dangerous: a subroutine call can invoke stat without your knowledge, blowing your buffer away. If you're careful, you can save yourself a few unneeded system calls, thereby making your program faster. Here's that example of finding files to put on the backup tapes again, using the new tricks you've learned:

```
my @original_files = qw/ fred barney betty wilma pebbles dino bamm-bamm /;
my @big_old_files;                     # The ones we want to put on backup tapes
foreach (@original_files) {
  push @big_old_files, $_
    if (-s) > 100_000 and -A _ > 90;   # More efficient than before
}
```

We used the default of $_ for the first test; this is as more efficient (except perhaps for the programmer), and it gets the data from the operating system. The second test uses the magic _ filehandle. For this test, the data left around after getting the file's size are used, which are what we want.

---

* Because it is. Asking the system for information is relatively slow.

Testing the _ filehandle is different from allowing the operand of a file test, stat, or lstat to default to testing $_. Using $_ would be a fresh test each time on the current file named by the contents of $_, but using _ saves the trouble of calling the system again. Here is another case where similar names were chosen for radically different functions.

Exercises

See Appendix A for answers to the following exercises:

1. [15] Make a program that takes a list of files named on the command line and reports for each one whether it's readable, writable, executable, or doesn't exist. (Hint: It may be helpful to have a function that will do all of the file tests for one file at a time.) What does it report about a file which has been chmod'ed to 0? (That is, if you're on a Unix system, use the command chmod 0 *some_file* to mark that file as neither being readable, writable, nor executable.) In most shells, use a star as the argument to mean all of the normal files in the current directory. That is, you could type something like ./ex11-1 * to ask the program for the attributes of many files at once.

2. [10] Make a program to identify the oldest file named on the command line and report its age in days. What does it do if the list is empty (that is, if no files are mentioned on the command line)?

CHAPTER 12
Directory Operations

The files we created in the previous chapter were generally in the same place as our program. But modern operating systems let us organize files into directories, allowing us to keep our Beatles MP3s away from our important Llama book chapter sources so we don't accidentally send an MP3 file to the publisher. Perl lets you manipulate these directories directly, in ways that are even fairly portable from one operating system to another.

Moving Around the Directory Tree

Your program runs with a working directory, which is the starting point for relative pathnames. That is, if you refer to the file fred, that means "fred in the current working directory."

The chdir operator changes the working directory. It's just like the Unix shell's cd command:

```
chdir "/etc" or die "cannot chdir to /etc: $!";
```

Because this is a system request, the value of $! will be set if an error occurs. You should normally check $! when a false value is returned from chdir since that indicates that something has not gone as requested.

The working directory is inherited by all processes that Perl starts (we'll talk more about that in Chapter 14). However, the change in working directory cannot affect the process that invoked Perl, such as the shell.* So, you can't make a Perl program to replace your shell's cd command.

If you omit the parameter, Perl determines your home directory as best as possible and attempts to set the working directory to your home directory, similar to using

---

* This isn't a limitation on Perl's part; it's a feature of Unix, Windows, and other systems. If you need to change the shell's working directory, see the documentation of your shell.

the `cd` command at the shell without a parameter. This is one of the few places where omitting the parameter doesn't use `$_`.

Some shells permit you to use a tilde-prefixed path with `cd` to use another user's home directory as a starting point (such as `cd ~merlyn`). This is a function of the shell, not the operating system, and Perl is calling the operating system directly. Thus, a tilde prefix will not work with `chdir`.

Globbing

Normally, the shell expands any filename patterns on each command line into the matching filenames. This is called *globbing*. For example, if you give a filename pattern of `*.pm` to the `echo` command, the shell expands this list to a list of names that match:

```
$ echo *.pm
barney.pm dino.pm fred.pm wilma.pm
$
```

The echo command doesn't have to know anything about expanding `*.pm` because the shell has expanded it. This works for your Perl programs:

```
$ cat >show-args
foreach $arg (@ARGV) {
  print "one arg is $arg\n";
}
^D
$ perl show-args *.pm
one arg is barney.pm
one arg is dino.pm
one arg is fred.pm
one arg is wilma.pm
$
```

`show-args` didn't need to know anything about globbing—the names were already expanded in `@ARGV`.

Sometimes we end up with a pattern such as `*.pm` inside our Perl program. Can we expand this pattern into the matching filenames without working hard? Sure—just use the glob operator:

```
my @all_files = glob "*";
my @pm_files = glob "*.pm";
```

Here, `@all_files` gets all the files in the current directory, alphabetically sorted, and not including the files beginning with a period, like the shell. And `@pm_files` gets the same list as we got before by using `*.pm` on the command line.

Anything you can say on the command line, you can put as the (single) argument to glob, including multiple patterns separated by spaces:

```
my @all_files_including_dot = glob ".* *";
```

Here, we've included an additional "dot star" parameter to get the filenames that begin with a dot as well as the ones that don't. The space between these two items inside the quoted string is significant since it separates two different items you want to glob.[*] The reason this works as the shell does is that prior to Perl Version 5.6, the glob operator called */bin/csh*[†] behind the scenes to perform the expansion. Because of this, globs were time-consuming and could break in large directories or in other cases. Conscientious Perl hackers avoided globbing in favor of directory handles, which we will discuss later in this chapter. However, if you're using a modern version of Perl, you should no longer be concerned about such things.

An Alternate Syntax for Globbing

Though we use the term globbing freely, and we talk about the glob operator, you might not see the word glob in many of the programs that use globbing. Why not? Well, most legacy code was written before the glob operator was given a name. Instead, it was called up by the angle-bracket syntax, similar to reading from a filehandle:

```
my @all_files = <*>; ## exactly the same as my @all_files = glob "*";
```

The value between the angle brackets is interpolated similarly to a double-quoted string, which means that Perl variables are expanded to their current Perl values before being globbed:

```
my $dir = "/etc";
my @dir_files = <$dir/* $dir/.*>;
```

Here, we've fetched all the non-dot and dot files from the designated directory because $dir has been expanded to its current value.

Since using angle brackets means both filehandle reading and globbing, how does Perl decide which of the two operators to use? Well, a filehandle has to be a Perl identifier. If the item between the angle brackets is strictly a Perl identifier, it'll be a filehandle read; otherwise, it'll be a globbing operation, as in this example:

```
my @files = <FRED/*>;  ## a glob
my @lines = <FRED>;     ## a filehandle read
my $name = "FRED";
my @files = <$name/*>; ## a glob
```

---

[*] Windows users may be accustomed to using a glob of *.* to mean "all files," but that means "all files with a dot in their names," even in Perl on Windows.

[†] Or a valid substitute if a C-shell wasn't available.

The one exception is if the contents are a simple scalar variable (not an element of a hash or array), then it's an *indirect filehandle read,** where the variable contents give the name of the filehandle you want to read:

```
my $name = "FRED";
my @lines = <$name>; ## an indirect filehandle read of FRED handle
```

Determining if it's a glob or a filehandle read is done at compile time so it's independent of the content of the variables.

If you want, you can get the operation of an indirect filehandle read using the readline operator,† which makes it clearer:

```
my $name = "FRED";
my @lines = readline FRED;  ## read from FRED
my @lines = readline $name; ## read from FRED
```

But the readline operator is rarely used, as indirect filehandle reads are uncommon and are generally performed against a simple scalar variable anyway.

Directory Handles

Another way to get a list of names from a given directory is with a *directory handle*. A directory handle looks and acts like a filehandle. You open it (with opendir instead of open), you read from it (with readdir instead of readline), and you close it (with closedir instead of close). Instead of reading the contents of a file, you're reading the names of files (and other things) in a directory as in this example:

```
my $dir_to_process = "/etc";
opendir DH, $dir_to_process or die "Cannot open $dir_to_process: $!";
foreach $file (readdir DH) {
  print "one file in $dir_to_process is $file\n";
}
closedir DH;
```

Like filehandles, directory handles are automatically closed at the end of the program or if the directory handle is reopened onto another directory.

Unlike globbing, which in older versions of Perl fired off a separate process, a directory handle never fires off another process, which makes it more efficient for applications that demand every ounce of power from the machine. However, it's a lower-level operation, meaning that we have to do more of the work ourselves.

For example, the names are returned in no particular order.‡ The list includes all files, not just those matching a particular pattern (such as *.pm from our globbing

---

* If the indirect handle is a text string, then it's subject to the "symbolic reference" test that is forbidden under use strict. However, the indirect handle might be a typeglob or reference to an I/O object, which means it would work under use strict.

† If you're using Perl 5.005 or later.

‡ It's the unsorted order of the directory entries, similar to the order you get from ls -f or find.

examples). And the list includes all files, especially the dot files and the dot and dot-dot entries.* So, if we wanted only the *pm*-ending files, we could use a skip-over function inside the loop:

```
while ($name = readdir DIR) {
  next unless $name =~ /\.pm$/;
  ... more processing ...
}
```

The syntax is that of a regular expression and not a glob. If we wanted all the non-dot files and we could say that:

```
next if $name =~ /^\./;
```

If we wanted everything but the common dot (current directory) and dot-dot (parent directory) entries, we could explicitly say the following:

```
next if $name eq "." or $name eq "..";
```

Now we'll look at the part that confuses most people, so pay attention. The filenames returned by the readdir operator have no pathname component, but are the name within the directory. So, we're not looking at */etc/passwd* but are looking at *passwd*. Because this is another difference from the globbing operation, it's easy to see how people get confused.

You'll need to patch up the name to get the full name:

```
opendir SOMEDIR, $dirname or die "Cannot open $dirname: $!";
while (my $name = readdir SOMEDIR) {
  next if $name =~ /^\./; # skip over dot files
  $name = "$dirname/$name"; # patch up the path
  next unless -f $name and -r $name; # only readable files
  ...
}
```

Without the patch, the file tests would have been checking files in the current directory, rather than in the directory named in $dirname. This is the single most common mistake when using directory handles.

Recursive Directory Listing

You probably won't need recursive directory access for the first few dozen hours of your Perl programming career. Rather than distract you with the possibility of replacing all those ugly *find* scripts with Perl right now, we'll entice you by saying that Perl comes with a library called File::Find, which you can use for recursive directory processing. We're saying this to keep you from writing your own routines,

---

* Do not make the mistake of many old Unix programs and presume dot and dot-dot are always returned as the first two entries (sorted or not). If that hadn't even occurred to you, pretend we never said it because it's a false presumption. In fact, we're now sorry for bringing it up.

which everyone seems to want to do after those first few dozen hours of programming and then getting puzzled about things like "local directory handles" and "how do I change my directory back?"

Manipulating Files and Directories

Perl is commonly used to wrangle files and directories. Because Perl grew up in a Unix environment and still spends most of its time there, most of the description in this chapter may seem Unix-centric. But the nice thing is that to whatever degree possible, Perl works the same way on non-Unix systems.

Removing Files

Most of the time, we make files so the data can stay around for a while. But when a file is no longer needed, it's time to make it go away. At the Unix shell level, we'd type an rm command to remove a file or files:

```
$ rm slate bedrock lava
```

In Perl, we use the unlink operator:

```
unlink "slate", "bedrock", "lava";
```

This sends the three named files away to bit heaven, never to be seen again.

Since unlink takes a list, and the glob function returns a list, we can combine the two to delete many files at once:

```
unlink glob "*.o";
```

This is similar to rm *.o at the shell, except that we didn't have to fire off a separate rm process. So, we can make those important files go away that much faster.

The return value from unlink tells us how many files have been successfully deleted. Back to the first example, we can check its success:

```
my $successful = unlink "slate", "bedrock", "lava";
print "I deleted $successful file(s) just now\n";
```

Sure, if this number is 3, we know it removed all of the files, and if it's 0, then we removed none of them. But what if it's 1 or 2? Well, there's no clue which ones were removed. If you need to know, do them one at a time in a loop:

```
foreach my $file (qw(slate bedrock lava)) {
  unlink $file or warn "failed on $file: $!\n";
}
```

Here, each file being deleted one at a time means the return value will be 0 (failed) or 1 (succeeded), which happens to look like a nice Boolean value, controlling the execution of warn. Using or warn is similar to or die, except that it's not fatal (see

Chapter 5). In this case, we put the newline on the end of the message to warn because it's not a bug in our program causing the message.

When a particular unlink fails, the $! variable is set to something related to the operating system error, which we've included in the message. This makes sense to use only when doing one filename at a time because the next operating system failed request resets the variable. You can't remove a directory with unlink (just like you can't remove a directory with the simple rm invocation either). Look for the rmdir function coming up shortly for that.

Here's a little-known Unix fact. You can have a file that you can't read, write, or execute, maybe you don't even own the file—that is, it's somebody else's file altogether—but you can still delete the file. That's because the permission to unlink a file doesn't depend upon the permission bits on the file; it's the permission bits on the directory that contains the file that matter.

We mention this because it's normal for a beginning Perl programmer, in the course of trying out unlink, to make a file, chmod it to 0 (so that it's not readable or writable), and check if this makes unlink fail. Instead, it vanishes without so much as a whimper.* If you want to see a failed unlink, try to remove */etc/passwd* or a similar system file. Since that's a file controlled by the system administrator, you won't be able to remove it.†

Renaming Files

Giving an existing file a new name is simple with the rename function:

```
rename "old", "new";
```

This is similar to the Unix mv command, taking a file named *old* and giving it the name *new* in the same directory. You can even move things around:

```
rename "over_there/some/place/some_file", "some_file";
```

This moves a file called some_file from another directory into the current directory, provided the user running the program has the appropriate permissions.‡ Like most functions that request something of the operating system, rename returns false if it fails, and sets $! with the operating system error, so you can (and often should) use or die (or or warn) to report this to the user.

---

* Some of these folks know that rm would generally ask before deleting such a file. But rm is a command, and unlink is a system call. System calls never ask permission, and they never say they're sorry.

† Of course, if you're silly enough to try this when you are logged in as the system administrator, you deserve what you get.

‡ And the files must reside on the same filesystem. You'll see why this rule exists a little later in this chapter.

One frequent* question in the Unix shell-usage newsgroups is how to rename everything that ends with *.old* to the same name with *.new*. Here's how to do it in Perl:

```
foreach my $file (glob "*.old") {
  my $newfile = $file;
  $newfile =~ s/\.old$/.new/;
  if (-e $newfile) {
    warn "can't rename $file to $newfile: $newfile exists\n";
  } elsif (rename $file, $newfile) {
    ## success, do nothing
  } else {
    warn "rename $file to $newfile failed: $!\n";
  }
}
```

The check for the existence of $newfile is needed because rename will rename a file right over the top of an existing file, presuming the user has permission to remove the destination filename. We put the check in so that it's less likely that we'll lose information this way. If you wanted to replace existing files, like *wilma.new*, you wouldn't bother testing with -e first.

Those first two lines inside the loop can be combined (and often are):

```
(my $newfile = $file) =~ s/\.old$/.new/;
```

This works to declare $newfile, copy its initial value from $file, and modify $newfile with the substitution. You can read this as "transform $file to $newfile using this replacement on the right." And yes, because of precedence, those parentheses are required.

Some programmers seeing this substitution for the first time wonder why the backslash is needed on the left but not on the right. The two sides aren't symmetrical: the left part of a substitution is a regular expression, and the right part is a double-quoted string. So we use the pattern /\.old$/ to mean ".*old* anchored at the end of the string" (anchored at the end because we don't want to rename the *first* occurrance of *.old* in a file called *betty.old.old*), but on the right we can write *.new* to make the replacement.

Links and Files

To understand more about what's going on with files and directories, it helps to understand the Unix model of files and directories even if your non-Unix system doesn't work in this way. As usual, there's more to the story than we'll explain here, so check any good book on Unix internal details if you need the full story.

---

* This isn't just any old frequent question; the question of renaming a batch of files at once is the *most* frequent question asked in these newsgroups. And that's why it's the *first* question answered in the FAQs for those newsgroups. And yet, it stays in first place. Hmmm.

A *mounted volume* is a hard disk drive (or something else that works, more or less, like that, such as a disk partition, a floppy disk, a CD-ROM, or a DVD-ROM). It may contain any number of files and directories. Each file is stored in a numbered *inode*, which we can think of as a particular piece of disk real estate. One file might be stored in inode 613, and another in inode 7033.

To locate a particular file, we'll have to look it up in a directory. A directory is a special kind of file, maintained by the system. Essentially, it is a table of filenames and their inode numbers.* Along with the other things in the directory, there are two special directory entries. One is . (called "dot"), which is the name of that directory; and the other is .. ("dot-dot"), which is the directory one step higher in the hierarchy (i.e., the directory's parent directory).† Figure 12-1 provides an illustration of two inodes. One is for a file called *chicken*, and the other is Barney's directory of poems, */home/barney/poems*, which contains that file. The file is stored in inode 613 and the directory is stored in inode 919. (The directory's own name, *poems*, doesn't appear in the illustration because that's stored in another directory.) The directory contains entries for three files (including *chicken*) and two directories (one of which is the reference back to the directory itself, in inode 919), along with each item's inode number.

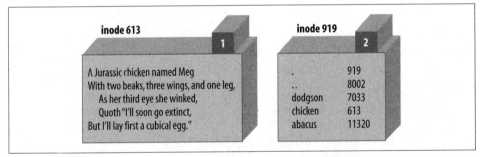

Figure 12-1. The chicken before the egg

When it's time to make a new file in a given directory, the system adds an entry with the file's name and the number of a new inode. How can the system tell that a particular inode is available? Each inode holds a number called its *link count*. The link count is always zero if the inode isn't listed in any directory, so any inode with a link count of zero is available for new file storage. When the inode is added to a directory, the link count is incremented; when the listing is removed, the link count is decremented. For the file *chicken* as illustrated above, the inode count of 1 is shown in the box above the inode's data.

---

* On Unix systems (others don't generally have inodes, hard links, and such), you can use the ls command's -i option to see files' inode numbers. Try a command like ls -ail. When two or more inode numbers are the same for multiple items on a given filesystem, there's only one file involved, one piece of the disk.

† The Unix system *root* directory has no parent. In that directory, .. is the same directory as ., which is the system *root* directory itself.

But some inodes have more than one listing. For example, we've seen that each directory entry includes ., which points back to that directory's own inode. The link count for a directory should always be at least two: its listing in its parent directory and its listing in itself. In addition, if it has subdirectories, each of those will add a link since each will contain ...* In Figure 12-1, the directory's inode count of 2 is shown in the box above its data. A link count is the number of true names for the inode.† Could an ordinary file inode have more than one listing in the directory? It certainly could. Suppose that, working in the directory shown above, Barney uses the Perl link function to create a new link:

```
link "chicken", "egg"
    or warn "can't link chicken to egg: $!";
```

This is similar to typing ln chicken egg at the Unix shell prompt. If link succeeds, it returns true. If it fails, it returns false and sets $!, which Barney is checking in the error message. After this runs, the name *egg* is another name for the file *chicken*, and vice versa; neither name is more real than the other, and (as you may have guessed) it would take some detective work to find out which came first. Figure 12-2 shows a picture of the new situation, where there are two links to inode 613.

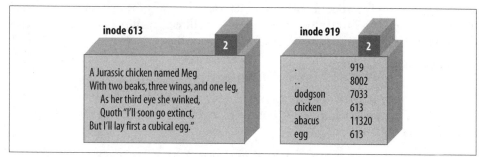

Figure 12-2. The egg is linked to the chicken

These two filenames are talking about the same place on the disk. If the file *chicken* holds 200 bytes of data, *egg* holds the same 200 bytes, for a total of 200 bytes (since it's the same file with two names). If Barney appends a new line of text to file *egg*, that line will also appear at the end of *chicken*.‡ If Barney were to delete *chicken* accidentally (or intentionally), that data would not be lost because it's still available

---

* This implies that the link count of a directory is always equal to two plus the number of directories it contains. On some systems that's true, but some other systems work differently.

† In the traditional output of ls -l, the number of hard links to the item appears to the right of the permission flags (such as -rwxr-xr-x). Now you know why this number is more than 1 for directories and nearly always 1 for ordinary files.

‡ If you experiment with making links and changing text files, be aware that most text editors don't edit the file "in place" but instead save a modified copy. If Barney were to edit *egg* with a text editor, he'd most likely end up with a new file called *egg* and the old file called *chicken*, two separate files, rather than two links to the same file.

under the name *egg*. If he were to delete *egg*, he'd still have *chicken*. Of course, if he deletes both of them, the data will be lost.* There's another rule about the links in directory listings: the inode numbers in a given directory listing refer to inodes on that same mounted volume.† This rule ensures that if the physical medium (the diskette, perhaps) is moved to another machine, all of the directories stick together with their files. That's why you can use `rename` to move a file from one directory to another, but only if both directories are on the same filesystem (mounted volume). If they were on different disks, the system would have to relocate the inode's data, which is too complex an operation for a simple system call.

Another restriction on links is they can't make new names for directories because the directories are arranged in a hierarchy. If you were able to change that, utility programs like *find* and *pwd* could become lost trying to find their way around the filesystem.

So, links can't be added to directories, and they can't cross from one mounted volume to another. Fortunately, there's a way to get around these restrictions on links by using a new and different kind of link: a *symbolic link*.‡ A symbolic link (also called a *soft link* to distinguish it from the true or *hard links* that we've been talking about up to now) is a special entry in a directory that tells the system to look elsewhere. Let's say that Barney (working in the same directory of poems as before) creates a symbolic link with Perl's `symlink` function, like this:

```
symlink "dodgson", "carroll"
  or warn "can't symlink dodgson to carroll: $!";
```

This is similar to what would happen if Barney used the command `ln -s dodgson carroll` from the shell. Figure 12-3 shows a picture of the result, including the poem in inode 7033.

Now if Barney chooses to read */home/barney/poems/carroll*, he gets the same data as if he had opened */home/barney/poems/dodgson* because the system follows the symbolic link automatically. That new name isn't the "real" name of the file because (as you can see in the diagram) the link count on inode 7033 is still just one. That's because the symbolic link tells the system, "If you got here looking for *carroll*, now you want to go off to find something called *dodgson* instead."

A symbolic link can freely cross mounted filesystems or provide a new name for a directory unlike a hard link. A symbolic link can point to any filename, one in this directory or in another one—even to a file that doesn't exist. But that means a soft link can't keep data from being lost as a hard link can since the symlink doesn't contribute

---

* Though the system won't necessarily overwrite this inode right away, there's no easy way to get the data back once the link count has gone to zero. Have you made a backup recently?

† The one exception is the special .. entry in the volume's *root* directory, which refers to the directory in which that volume is mounted.

‡ Some old Unix systems don't support symlinks, but those are rare nowadays.

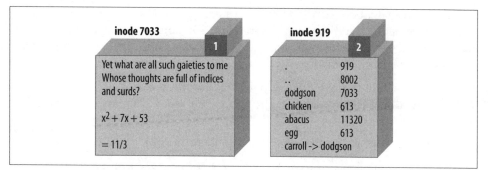

Figure 12-3. A symlink to inode 7033

to the link count. If Barney were to delete *dodgson*, the system could no longer follow the soft link.* Though there would be an entry called *carroll*, trying to read from it would give an error such as file not found. The file test -l 'carroll' would report true, but -e 'carroll' would be false. It's a symlink, but it doesn't exist.

Since a soft link could point to a file that doesn't exist, it could be used when creating a file as well. Barney has most of his files in his home directory, */home/barney*, but he also needs frequent access to a directory with a long name that is difficult to type: */usr/local/opt/system/httpd/root-dev/users/staging/barney/cgi-bin*. So, he sets up a symlink named */home/barney/my_stuff*, which points to that long name, and now it's easy for him to get to it. If he creates a file (from his home directory) called *my_stuff/ bowling*, that file's real name is */usr/local/opt/system/httpd/root-dev/users/staging/ barney/cgi-bin/bowling*. Next week, when the system administrator moves these files of Barney's to */usr/local/opt/internal/httpd/www-dev/users/staging/barney/cgi-bin*, Barney repoints the one symlink, and he and all of his programs can still find his files with ease.

It's normal for */usr/bin/perl*, */usr/local/bin/perl*, or both to be symbolic links to the true Perl binary on your system. This makes it easy to switch to a new version of Perl. Say you're the system administrator, and you've built the new Perl. Your older version is running, and you don't want to disrupt anything. When you're ready for the switch, you move a symlink or two, and every program that begins with #!/usr/bin/ perl will use the new version. In the unlikely case of a problem, you can replace the old symlinks and have the older Perl running the show again. (Like any good admin, notify your users to test their code with the new */usr/bin/perl-7.2* well in advance of the switch, and tell them they can keep using the older one during the next month's grace period by changing their programs' first lines to #!/usr/bin/perl-6.1, if they need to.)

---

* Deleting *carroll* would merely remove the symlink.

Perhaps suprisingly, both hard and soft links are useful. Many non-Unix operating systems have neither, and the lack is sorely felt. On some non-Unix systems, symbolic links may be implemented as a "shortcut" or an "alias." Check the perlport manpage for the latest details.

To find out where a symbolic link is pointing, use the readlink function. This will tell you where the symlink leads, or it will return undef if its argument wasn't a symlink:

```
my $where = readlink "carroll";           # Gives "dodgson"

my $perl = readlink "/usr/local/bin/perl"; # Maybe tells where perl is
```

You can remove either kind of link with unlink. Now, you see where that operation gets its name. unlink removes the directory entry associated with the given filename, decrementing the link count and possibly freeing the inode.

Making and Removing Directories

Making a directory inside an existing directory is easy. Invoke the mkdir function:

```
mkdir "fred", 0755 or warn "Cannot make fred directory: $!";
```

Again, true means success, and $! is set on failure.

But what's that second parameter, 0755? That's the initial permission setting[*] on the newly created directory (you can always change it later). The value here is specified as an octal value because the value will be interpreted as a Unix permission value, which has a meaning based on groups of three bits each, and octal values represent that nicely. Yes, even on Windows or MacPerl, you still need to know a little about Unix permissions values to use the mkdir function. Mode 0755 is a good one to use because it gives you full permission but lets everyone else have read access without permission to change anything.

The mkdir function doesn't require you to specify this value in octal. It's just looking for a numeric value (a literal or a calculation), but unless you can quickly figure that 0755 octal is 493 decimal in your head, it's easier to let Perl calculate that. And if you accidentally leave off the leading zero, you get 755 decimal, which is 1363 octal, a strange permission combination indeed.

As we saw in Chapter 2, a string value being used as a number is never interpreted as octal even if it starts with a leading 0. So this doesn't work:

```
my $name = "fred";
my $permissions = "0755"; # danger... this isn't working
mkdir $name, $permissions;
```

---

[*] The permission value is modified by the umask value in the usual way. See umask(2) for further information.

Oops, we created a directory with that bizarre 01363 permissions because 0755 was treated as decimal. To fix that, use the oct function, which forces octal interpretation of a string whether or not there's a leading zero:

```
mkdir $name, oct($permissions);
```

If you are specifying the permission value directly within the program, use a number instead of a string. The need for the extra oct function shows up most often when the value comes from user input. For example, suppose we take the arguments from the command line:

```
my ($name, $perm) = @ARGV;  # first two args are name, permissions
mkdir $name, oct($perm) or die "cannot create $name: $!";
```

The value here for $perm is interpreted as a string initially, and the oct function interprets the common octal representation properly.

To remove empty directories, use the rmdir function in a manner similar to the unlink function:

```
rmdir glob "fred/*";  # remove all empty directories below fred/

foreach my $dir (qw(fred barney betty)) {
  rmdir $dir or warn "cannot rmdir $dir: $!\n";
}
```

As with unlink, rmdir returns the number of directories removed, and if invoked with a single name, it sets $! in a reasonable manner on a failure.

The rmdir operator fails for non-empty directories. As a first pass, you can attempt to delete the contents of the directory with unlink, then try to remove what should now be an empty directory. For example, suppose we need a place to write many temporary files during the execution of a program:

```
my $temp_dir = "/tmp/scratch_$$";       # based on process ID; see the text
mkdir $temp_dir, 0700 or die "cannot create $temp_dir: $!";
...
# use $temp_dir as location of all temporary files
...
unlink glob "$temp_dir/* $temp_dir/.*"; # delete contents of $temp_dir
rmdir $temp_dir;                        # delete now-empty directory
```

The initial temporary directory name includes the current process ID, which is unique for every running process and is accessed with the $$ variable (similar to the shell). We do this to avoid colliding with any other processes as long as they also include their process ID as part of their pathname. (Using the program's name as well as the process ID is common, so if the program is called quarry, the directory would be something like /tmp/quarry_$$.)

At the end of the program, that last unlink should remove all the files in this temporary directory, and then the rmdir function can delete the empty directory. However, if we've created subdirectories under that directory, the unlink operator and the rmdir will fail. For a more robust solution, check out the rmtree function provided by the File::Path module of the standard distribution.

Modifying Permissions

The Unix chmod command changes the permissions on a file or directory. Similarly, Perl has the chmod function to perform this task:

```
chmod 0755, "fred", "barney";
```

As with many of the operating system interface functions, chmod returns the number of items successfully altered and, when used with a single argument, sets $! in a sensible way for error messages when it fails. The first parameter is the Unix permission value (even for non-Unix versions of Perl). For the same reasons we presented earlier in describing mkdir, this value is usually specified in octal.

Symbolic permissions (like +x or go=u-w) accepted by the Unix chmod command are not valid for the chmod function.*

Changing Ownership

If the operating system permits it, you may change the ownership and group membership of a list of files with the chown function. The user and group are changed simultaneously, and both have to be the numeric user-ID and group-ID values. For example:

```
my $user = 1004;
my $group = 100;
chown $user, $group, glob "*.o";
```

What if you have a username like merlyn instead of the number? Call the getpwnam function to translate the name into a number, and the corresponding getgrnam† to translate the group name into its number:

```
defined(my $user = getpwnam "merlyn") or die "bad user";
defined(my $group = getgrnam "users") or die "bad group";
chown $user, $group, glob "/home/merlyn/*";
```

The defined function verifies the return value is not undef, which will be returned if the requested user or group is invalid.

The chown function returns the number of files affected, and it sets $! on error.

---

* Unless you've installed and invoked the File::chmod module from CPAN, which can apparently upgrade the chmod operator to understand symbolic mode values.

† These two are among the ugliest function names known to mankind. But don't blame Larry for them; he's giving them the same names the folks at Berkeley did.

Changing Timestamps

In those rare cases when you want to lie to other programs about when a file was most recently modified or accessed, you can use the utime function to fudge the books a bit. The first two arguments give the new access time and modification time, and the remaining arguments are the list of filenames to alter to those timestamps. The times are specified in internal timestamp format (the same type of values returned from the stat function that we mentioned in Chapter 11).

One convenient value to use for the timestamps is "right now," returned in the proper format by the time function. To update all the files in the current directory to look as if they were modified a day ago but accessed now, we could do this:

```
my $now = time;
my $ago = $now - 24 * 60 * 60;   # seconds per day
utime $now, $ago, glob "*";      # set access to now, mod to a day ago
```

Nothing stops you from creating a file that is arbitrarily stamped far in the future or past (within the limits of the Unix timestamp values of 1970 to 2038 or whatever your non-Unix system uses until we get 64-bit timestamps). Maybe you could use this to create a directory where you keep your notes for that time travel novel you're writing.

The third timestamp (the ctime value) is always set to "now" whenever anything alters a file, so there's no way to set it (it would have to be reset to "now" after you set it) with the utime function. That's because it's primary purpose is for incremental backups: if the file's ctime is newer than the date on the backup tape, it's time to back it up again.

Exercises

The programs here are potentially dangerous. Test them in a mostly empty directory to make it difficult to accidentally delete something useful.

See Appendix A for answers to the following exercises:

1. [12] Write a program to ask the user for a directory name and change to that directory. If the user enters a line with nothing but whitespace, change to his or her home directory as a default. After changing, list the ordinary directory contents (not the items whose names begin with a dot) in alphabetical order. (Hint: Will that be easier to do with a directory handle or with a glob?) If the directory change doesn't succeed, alert the user but don't try show the contents.

2. [4] Modify the program to include all files and not just the ones that don't begin with a dot.

3. [5] If you used a directory handle for the previous exercise, rewrite it to use a glob. If you used a glob, try it now with a directory handle.

4. [6] Write a program that works like rm, deleting any files named on the command line. (You don't need to handle any of the options of rm.)

5. [10] Write a program that works like mv, renaming the first command-line argument to the second command-line argument. (You don't need to handle any of the options of mv or additional arguments.) Allow for the destination to be a directory; if it is, use the same original basename in the new directory.

6. [7] If your operating system supports it, write a program that works like ln, making a hard link from the first command-line argument to the second. (You don't need to handle options of ln or more arguments.) If your system doesn't have hard links, print out a message telling what operation you would perform if it were available. Hint: This program has something in common with the previous one and recognizing that could save you time in coding.

7. [7] If your operating system supports it, fix up the program from the previous exercise to allow an optional -s switch before the other arguments to indicate you want to make a soft link instead of a hard link. (Even if you don't have hard links, see whether you can at least make soft links with this program.)

8. [7] If your operating system supports it, write a program to find any symbolic links in the current directory and print out their values (like ls -l would: name -> value).

## CHAPTER 13

Strings and Sorting

Perl is designed to be good at solving programming problems that are about 90% working with text and 10% everything else. So it's no surprise that Perl has strong text-processing abilities, including all that we've done with regular expressions. But sometimes the regular expression engine is too fancy, and you need a simpler way of working with a string, as you'll see in this chapter.

Finding a Substring with index

Finding a substring depends on where you have lost it. If you happen to have lost it within a bigger string, you're in luck because the index function can help you out. Here's how it looks:

```
$where = index($big, $small);
```

Perl locates the first occurrence of the small string within the big string, returning an integer location of the first character. The character position returned is a zero-based value. If the substring is found at the beginning of the string, index returns 0. If it's one character later, the return value is 1, and so on. If the substring can't be found at all, the return value is -1.[*] In this example, $where gets 6:

```
my $stuff = "Howdy world!";
my $where = index($stuff, "wor");
```

Another way you could think of the position number is the number of characters to skip over before getting to the substring. Since $where is 6, we know we have to skip over the first six characters of $stuff before we find wor.

The index function always reports the location of the first found occurrence of the substring. But you can tell it to start searching at a later point than the start of the

---

[*] Former C programmers will recognize this as being like C's index function. Current C programmers ought to recognize it as well, but by this point in the book, you should really be a *former* C programmer.

string by using the optional third parameter, which tells index to start at that position:

```
my $stuff  = "Howdy world!";
my $where1 = index($stuff, "w");             # $where1 gets 2
my $where2 = index($stuff, "w", $where1 + 1); # $where2 gets 6
my $where3 = index($stuff, "w", $where2 + 1); # $where3 gets -1 (not found)
```

(You wouldn't normally search repeatedly for a substring without using a loop.) That third parameter is giving a minimum value for the return value; if the substring can't be found at that position or later, the return value will be -1.

Once in a while, you might prefer to have the last found occurrence of the substring.* You can get that with the rindex function. In this example, we can find the last slash, which turns out to be at position 4 in a string:

```
my $last_slash = rindex("/etc/passwd", "/"); # value is 4
```

The rindex function has an optional third parameter; in this case, it gives the maximum permitted return value:

```
my $fred = "Yabba dabba doo!";
my $where1 = rindex($fred, "abba");          # $where1 gets 7
my $where2 = rindex($fred, "abba", $where1 - 1); # $where2 gets 1
my $where3 = rindex($fred, "abba", $where2 - 1); # $where3 gets -1
```

Manipulating a Substring with substr

The substr operator works with only a part of a larger string. It looks like this:

```
$part = substr($string, $initial_position, $length);
```

It takes three arguments: a string value, a zero-based initial position (like the return value of index), and a length for the substring. The return value is the substring:

```
my $mineral = substr("Fred J. Flintstone", 8, 5);  # gets "Flint"
my $rock = substr "Fred J. Flintstone", 13, 1000;  # gets "stone"
```

As in the previous example, if the requested length (1000 characters, in this case) goes past the end of the string, there'll be no complaint from Perl, but you get a shorter string than you might have. If you want to be sure to go to the end of the string, however long or short it may be, omit that third parameter (the length) like this:

```
my $pebble = substr "Fred J. Flintstone", 13;  # gets "stone"
```

The initial position of the substring in the larger string can be negative, counting from the end of the string (that is, position -1 is the last character).† In this example,

---

* Well, it's not really the last one found. Perl starts searching from the other end of the string, and returns the first location it finds, which amounts to the same result. The return value is the same zero-based number as we always use for describing locations of substrings.

† This is analogous to what you saw with array indices in Chapter 3. As arrays may be indexed from 0 (the first element) upward or from -1 (the last element) downward, substring locations may be indexed from position 0 (at the first character) upward or from position -1 (at the last character) downward.

position -3 is three characters from the end of the string, which is the location of the letter i:

```perl
my $out = substr("some very long string", -3, 2);  # $out gets "in"
```

index and substr work well together. In this example, we can extract a substring that starts at the location of the letter l:

```perl
my $long = "some very very long string";
my $right = substr($long, index($long, "l") );
```

Now here's something really cool: The selected portion of the string can be changed if the string is a variable:*

```perl
my $string = "Hello, world!";
substr($string, 0, 5) = "Goodbye";  # $string is now "Goodbye, world!"
```

The assigned (sub)string doesn't have to be the same length as the substring it's replacing. The string's length is adjusted to fit. If that isn't cool enough to impress you, you could use the binding operator (=~) to restrict an operation to work with part of a string. This example replaces fred with barney wherever possible within the last twenty characters of a string:

```perl
substr($string, -20) =~ s/fred/barney/g;
```

We've never needed that functionality in any of our own code, and chances are you'll never need it either. But it's nice to know that Perl can do more than you'll need, isn't it?

Much of the work that substr and index do could be done with regular expressions. Use those where they're appropriate. substr and index are often faster since they don't have the overhead of the regular expression engine: they're never case-insensitive, they have no metacharacters to worry about, and they don't set any of the memory variables.

Besides assigning to the substr function (which can look a little weird at first glance), you can use substr in a more traditional manner† with the four-argument version, in which the fourth argument is the replacement substring:

```perl
my $previous_value = substr($string, 0, 5, "Goodbye");
```

The previous value comes back as the return value, though you can use this function in a void context to discard it.

---

* Well, technically, it can be any *lvalue*. What that term means precisely is beyond the scope of this book, but you can think of it as anything that can be put on the left side of the equals sign (=) in a scalar assignment. That's usually a variable, but it can (as you see here) be an invocation of the substr operator.

† By traditional, we mean in the "function invocation" sense but not in the "Perl" sense since this feature was introduced to Perl relatively recently.

Formatting Data with sprintf

The `sprintf` function takes the same arguments as `printf` (except for the optional filehandle), but it returns the requested string instead of printing it. This is handy if you want to store a formatted string into a variable for later use or if you want more control over the result than `printf` provides:

```
my $date_tag = sprintf
  "%4d/%02d/%02d %2d:%02d:%02d",
  $yr, $mo, $da, $h, $m, $s;
```

In that example, `$date_tag` gets something like `"2038/01/19 3:00:08"`. The format string (the first argument to `sprintf`) uses a leading zero on some of the format numbers, which we didn't mention when we talked about `printf` formats in Chapter 5. The leading zero on the format number means to use leading zeroes as needed to make the number as wide as requested. Without a leading zero in the formats, the resulting date-and-time string would have unwanted leading spaces instead of zeroes, looking like `"2038/ 1/19 3: 0: 8"`.

Using sprintf with "Money Numbers"

One popular use for `sprintf` is when you want to format a number with a certain number of places after the decimal point, such as when you want to show an amount of money as `2.50` and not `2.5` and certainly not as `2.49997`! That's easy to accomplish with the `"%.2f"` format:

```
my $money = sprintf "%.2f", 2.49997;
```

The full implications of rounding are numerous and subtle, but in most cases, you should keep numbers in memory with all of the available accuracy, rounding off only for output.

If you have a "money number" that is large enough to need commas to show its size, you might find it handy to use a subroutine like this one.[*]

```
sub big_money {
    my $number = sprintf "%.2f", shift @_;
    # Add one comma each time through the do-nothing loop
    1 while $number =~ s/^(-?\d+)(\d\d\d)/$1,$2/;
    # Put the dollar sign in the right place
    $number =~ s/^(-?)/$1\$/;
    $number;
}
```

---

[*] Yes, we know that not everywhere in the world are commas used to separate groups of digits, not everywhere are the digits grouped by threes, and not everywhere the currency symbol appears as it does for U.S. dollars. But this is a good example anyway, so there!

This subroutine uses some techniques you haven't seen yet, but they logically follow from what we've shown you. The first line of the subroutine formats the first (and only) parameter to have two digits after the decimal point. That is, if the parameter were the number 12345678.9, our $number would be the string "12345678.90".

The next line of code uses a while modifier. As we mentioned when we covered that modifier in Chapter 10, that can be rewritten as a traditional while loop:

```
while ($number =~ s/^(-?\d+)(\d\d\d)/$1,$2/) {
    1;
}
```

What does that say to do? As long as the substitution returns a true value (signifying success), the loop body should run. But the loop body does nothing. That's okay with Perl, but it tells us that the purpose of that statement is to do the conditional expression (the substitution) rather than the useless loop body. The value 1 is traditionally used as this kind of a placeholder though any other value would be equally useful.* This works as well as the loop above:

```
'keep looping' while $number =~ s/^(-?\d+)(\d\d\d)/$1,$2/;
```

Now we know that the substitution is the real purpose of the loop, but what is the substitution doing? $number will be some string like "12345678.90" at this point. The pattern will match the first part of the string, but it can't get past the decimal point. (Do you see why it can't?) Memory $1 will get "12345", and $2 will get "678", so the substitution will make $number into "12345,678.90". (Remember, it couldn't match the decimal point, so the last part of the string is left untouched.)

Do you see what the dash is doing near the start of that pattern? (Hint: The dash is allowed at only one place in the string.) We'll tell you at the end of this section in case you haven't figured it out.

We're not done with that substitution statement: since the substitution succeeded, the do-nothing loop goes back to try again. This time, the pattern can't match anything from the comma onward, so $number becomes "12,345,678.90". The substitution adds a comma to the number each time through the loop.

Speaking of the loop, it's still not done. Since the previous substitution was a success, we're back around the loop to try again. But this time, the pattern can't match at all since it has to match at least four digits at the start of the string, so that is the end of the loop.

Why couldn't we have used the /g modifier to do a "global" search-and-replace to save the trouble and confusion of the 1 while? We couldn't use that because we're working backward from the decimal point rather than forward from the start of the

---

* Which is to say, useless. By the way, Perl optimizes away the constant expression so it doesn't take up any runtime.

string. Putting the commas in a number like this can't be done only with the s///g substitution.* Did you figure out the dash? It's allowing for a possible minus sign at the start of the string. The next line of code makes the same allowance, putting the dollar sign in the right place so $number is something like "$12,345,678.90" or perhaps "-$12,345,678.90" if it's negative. The dollar sign isn't necessarily the first character in the string, or that line would be a lot simpler. Finally, the last line of code returns a formatted money number you can print in the annual report.

Advanced Sorting

In Chapter 3, we showed you could sort a list in ascending ASCIIbetical order by using the built-in sort operator. What if you want a numeric sort or a case-insensitive sort? Maybe you want to sort items according to information stored in a hash. Well, Perl lets you sort a list in whatever order you need; you'll see all of those examples by the end of the chapter.

You tell Perl what order you want by making a *sort-definition subroutine*, or *sort subroutine* for short. When you hear the term "sort subroutine," if you've been through any computer science courses, visions of bubble sort, shell sort, and quick sort race through your head, and you say, "No, never again!" Don't worry because it's not that bad. In fact, it's simple. Perl knows how to sort a list of items, but it doesn't know which order you want. So the sort subroutine tells it the order.

Why is this necessary? Well, if you think about it, sorting is putting a bunch of things in order by comparing them all. Since you can't compare them all at once, you need to compare two at a time, eventually using what you find out about each pair's order to put the whole kit and caboodle in line. Perl understands all of those steps except for the part about how you'd like to compare the items, so that's all you have to write.

This means that the sort subroutine doesn't need to sort many items after all. It merely has to be able to compare two items. If it can put two items in the proper order, Perl will be able to tell (by repeatedly consulting the sort subroutine) what order you want for your data.

The sort subroutine is defined like an ordinary subroutine (well, almost). This routine will be called repeatedly, each time checking on a pair of elements from the list you're sorting.

Now, if you were writing a subroutine that's expecting to get two parameters that need sorting, you might write something like this to start:

```
sub any_sort_sub {  # It doesn't really work this way
  my($a, $b) = @_;  # Get and name the two parameters
```

---

* At least, it can't be done without some more advanced regular expression techniques than we've shown you. Those darn Perl developers keep making it harder to write Perl books that use the word "can't."

```
  # start comparing $a and $b here
  ...
}
```

But the sort subroutine will be called repeatedly, often hundreds or thousands of times. Declaring the variables $a and $b and assigning them values at the top of the subroutine will take just a little time, but multiply that by the thousands of times the routine will be called, and you can see it will contribute significantly to the overall execution speed.

We don't do it like that. (In fact, if you did it that way, it wouldn't work.) Instead, it is as if Perl has done this for us, before our subroutine's code has started. You'll write a sort subroutine without that first line; $a and $b have been assigned for you. When the sort subroutine starts running, $a and $b are two elements from the original list.

The sort subroutine returns a coded value describing how the elements compare (like C's qsort(3) does, but it's Perl's own internal sort implementation). If $a should appear before $b in the final list, the sort subroutine returns -1 to say so. If $b should appear before $a, it returns 1.

If the order of $a and $b doesn't matter, the subroutine returns 0. Why would it not matter? Perhaps you're doing a case-insensitive sort and the two strings are fred and Fred. Perhaps you're doing a numeric sort, and the two numbers are equal.

We could write a numeric sort subroutine like this:

```
sub by_number {
  # a sort subroutine, expect $a and $b
  if ($a < $b) { -1 } elsif ($a > $b) { 1 } else { 0 }
}
```

To use the sort subroutine, put its name (without an ampersand) between the keyword sort and the list you're sorting. This example puts a numerically sorted list of numbers into @result:

```
my @result = sort by_number @some_numbers;
```

We called the subroutine by_number because that describes how it's sorting. But more importantly, you can read the line of code that uses it with sort as saying "sort by number," as you would in English. Many sort subroutine names begin with by_ to describe how they sort. We could have called this one numerically for a similar reason, but that's more typing and more chance to mess something up.

We don't have to do anything in the sort subroutine to declare $a and $b, and to set their values. If we did, the subroutine wouldn't work right. We let Perl set up $a and $b for us, and all we need to write is the comparison.

In fact, we can make it simpler and more efficient. Since this kind of three-way comparison is frequent, Perl has a convenient shortcut to use to write it. In this case, we use the spaceship operator (<=>).* This operator compares two numbers and returns -1, 0, or 1 as needed to sort them numerically. So, we could have written that sort subroutine better like this:

```
sub by_number { $a <=> $b }
```

Since the spaceship compares numbers, you may have guessed there's a corresponding three-way string comparison operator: cmp. These two are easy to remember and keep straight. The spaceship has a family resemblance to the numeric comparison operators like >=, but it's three characters long instead of two because it has three possible return values instead of two. And cmp has a family resemblance to the string comparison operators like ge, but it's three characters long instead of two because it has three possible return values instead of two.† Of course, cmp provides the same order as the default sort. You'll never need to write this subroutine, which yields merely the default sort order:‡

```
sub ASCIIbetically { $a cmp $b } my @strings = sort ASCIIbetically @any_strings;
```

But you can use cmp to build a more complex sort order, like a case-insensitive sort:

```
sub case_insensitive { "\L$a" cmp "\L$b" }
```

In this case, we're comparing the string from $a (forced to lowercase) against the string from $b (forced to lowercase), giving a case-insensitive sort order.

We're not modifying the elements themselves; we're using their values. That's important: for efficiency reasons, $a and $b aren't copies of the data items. They're new, temporary aliases for elements of the original list, so if we changed them we'd be mangling the original data. Don't do that—it's neither supported nor recommended.

When your sort subroutine is as simple as the ones we show here (most of the time, it is), you can make the code simpler by replacing the name of the sort routine with the entire sort routine "in line," like this:

```
my @numbers = sort { $a <=> $b } @some_numbers;
```

In modern Perl, you'll hardly ever see a separate sort subroutine, but you'll frequently find sort routines written inline as we've done here.

Suppose you want to sort in descending numeric order. That's easy enough to do with the help of reverse:

```
my @descending = reverse sort { $a <=> $b } @some_numbers;
```

But here's a neat trick. The comparison operators (<=> and cmp) are nearsighted in that they can't see which operand is $a and which is $b. They can only see which

---

* We call it that because it looks like one of the Tie-fighters from *Star Wars*. Well, it looks like that to us.

† This is no accident. Larry does things like this on purpose to make Perl easier to learn and remember. He's a linguist at heart, so he's studied how people think of languages.

‡ You'd never need to write this unless you were writing an introductory Perl book and needed it for an example.

value is on the left and which is on the right. If $a and $b were to swap places, the comparison operator would get the results backward every time. That means this is another way to get a reversed numeric sort:

```
my @descending = sort { $b <=> $a } @some_numbers;
```

With a little practice, you can read this at a glance. It's a descending-order comparison (because $b comes before $a, which is descending order), and it's a numeric comparison (because it uses the spaceship instead of cmp). So, it's sorting numbers in reverse order. In modern Perl versions it doesn't matter much which one of those you do, because reverse is recognized as a modifier to sort, and special shortcuts are taken to avoid sorting it one way just to have to turn it around the other way.

Sorting a Hash by Value

Once you've been sorting lists for a while, you'll run into a situation where you want to sort a hash by value. For example, three of our characters went out bowling last night, and we've got their bowling scores in the following hash. You want to be able to print out the list in the proper order, with the game winner at the top, so we want to sort the hash by score:

```
my %score = ("barney" => 195, "fred" => 205, "dino" => 30);
my @winners = sort by_score keys %score;
```

You aren't really going to be able to sort the hash by score; that's just a verbal shortcut. You can't sort a hash. But when we've used sort with hashes before, we sorted the keys of the hash (in ASCIIbetical order). Now you're going to sort the keys of the hash, but the order will be defined by their corresponding values from the hash. In this case, the result should be a list of our three characters' names in order, according to their bowling scores.

Writing this sort subroutine is fairly easy. What we want is to use a numeric comparison on the scores rather than the names. Instead of comparing $a and $b (the players' names), we want to compare $score{$a} and $score{$b} (their scores). If you think of it that way, it almost writes itself, as in:

```
sub by_score { $score{$b} <=> $score{$a} }
```

Let's step through this and see how it works. Imagine the first time it's called, Perl has set $a to barney and $b to fred. The comparison is $score{"fred"} <=> $score{"barney"}, which (as we can see by consulting the hash) is 205 <=> 195. The spaceship is nearsighted, so when it sees 205 before 195, it says: "No, that's not the right numeric order; $b should come before $a." It tells Perl that fred should come before barney.

Maybe the next time the routine is called, $a is barney again and $b has become dino. The nearsighted numeric comparison sees 30 <=> 195, so it reports that they're in the right order: $a does indeed sort in front of $b. That is, barney comes before dino. At this point, Perl has enough information to put the list in order: fred is the winner, and barney is in second place, and dino is in third place.

Why did the comparison use the $score{$b} before the $score{$a} instead of the other way around? That's because we want bowling scores arranged in descending order, from the highest score of the winner down. You can (after a little practice) read this one at sight as well: $score{$b} <=> $score{$a} means to sort according to the scores in reversed numeric order.

Sorting by Multiple Keys

We forgot to mention the fourth player bowling last night with the other three, so the hash looked like this:

```
my %score = (
  "barney" => 195, "fred" => 205,
  "dino" => 30, "bamm-bamm" => 195,
);
```

bamm-bamm has the same score as barney. Which one will be first in the sorted list of players? There's no telling because the comparison operator (seeing the same score on both sides) will have to return zero when checking those two.

Maybe that doesn't matter, but we prefer to have a well-defined sort. If several players have the same score, we want them to be together in the list, but within that group, the names should be in ASCIIbetical order. How can we write the sort subroutine to say that? Again, this turns out to be easy:

```
my @winners = sort by_score_and_name keys %score;

sub by_score_and_name {
  $score{$b} <=> $score{$a}    # by descending numeric score
    or
  $a cmp $b                    # ASCIIbetically by name
}
```

How does this work? If the spaceship sees two different scores, that's the comparison we want to use. It returns -1 or 1, a true value, so the low-precedence short-circuit or will mean that the rest of the expression will be skipped, and the comparison we want is returned. (Remember, the short-circuit or returns the last expression evaluated.) If the spaceship sees two identical scores, it returns 0, a false value, and the cmp operator gets its turn at bat, returning an appropriate ordering value considering the keys as strings. That is, if the scores are the same, the string-order comparison breaks the tie.

We know that when we use the by_score_and_name sort subroutine like this, it will never return 0. (Do you see why it won't? The answer is in the footnote.*) We know the sort order is always well-defined; that is, we know the result today will be the same as the result with the same data tomorrow.

Your sort subroutine does not have to be limited to two levels of sorting. Here the Bedrock library program puts a list of patron ID numbers in order according to a five-level sort.† This example sorts according to the amount of each patron's outstanding fines (as calculated by a subroutine &fines, not shown here), the number of items they currently have checked out (from %items), their name (in order by family name, then by personal name, both from hashes), and finally by the patron's ID number, in case everything else is the same:

```
@patron_IDs = sort {
  &fines($b) <=> &fines($a) or
  $items{$b} <=> $items{$a} or
  $family_name{$a} cmp $family_name{$a} or
  $personal_name{$a} cmp $family_name{$b} or
  $a <=> $b
} @patron_IDs;
```

Exercises

See Appendix A for answers to the following exercises:

1. [10] Write a program to read in a list of numbers and sort them numerically, printing out the resulting list in a right-justified column. Try it out on this sample data, or use the file *numbers* from the O'Reilly web site (see the Preface):

   ```
   17 1000 04 1.50 3.14159 -10 1.5 4 2001 90210 666
   ```

2. [15] Make a program that will print the following hash's data sorted in case-insensitive alphabetical order by last name. When the last names are the same, sort those by first name (without regard for case). That is, the first name in the output should be Fred's, and the last one should be Betty's. All of the people with the same family name should be grouped together. Don't alter the data. The names should be printed with the same capitalization as shown here. (You can find the source code to create a hash like this in the file *sortable_hash* with the other downloaded files.)

   ```
   my %last_name = qw{
     fred flintstone Wilma Flintstone Barney Rubble
   ```

---

* The only way it could return 0 would be if the two strings were identical, and (since the strings are keys of a hash) we know they're different. If you passed a list with duplicate (identical) strings to sort, it would return 0 when comparing those, but we're passing a list of hash keys.

† It's not unusual in the modern world to need a five-level sort like this, although it was quite infrequent in prehistoric times.

```
    betty rubble Bamm-Bamm Rubble PEBBLES FLINTSTONE
};
```

3. [15] Make a program that looks through a given string for every occurrence of a given substring, printing out the positions where the substring is found. For example, given the input string "This is a test." and the substring "is", it should report positions 2 and 5. If the substring were "a", it should report 8. What does it report if the substring is "t"?

## CHAPTER 14

Process Management

One of the best parts of being a programmer is launching someone else's code so you don't have to write it yourself. It's time to learn how to manage your children* by launching other programs directly from Perl.

Like everything else in Perl, There's More Than One Way To Do It, with lots of overlap, variations, and special features. If you don't like the first way, read on for another page or two for a solution more to your liking.

Perl is very portable. Most of the rest of this book doesn't need many notes saying that it works this way on Unix systems, that way on Windows, and the other way on VMS. But when you're starting other programs on your machine, different programs are available on a Macintosh than you'll likely find on a Cray. The examples in this chapter are primarily Unix-based; if you have a non-Unix system, expect to see some differences.

The system Function

The simplest way to launch a child process in Perl to run a program is the system function. For example, to invoke the Unix date command from within Perl, it looks like this:

```
system "date";
```

The child process runs the date command, which inherits Perl's standard input, standard output, and standard error. This mean the normal short date-and-time string generated by date ends up wherever Perl's STDOUT was going.

The parameter to the system function is generally whatever you'd normally type at the shell. If it were a more complicated command, like "ls -l $HOME", we'd just have put all that into the parameter:

```
system 'ls -l $HOME';
```

---

* Child processes, that is.

We had to switch here from double quotes to single quotes since $HOME is the shell's variable. Otherwise, the shell would never have seen the dollar sign since that's an indicator for Perl to interpolate. Alternatively, we could write this:

```
system "ls -l \$HOME";
```

But that can become unwieldly.

The date command is output-only, but say it had been a chatty command, asking first "for which time zone do you want the time?"* That'll end up on standard output, and then the program will listen on standard input (inherited from Perl's STDIN) for the response. You'll see the question, type in the answer (like "Zimbabwe time"), and date will finish its duty.

While the child process is running, Perl is patiently waiting for it to finish. If the date command took 37 seconds, then Perl is paused for those 37 seconds. You can use the shell's facility to launch a background process†:

```
system "long_running_command with parameters &";
```

Here the shell launches, notices the ampersand at the end of the command line, and puts long_running_command into the background. And then the shell exits quickly, which Perl notices and moves on. In this case, the long_running_command is a grand-child of the Perl process, to which Perl has no direct access or knowledge.

When the command is "simple enough," no shell gets involved. For the date and ls commands, the requested command is launched directly by Perl, which searches the inherited PATH‡ to find the command if necessary. But if there's anything weird in the string (such as shell metacharacters like the dollar sign, semicolon, or vertical bar), Perl invokes the standard Bourne Shell (*/bin/sh*§) to work through the complicated stuff. In that case, the shell is the child process, and the requested commands are grandchildren (or further offspring). For example, you can write an entire little shell script in the following argument:

```
system 'for i in *; do echo == $i ==; cat $i; done';
```

Here again, we're using single quotes because the dollar signs are meant for the shell and not for Perl. Double quotes would have permitted Perl to expand $i to its current Perl value and not let the shell expand it to its own value.** By the way, that little shell

---

* As far as we know, no one has made a date command that works like this.

† See what we mean about this depending upon your system? The Unix shell (*/bin/sh*) lets you use the ampersand on this kind of command to make a background process. If your non-Unix system doesn't support this way to launch a background process, then you can't do it this way.

‡ The PATH can be changed by adjusting $ENV{'PATH'} at any time. Initially, this is the environment variable inherited from the parent process (usually the shell). Changing this value affects new child processes but cannot affect any preceding parent processes. The PATH is the list of directories where executable programs (commands) are found, even on some non-Unix systems.

§ Or whatever was determined when Perl was built. Practically, this is */bin/sh* on Unix-like systems.

** If you set $i = '$i', it would work anyway until a maintenance programmer came along and "fixed" that line out of existence.

script goes through all of the normal files in the current directory, printing out each one's name and contents; you can try it if you don't believe us.

Avoiding the Shell

The system operator may be invoked with more than one argument,[*] in which case a shell doesn't get involved no matter how complicated the text:

```
my $tarfile = "something*wicked.tar";
my @dirs = qw(fred|flintstone <barney&rubble> betty );
system "tar", "cvf", $tarfile, @dirs;
```

In this case, the first parameter ("tar" here) gives the name of a command found in the normal PATH-searching way, and the remaining arguments are passed, one by one, directly to that command. Even if the arguments have shell-significant characters, such as the name in $tarfile or the directory names in @dirs, the shell never gets a chance to mangle the string. So, that tar command will get five parameters. Compare this with:

```
system "tar cvf $tarfile @dirs";  # Oops!
```

Here, we've now piped a bunch of stuff into a flintstone command, put it into the background, and opened *betty* for output.

That's a bit scary,[†] especially if those variables are from user input, such as from a web form or something. So, if you can arrange things to use the multiple-argument version of system, you probably should use that way to launch your subprocess. (You'll have to give up the ability to have the shell do the work for you to set up I/O redirection, background processes, and the like, though. There's no such thing as a free launch.)

Note that redundantly, a single-argument invocation of system is nearly equivalent to the proper multiple-argument version of system:

```
system $command_line;
system "/bin/sh", "-c", $command_line;
```

But nobody writes the latter unless you want things processed by a different shell, like the C-shell:

```
system "/bin/csh", "-fc", $command_line;
```

---

[*] Or with a parameter in the indirect-object slot, like system { 'fred' } 'barney';, which runs the program barney, but lies to it so it thinks it's called 'fred'. See the perlfunc manpage.

[†] Unless you're using taint checking and have done all the right things to prescan your data to ensure that the user isn't pulling a fast one on you.

Even this is rare since the One True Shell* seems to have a lot more flexibility, especially for scripted items.

The return value of the system operator is based upon the exit status of the child command†. In Unix, an exit value of 0 means that everything is all right, and a nonzero exit value usually indicates that something went wrong:

```
unless (system "date") {
  # Return was zero - meaning success
  print "We gave you a date, OK!\n";
}
```

This is backward from the normal "true is good—false is bad" strategy for most of the operators, so to write a typical "do this or die" style, we'll need to flip false and true. The easiest way is to prefix the system operator with a bang (the logical-not operator):

```
!system "rm -rf files_to_delete" or die "something went wrong";
```

In this case, including $! in the error message would be inappropriate because the failure is most likely somewhere within the experience of the rm command, and it's not a system-call related error within Perl that $! can reveal.

The exec Function

Everything we've said about system syntax and semantics is also true about the exec function except for one (very important) thing. The system function creates a child process, which scurries off to perform the requested action while Perl naps. The exec function causes the Perl process itself to perform the requested action. Think of it as more like a "goto" than a subroutine call.

For example, suppose we wanted to run the bedrock command in the /tmp directory, passing it arguments of -o args1 followed by whatever arguments our own program was invoked with. That'd look like this:

```
chdir "/tmp" or die "Cannot chdir /tmp: $!";
exec "bedrock", "-o", "args1", @ARGV;
```

When we reach the exec operation, Perl locates bedrock, and "jumps into it." At that point, the Perl process is gone,‡ only the process running the bedrock command

---

* That's /bin/sh, or whatever your Unix system has installed as the most Bourne-like shell. If you don't have a One True Shell, Perl figures out how to invoke some other command-line interpreter, with notable consequences. See the documentation for that Perl port.

† It's the "wait" status, which is the child exit code times 256, plus 128 if core was dumped, plus the signal number triggering termination if any. But we rarely check the specifics of that, and a true/false value suffices for nearly all applications.

‡ Actually, it's the same process, having performed the Unix exec(2) system call (or equivalent). The process ID remains the same.

remains. When bedrock is finished, there's no Perl to come back to, so we'd get a prompt back if we invoked this program from the command line.

Why is this useful? If the purpose of this Perl program were to set up a particular environment to run another program, the purpose is fulfilled as soon as the other program has started. If we'd used system instead of exec, we'd have a Perl program standing around tapping its toes waiting for the other program to complete, so Perl could finally exit as well. That's a wasted resource.

Having said that, using exec is rare except in combination with fork (which you'll see later). If you are puzzling over system versus exec, pick system, and you'll be fine most of the time.

Because Perl is no longer in control once the requested command has started, it doesn't make any sense to have any Perl code following the exec except for handling the error when the requested command cannot be started:

```
exec "date";
die "date couldn't run: $!";
```

If you have warnings turned on, and if you have any code after the exec other than a die,* you'll get notified.

The Environment Variables

When you're starting another process (with any of the methods discussed here), you may need to set up its environment in one way or another. You could start the process with a certain working directory, which it inherits from your process. Another common configuration detail is the environment variables.

One of the best-known environment variables is PATH. (If you've never heard of it, you probably haven't used a system that has environment variables.) On Unix and similar systems, PATH is a colon-separated list of directories that may hold programs. When you type a command such as rm fred, the system will look for the rm command in that list of directories in order. Perl (or your system) will use PATH whenever it needs to find the program to run. If the program runs other programs, those may also be found along the PATH. (If you give a complete name for a command, such as /bin/echo, there'll be no need to search PATH. But that's less convenient.)

In Perl, the environment variables are available via the special %ENV hash, and each key in this hash represents one environment variable. At the start of your program's execution, %ENV holds values it has inherited from its parent process (generally the shell). Modifying this hash changes the environment variables, which will be inherited by new processes and possibly used by Perl as well. For example, suppose you

---

* Or exit. Or if it's at the end of a block. This may change in a new release of Perl, too.

wished to run the system's make utility (which typically runs other programs), and you want to use a private directory as the first place to look for commands (including make). And let's say you don't want the IFS environment variable to be set when you run the command because that might cause make or some subcommand do the wrong thing. Here we go:

```
$ENV{'PATH'} = "/home/rootbeer/bin:$ENV{'PATH'}";
delete $ENV{'IFS'};
my $make_result = system "make";
```

Newly created processes will generally inherit from their parent the environment variables, the current working directory, the standard input, output, and error streams, and more esoteric items. See the documentation about programming on your system for more details. (On most systems, your program can't change the environment for the shell or other parent process that started it.)

Using Backquotes to Capture Output

With system and exec, the output of the launched command ends up wherever Perl's standard output is going. Sometimes, it's interesting to capture that output as a string value to perform further processing. That's done by creating a string using backquotes instead of single or double quotes:

```
my $now = `date`;           # grab the output of date
print "The time is now $now"; # newline already present
```

Normally, this date command spits out a string approximately 30 characters long to its standard output, giving the current date and time followed by a newline. When we've placed date between backquotes, Perl executes the date command, arranging to capture its standard output as a string value and, in this case, assigned to the $now variable.

This is similar to the Unix shell's meaning for backquotes. However, the shell performs the additional job of ripping off the final end-of-line to make it easier to use the value as part of other things. Perl is honest; it gives the real output. To get the same result in Perl, add an additional chomp operation on the result:

```
chomp(my $no_newline_now = `date`);
print "A moment ago, it was $no_newline_now, I think.\n";
```

The value beween backquotes is like the single-argument form of system* and is interpreted as a double-quoted string, meaning that backslash-escapes and variables are expanded appropriately.† For example, to fetch the Perl documentation on a list

---

* That is, it's always interpreted by the One True Shell (*/bin/sh*) or an alternative, as with system.

† If you want to pass a real backslash to the shell, you'll need to use two. If you need to pass two (which happens frequently on Windows systems), you'll need to use four.

---

of Perl functions, we might invoke the perldoc command repeatedly, each time with a different argument:

```
my @functions = qw{ int rand sleep length hex eof not exit sqrt umask };
my %about;

foreach (@functions) {
  $about{$_} = `perldoc -t -f $_`;
}
```

$_ will be a different value for each invocation, letting us grab the output of a different command varying only in one of its parameters. If you haven't seen some of these functions, it might be useful to look them up in the documentation to see what they do.

There's no easy equivalent of single quotes for backquotes;[*] variable references and backslash items are always expanded. There's no easy equivalent of the multiple-argument version of system where a shell is never involved. If the command inside the backquotes is complex enough, a Unix Bourne Shell (or whatever your system uses) is invoked to interpret the command automatically.

At the risk of introducing the behavior by demonstrating how not to do it, we'd like to suggest you avoid using backquotes in a place where the value isn't being captured[†] as in this example:

```
print "Starting the frobnitzigator:\n";
`frobnitz -enable`; # please don't do this!
print "Done!\n";
```

The problem is that Perl has to work harder to capture the output of this command, even when you're throwing it away. Also, you lose the option to use multiple arguments to system to control the argument list. So from both a security standpoint and an efficiency viewpoint, use system instead.

Standard error of a backquoted command is inherited from Perl's current standard error output. If the command spits out error messages to standard error, you'll probably see them on the terminal, which could be confusing to the user who hasn't invoked the frobnitz command. If you want to capture error messages with standard output, you can use the shell's normal "merge standard error to the current standard output," which is spelled 2>&1 in the normal Unix shell:

```
my $output_with_errors = `frobnitz -enable 2>&1`;
```

This will make the standard error output intermingled with the standard output, much as it appears on the terminal, though possibly in a different sequence because

---

[*] For harder methods, you can place your string inside qx'...' delimiters, or you can put it all in a variable using a single-quoted string and interpolate that string into a backquoted string since the interpolation will be only one level.

[†] This is called a "void" context.

of buffering. If you need the output and the error output separated, you will find harder-to-type solutions.* Similarly, standard input is inherited from Perl's current standard input. The commands we typically use with backquotes don't read standard input, so that's rarely a problem. However, let's say the date command asked which time zone (as we imagined earlier). That'll be a problem because the prompt for "which time zone" will be sent to standard output, which is being captured as part of the value. Then, the date command will want to read from standard input. Since the user has never seen the prompt, he doesn't know he should be typing anything. Soon, the user calls you up and tells you your program is stuck.

So, stay away from commands that read standard input. If you're not sure whether something reads from standard input, add a redirection from */dev/null* for input like this:

```
my $result = `some_questionable_command arg arg argh </dev/null`;
```

The child shell will redirect input from */dev/null*, and the grandchild questionable command will at worst read and immediately get an end-of-file.

Using Backquotes in a List Context

If the output from a command has multiple lines, the scalar use of backquotes returns it as a single long string containing newline characters. However, using the same backquoted string in a list context yields a list containing one line of output per element.

For example, the Unix who command normally spits out a line of text for each current login on the system as follows:

```
merlyn     tty/42     Dec 7  19:41
rootbeer   console    Dec 2  14:15
rootbeer   tty/12     Dec 6  23:00
```

The left column is the username, the middle column is the tty name (that is, the name of the user's connection to the machine), and the rest of the line is the date and time of login (and possibly remote login information but not in this example). In a scalar context, we get all that at once, which we would need to split up:

```
my $who_text = `who`;
```

But in a list context, we automatically get the data broken up by lines:

```
my @who_lines = `who`;
```

We'll have a number of separate elements in @who_lines, each one terminated by a newline. Adding a chomp around the outside of that will rip off those newlines, but

---

* Such as IPC::Open3 in the standard Perl library, or writing your own forking code as you will see later.

let's go in a different direction. If we put that as part of the value for a foreach, we'll iterate over the lines automatically, placing each one in $_:

```
foreach (`who`) {
  my($user, $tty, $date) = /(\S+)\s+(\S+)\s+(.*)/;
  $ttys{$user} .= "$tty at $date\n";
}
```

This loop will iterate three times for the data above. (Your system will probably have more than three active logins at any given time.) The first statement in the loop is a regular expression match, and in the absence of the binding operator (=~), that's matching against $_, which is good because that's where the data is.

The regular expression is looking for a nonblank word, some whitespace, a non-blank word, some whitespace, and the rest of the line up to, but not including, the newline (since dot doesn't match newline by default).* That's good because that's what $_ looks like each time through the loop. That'll make $1 be "merlyn", $2 be "tty/42", and $3 be "Dec 7 19:41" as a successful match on the first time through the loop.

However, this regular expression match is in a list context, so we'll get the list of memories instead of the true/false "did it match" value, as described in Chapter 8. So, $user ends up being "merlyn", and so on.

The second statement inside the loop stores away the tty and date information, appending to a (possibly undef) value in the hash because a user might be logged in more than once as user "rootbeer" was in our example.

Processes as Filehandles

So far, we've been looking at ways to deal with synchronous processes, where Perl stays in charge, launches a command, (usually) waits for it to finish, and possibly grabs its output. But Perl can also launch a child process that stays alive, communicating† to Perl on an ongoing basis until the task is complete.

The syntax for launching a concurrent (parallel) child process is to put the command as the "filename" for an open call and to precede or follow the command with a vertical bar, which is the "pipe" character. For that reason, this is often called a *piped open*:

```
open DATE, "date|" or die "cannot pipe from date: $!";
open MAIL, "|mail merlyn" or die "cannot pipe to mail: $!";
```

---

* Now you can see why dot doesn't match newline by default. It makes it easy to write patterns like this one in which we don't have to worry about a newline at the end of the string.

† Via pipes or whatever your operating system provides for interprocess communication.

In the first example, with the vertical bar on the right, the command is launched with its standard output connected to the DATE filehandle opened for reading, similar to the way that the command date | your_program would work from the shell. In the second example, with the vertical bar on the left, the command's standard input is connected to the MAIL filehandle opened for writing, similar to what happens with the command your_program | mail merlyn. In either case, the command launches and continues independently of the Perl process.* The open fails if the child process cannot be created. If the command doesn't exist or exits erroneously, this will (generally) not be seen as an error when opening but as an error when closing. We'll get to that in a moment.

For all intents and purposes, the rest of the program doesn't know, doesn't care, and would have to work hard to figure out that this is a filehandle opened on a process rather than on a file. So, to get data from a filehandle opened for reading, we'll do the normal read:

```
my $now = <DATE>;
```

To send data to the mail process (waiting for the body of a message to deliver to *merlyn* on standard input), a simple print-with-a-filehandle will do:

```
print MAIL "The time is now $now"; # presume $now ends in newline
```

In short, you can pretend that these filehandles are hooked up to magical files, one that contains the output of the date command and one that will automatically be mailed by the mail command.

If a process is connected to a filehandle, open for reading, and then it exits, the filehandle returns end-of-file, just like reading up to the end of a normal file. When you close a filehandle open for writing to a process, the process will see end-of-file. So, to finish sending the email, close the handle:

```
close MAIL;
die "mail: nonzero exit of $?" if $?;
```

If you close a filehandle attached to a process, Perl waits for the process to complete so it can get the process's exit status. The exit status is then available in the $? variable (reminiscent of the same variable in the Bourne Shell) and is the same kind of number as the value returned by the system function: zero for success and nonzero for failure. Each new exited process overwrites the previous value though, so save it quickly if you want it. (The $? variable also holds the exit status of the most recent system or backquoted command, if you're curious.)

The processes are synchronized like a pipelined command. If you try to read with no data available, the process is suspended (without consuming additional CPU time)

---

* If the Perl process exits before the command is complete, a command that's been reading will see end-of-file, while a command that's been writing will get a "broken pipe" error signal on the next write by default.

until the sending program has started speaking again. Similarly, if a writing process gets ahead of the reading process, the writing process slows down until the reader starts to catch up. There's a buffer (usually 8KB or so) in between so they don't have to stay in lockstep.

Why use processes as filehandles? Well, it's the only easy way to write to a process based on the results of a computation. If you're only reading, backquotes can be easier to manage unless you want to have the results as they come in.

For example, the Unix find command locates files based on their attributes, and it can take a while if used on a fairly large number of files (such as starting from the *root* directory). You can put a find command inside backquotes, but it's often nicer to see the results as they are found:

```
open F, "find / -atime +90 -size +1000 -print|" or die "fork: $!";
while (<F>) {
  chomp;
  printf "%s size %dK last accessed on %s\n",
    $_, (1023 + -s $_)/1024, -A $_;
}
```

The find command in the previous example is looking for all the files not accessed within the past 90 days and larger than 1,000 blocks. (These are good candidates to move to longer-term storage.) While find is searching, Perl can wait. As each file is found, Perl responds to the incoming name and displays some information about that file for further research. Had this been written with backquotes, we wouldn't have seen any output until the find commmand had finished. It's comforting to see that it's actually doing the job before it's done.

Getting Down and Dirty with fork

In addition to the high-level interfaces described, Perl provides nearly direct access to the low-level process management system calls of Unix and some other systems so far. If you've never done this before,* you will probably want to skip this section. While it's a bit much to cover all this stuff in a chapter like this, let's at least look at a quick reimplementation of this:

```
system "date";
```

Look at how that would be done using the low-level system calls:

```
defined(my $pid = fork) or die "Cannot fork: $!";
unless ($pid) {
  # Child process is here
  exec "date";
  die "cannot exec date: $!";
```

---

* Or if you're not running on a system that has support for forking. But the Perl developers are working hard to add forking even on systems whose underlying process model is very different than the one in Unix.

```
    }
    # Parent process is here
    waitpid($pid, 0);
```

Here, we've checked the return value from fork, which will be undef if it failed. Usually it will succeed, causing two separate processes to continue to the next line, but only the parent process has a nonzero value in $pid, so only the child process executes the exec function. The parent process skips over that and executes the waitpid function, waiting for that particular child to finish (if others finish in the meantime, they are ignored). If that all sounds like gobbledygook, just remember that you can continue to use the system function without being laughed at by your friends.

When you go to this extra trouble, you will have full control over arbitary pipe creation, rearranging filehandles and noticing your process ID and your parent's process ID (if knowable). But again, that's all a bit complicated for this chapter, so see the details in the perlipc manpage (and in any good book on application programming on your system) for further information.

Sending and Receiving Signals

A Unix signal is a tiny message sent to a process. It can't say much; it's like a car horn honking: does that honk you hear mean "look out—the bridge collapsed," "the light has changed—get going," "stop driving—you've got a baby on the roof," or "hello, world"? Fortunately, Unix signals are easier to interpret than that because there's a different one for each of these situations.* Different signals are identified by a name (such as SIGINT, meaning "interrupt signal") and a corresponding small integer (in the range from 1 to 16, 1 to 32, or 1 to 63, depending on your Unix flavor). Signals are typically sent when a significant event happens, such as pressing the interrupt character (typically Ctrl-C) on the terminal, which sends a SIGINT to all the processes attached to that terminal.† Some signals are sent automatically by the system, but they can come from another process.

You can send signals from your Perl process to another process, but you have to know the target's process ID number. How to figure that out is a bit complicated,‡ but say you know that you want to send a SIGINT to process 4201. That's easy enough:

```
    kill 2, 4201 or die "Cannot signal 4201 with SIGINT: $!";
```

---

* Well, not exactly these situations but analogous, Unix-like ones. For these, the signals are SIGHUP, SIGCONT, SIGINT, and the fake SIGZERO (signal number zero).

† And you thought that pressing Ctrl-C stopped your program. Actually, it simply sends the SIGINT signal, and that stops the program by default. As you'll see later in this chapter, you can make a program that does something different when SIGINT comes in rather than stopping at once.

‡ Usually, you have the process ID because it's a child process you produced with fork, or you found it in a file or from an external program. Using an external program can be difficult and problematic, which is why many long-running programs save their own current process ID into a file, usually described in the program's documentation.

It's named "kill" because one of the primary purposes of signals is to stop a process that's gone on long enough. You can use the string `'INT'` in place of the 2 there because signal number 2 is SIGINT. If the process no longer exists,* you'll get a false return value, so you can use this technique to see if a process is alive. A special signal number of 0 says, "Check to see whether I could send a signal if I wanted to, but I don't want to, so don't actually send anything." A process probe might look like:

```
unless (kill 0, $pid) {
  warn "$pid has gone away!";
}
```

Perhaps more interesting than sending signals is catching signals. Why might you want to do this? Suppose you have a program that creates files in */tmp*, and you normally delete those files at the end of the program. If someone presses Ctrl-C during the execution, that leaves trash in */tmp*, an impolite thing to do. To fix this, create a signal handler that takes care of the cleanup:

```
my $temp_directory = "/tmp/myprog.$$"; # create files below here
mkdir $temp_directory, 0700 or die "Cannot create $temp_directory: $!";

sub clean_up {
  unlink glob "$temp_directory/*";
  rmdir $temp_directory;
}

sub my_int_handler {
  &clean_up;
  die "interrupted, exiting...\n";
}

$SIG{'INT'} = 'my_int_handler';

.   # Time passes, the program runs, creates some temporary
.   # files in the temp directory, maybe someone presses Ctrl-C
.
# Now it's the end of normal execution
&clean_up;
```

The assignment into the special %SIG hash activates the handler until revoked. The key is the name of the signal without the constant SIG prefix, and the value is a string† naming the subroutine without the ampersand. From then on, if a SIGINT comes along, Perl will stop whatever it's doing and jump to the subroutine. Our subroutine cleans up the temp files and exits. (If nobody presses Ctrl-C, we'll still call &clean_up at the end of normal execution.)

---

* Sending a signal will also fail if you're not the superuser and it's someone else's process. It would be rude to send SIGINT to someone else's programs, anyway.

† The value can be a subroutine reference, but we're not doing those here.

If the subroutine returns rather than exiting, execution will resume right where it was interrupted. This can be useful if the interrupt needs to interrupt something rather than causing it to stop. For example, suppose processing each line of a file takes a few seconds, which is slow, and you want to abort the overall processing when an interrupt is processed but not in the middle of processing a line. Set a flag in the interrupt procedure and check it at the end of each line's processing:

```perl
my $int_count;
sub my_int_handler { $int_count++ }
$SIG{'INT'} = 'my_int_handler';
...
$int_count = 0;
while (<SOMEFILE>) {
  ... some processing that takes a few seconds ...
  if ($int_count) {
    # interrupt was seen!
    print "[processing interrupted...]\n";
    last;
  }
}
```

As each line is processed, the value of $int_count will be 0 if no one has pressed Ctrl-C, so the loop continues to the next item. However, if an interrupt comes in, the interrupt handler increments the $int_count flag, breaking out of the loop when checked at the end.

So, you can set a flag or break out of the program, and that covers most of what you'll need from catching signals. The current implementation of signal handlers is not entirely without faults,[*] however, so keep the stuff you're doing in there to a minimum, or your program may end up blowing up sometime when you least expect it.

Exercises

See Appendix A for answers to the following exercises:

1. [6] Write a program that changes to some particular (hardcoded) directory, like the system's *root* directory, and executes the ls -l command to get a long-format directory listing in that directory. (If you use a non-Unix system, use your own system's command to get a detailed directory listing.)

2. [10] Modify the previous program to send the output of the command to a file called *ls.out* in the current directory. The error output should go to a file called

---

[*] This is one of the top items on the Perl developers' list of things to fix, so we expect reliable signal handling to be one of the first items on the new feature list for Perl 6. The problem is that a signal may come in at any time, even when Perl isn't ready for one. For example, if Perl is in the middle of allocating some memory when a signal comes in, the signal handler can accidentally allocate some memory and your program is dead. You can't control when your Perl code will allocate memory, but XSUB code (usually written in C) can safely handle signals. See the Perl documentation for more information about this advanced topic.

ls.err. (You don't need to do anything special about the fact that either of these files may end up being empty.)

3. [8] Write a program to parse the output of the date command to determine the current day of the week. If the day of the week is a weekday, print get to work; otherwise, print go play. The output of the date command begins with Mon on a Monday.[*] If you don't have a date command on your non-Unix system, make a fake program that prints a string similar to one that date might print. We'll give you this two-line program if you promise not to ask us how it works:

```
#!/usr/bin/perl
print localtime() . "\n";
```

---

[*] At least when the days of the week are being given in English. You might have to adjust accordingly if that's not the case on your system.

CHAPTER 15

Perl Modules

There is a lot more to Perl than what we're able to show you in this book, and there are a lot of people doing a lot of interesting things with Perl. If there is a problem to solve, then somebody has probably already solved it and made their solution available on the Comprehensive Perl Archive Network (CPAN), which is a worldwide collection of servers and mirrors containing thousands of modules of reusable Perl code.

If you want to learn how to write modules, consult the Alpaca book. In this chapter, we'll show you how to use modules that already exist.

Finding Modules

Modules come in two types: those that come with Perl and those that you can get from CPAN to install yourself. Unless we say otherwise, the modules we discuss come with Perl.

To find modules that don't come with Perl, start at CPAN Search, *http://search.cpan.org*, or Kobes' Search, *http://kobesearch.cpan.org*.[*] You can browse through the categories or search directly.

Either of those resources are great since you can read the module documentation before you download the entire package. You can also browse the distribution and have a peek at the files without bothering to install the modules.

Before you go looking for a module, check if it has been installed already. One way is to just try to read the documentation with perldoc. The *CGI.pm* module comes with Perl (and we'll discuss it later in this chapter), so you should be able to read its documentation.

```
$ perldoc CGI
```

---

[*] Yes, there should be two *s*'s in that URL, but there aren't and nobody ever fixed it.

Try it with a module that doesn't exist, and you'll get an error message.

```
$ perldoc Llamas
$ No documentation found for "Llamas".
```

The documentation may be available in other formats, such as HTML, on your system, too.*

Installing Modules

When you want to install a module you don't have, sometimes you can simply download the distribution, unpack it, and run a series of commands from the shell. Check for a *README* or *INSTALL* file that gives you more information. If the module uses MakeMaker,† the sequence will be something like this:

```
$ perl Makefile.PL
$ make install
```

If you can't install modules in the system-wide directories, you can specify another directory with a PREFIX argument to *Makefile.PL*.

```
$ perl Makefile.PL PREFIX=/Users/fred/lib
```

Some Perl module authors use another module, Module::Build, to build and install their creations. That sequence will be something like this:

```
$ perl Build.PL
$ ./Build install
```

Some modules depend on other modules, and they won't work unless you install yet more modules. Instead of doing all that work ourselves, we can use one of the modules that come with Perl: *CPAN.pm*.‡ From the command line, you can start up the *CPAN.pm* shell, from which you can issue commands.

```
$ perl -MCPAN -e shell
```

Even this can be complicated, so a while ago one of our authors wrote a little script called cpan, which comes with Perl and is usually installed with *perl* and its tools. Just call the script with a list of the modules you want to install.

```
$ cpan Module::CoreList LWP CGI::Prototype
```

"I don't have a command line!" you might be saying. If you are using the ActiveState port of Perl (for Windows, Linux, or Solaris), you can use the Perl Package Manager

---

* We cover Perl documentation in the Alpaca; most module documentation is in the same file as the actual code.

† That's the Perl module ExtUtils::MakeMaker, which comes with Perl. It handles all of the stuff to create the file that will have the installation instructions appropriate for your system and installation of Perl.

‡ The *.pm* file extension stands for "Perl Module," and some popular modules are pronounced with the ".pm" to distinguish them from something else. In this case, CPAN the archive is different than CPAN the module, so the latter is said "*CPAN.pm*."

(PPM),* which installs modules for you. You can even get the ActiveState ports on CD or DVD.† Your particular operating system may also have ways to install software, including Perl modules.

Using Simple Modules

Suppose that you've got a long filename like */usr/local/bin/perl* in your program, and you need to determine the *basename*. That's easy enough since the basename is everything after the last slash (in this case, *perl*):

```
my $name = "/usr/local/bin/perl";
(my $basename = $name) =~ s#.*/##;   # Oops!
```

As you saw earlier, first Perl does the assignment inside the parentheses, and then it does the substitution. The substitution is supposed to replace any string ending with a slash (that is, the directory name portion) with an empty string, leaving the basename.

If you try this, it will seem to work. Well, it will seem to, but there are three problems.

First, a Unix file or directory name could contain a newline character. (It's not something that's likely to happen by accident, but it's permitted.) Since the regular expression dot (.) can't match a newline, a filename like the string "/home/fred/ flintstone\n/brontosaurus" won't work right because that code will think the basename is "flintstone\n/brontosaurus". You could fix that with the /s option to the pattern (if you remembered about this subtle and infrequent case), making the substitution look like this: s#.*/##s. The second problem is this is Unix-specific. It assumes the forward slash will be the directory separator as it is on Unix and not the backslash or colon that some systems use.

The third (and biggest) problem with this is we're trying to solve a problem someone else has solved. Perl comes with a number of modules, which are smart extensions to Perl that add to its functionality. If those aren't enough, many other useful modules are available on CPAN, with new ones being added every week. You (or, better yet, your system administrator) can install them if you need their functionality.

In the rest of this section, we'll show you how to use the features of some of the modules that come with Perl. (There's more that these modules can do. This is just an overview to illustrate the general principles of how to use a module.)

We can't show you everything you'd need to know about using modules since you'd have to understand advanced topics like references and objects to use some modules.‡

---

* *http://aspn.activestate.com/ASPN/docs/ActivePerl/faq/ActivePerl-faq2.html.*

† You can make your own CDs or DVDs, too, by creating a local repository. Though CPAN is almost 3GB by now, a "minicpan" (again, by one of the authors) pares it down to the latest versions of everything, which is about 500 MB. See the CPAN::Mini module.

‡ As we'll see in the next few pages, you may be able to use a module that uses objects and references without having to understand those advanced topics.

Those topics, including how to create a module, will be covered in detail in the Alpaca. Further information on some interesting and useful modules is included in Appendix B.

The File::Basename Module

In the previous example, we found the basename of a filename in a way that's not portable. We showed that something that seemed straightforward was susceptible to subtle, mistaken assumptions. (The assumption was that newlines would never appear in file or directory names.) And we were re-inventing the wheel, solving a problem that others have solved (and debugged) many times before us.

Here's a better way to extract the basename of a filename. Perl comes with a module called File::Basename. With the command perldoc File::Basename, or with your system's documentation system, you can read about what it does, which is the first step when using a new module. (It's often the third and fifth step, as well.)

When you're ready to use it, declare it with a use directive near the top of your program:*

```
use File::Basename;
```

During compilation, Perl sees that line and loads up the module. Now it's as if Perl has some new functions you can use in the remainder of your program.† The one we wanted in the earlier example is the basename function:

```
my $name = "/usr/local/bin/perl";
my $basename = basename $name;  # gives 'perl'
```

Well, that worked for Unix. What if our program were running on MacPerl, Windows, or VMS, to name a few? There's no problem because this module can tell which kind of machine you're using, and it uses that machine's filename rules by default. (In that case, you'd have that machine's kind of filename string in $name, in that case.)

This module provides other related functions. One is the dirname function, which pulls the directory name from a full filename. The module also lets you separate a filename from its extension or change the default set of filename rules.‡

---

* It's traditional to declare modules near the top of the file since that makes it easy for the maintenance programmer to see which modules you'll be using. That greatly simplifies matters when it's time to install your program on a new machine, for example.

† You guessed it: there's more to the story, having to do with packages and fully qualified names. When your programs are growing beyond a few hundred lines in the main program (not counting code in modules), which is quite large in Perl, you should probably investigate these advanced features. Start with the perlmod manpage.

‡ You might need to change the filename rules if you're working with a Unix machine's filenames from a Windows machine, perhaps while sending commands over an FTP connection, for example.

Using Only Some Functions from a Module

Suppose that when you went to add the `File::Basename` module to your existing program, you discovered a subroutine called &dirname. That is, you have a subroutine with the same name as one of the module's functions.[*] The trouble is the new dirname has been implemented as a Perl subroutine (inside the module). What do you do?

Give `File::Basename`, in your use declaration, an *import list* showing which function names it should give you, and it'll supply those and no others. Here, we'll get nothing but basename:

```
use File::Basename qw/ basename /;
```

Here, we'll ask for no new functions at all:

```
use File::Basename qw/ /;
```

This is frequently written as:

```
use File::Basename ( );
```

Why would you want to do that? Well, this directive tells Perl to load `File::Basename` as before but not to *import* any function names. Importing lets us use the short, simple function names such as basename and dirname. However, if we don't import those names, we can still use the functions. When they're not imported, we have to call them by their full names:

```
use File::Basename qw/ /;                      # import no function names

my $betty = &dirname($wilma);                  # uses our own subroutine &dirname
                                               # (not shown)

my $name = "/usr/local/bin/perl";
my $dirname = File::Basename::dirname $name;   # dirname from the module
```

The full name of the dirname function from the module is `File::Basename::dirname`. We can always use the function's full name, once we've loaded the module, whether we've imported the short name dirname or not.

Most of the time, you'll want to use a module's default import list. But you can override that with a list of your own if you want to leave out some of the default items. Another reason to supply your own list would be if you wanted to import some function not on the default list since most modules include some (infrequently needed) functions not on the default import list.

Some modules will, by default, import more symbols than others. Each module's documentation should make it clear which symbols it imports, if any, but you are

---

[*] Well, it's not likely you would have a &dirname subroutine you use for another purpose, but this is an example. Some modules offer hundreds of new functions, making name collisions more frequent.

always free to override the default import list by specifying one of your own as we did with `File::Basename`. Supplying an empty list imports no symbols.

The File::Spec Module

Now you can find out a file's basename. That's useful, but you'll often want to put that together with a directory name to get a full filename. For example, we want to take a filename like */home/rootbeer/ice-2.1.txt* and add a prefix to the basename:

```
use File::Basename;

print "Please enter a filename: ";
chomp(my $old_name = <STDIN>);

my $dirname = dirname $old_name;
my $basename = basename $old_name;

$basename =~ s/^/not/;  # Add a prefix to the basename
my $new_name = "$dirname/$basename";

rename($old_name, $new_name)
  or warn "Can't rename '$old_name' to '$new_name': $!";
```

Do you see the problem here? Once again, we're making the assumption that filenames will follow the Unix conventions and use a forward slash between the directory name and the basename. Fortunately, Perl comes with a module to help with this problem, too.

The `File::Spec` module is used for manipulating *file specifications*, which are the names of files, directories, and the other things that are stored on filesystems. Like `File::Basename`, it understands what kind of system it's running on, and it chooses the right set of rules every time. Unlike `File::Basename`, `File::Spec` is an object-oriented (often abbreviated "OO") module.

If you've never caught the fever of OO, don't worry. If you understand objects, that's great; you can use this OO module. If you don't understand objects, that's okay, too. Type the symbols as we show you, and it will work as if you knew what you were doing.

In this case, we learn from reading the documentation for `File::Spec` that we want to use a *method* called `catfile`. What's a method? It's just a different kind of function, as far as we're concerned here. The difference is that you'll always call the methods from `File::Spec` with their full names, like this:

```
use File::Spec;

.
.  # Get the values for $dirname and $basename as above
.

my $new_name = File::Spec->catfile($dirname, $basename);
```

```
rename($old_name, $new_name)
    or warn "Can't rename '$old_name' to '$new_name': $!";
```

The full name of a method is the name of the module (called a *class*, here), a small arrow (->), and the short name of the method. Use the small arrow rather than the double-colon that we used with File::Basename.

Since we're calling the method by its full name, what symbols does the module import? None of them. That's normal for OO modules. You don't have to worry about having a subroutine with the same name as one of the many methods of File::Spec.

Should you bother using modules like these? If you're sure your program will never be run anywhere but on a Unix machine and you're sure you completely understand the rules for filenames on Unix, then you may prefer to hardcode your assumptions into your programs. But these modules give you an easy way to make your programs more robust in less time and and more portable at no extra charge.

CGI.pm

If you need to create CGI programs (which we don't cover in this book), use the *CGI.pm* module. You don't need to handle the interface and input parsing portion of the script which gets so many other people into trouble. The *CGI.pm* author, Lincoln Stein, spent a lot of time ensuring the module would work with most servers and operating systems. Use the module and focus on the interesting parts of your script.

The CGI module has two flavors: the plain old functional interface and the OO interface. We'll use the first one. As before, you can follow the examples in the *CGI.pm* documentation. Our simple CGI script parses the CGI input and displays the input names and values as a plain text document. In the import list, we use :all, which is an *export tag* that specifies a group of functions rather than a single function as you saw in the previous modules.[*]

```
#!/usr/bin/perl

use CGI qw(:all);

print header("text/plain");

foreach my $param ( param() )
        {
        print "$param: " . param($param) . "\n";
        }
```

---

[*] The module has several other export tags to select different groups of functions. For instance, if you want the ones that deal with the CGI, you can use :cgi, or if you want the HTML generation functions, you can use :html4. See the *CGI.pm* documentation for more details.

We can get fancier because we want to output HTML, and *CGI.pm* has many convenience functions to do that. It handles the CGI header, the beginning parts of HTML with start_html( ), and many HTML tags with functions of the same name, such as h1( ) for the <H1> tag.

```
#!/usr/bin/perl

use CGI qw(:all);

print header( ),
        start_html("This is the page title"),
        h1( "Input parameters" );

my $list_items;
foreach my $param ( param( ) )
        {
        $list_items .= li( "$param: " . param($param) );
        }

print ul( $list_items );

print end_html( );
```

Wasn't that easy? You don't have to know how *CGI.pm* is doing all this stuff: you just have to trust that it does it correctly. Once you let *CGI.pm* do all the hard work, you get to focus on the interesting parts of your program.

The *CGI.pm* module does a lot more, such as handle cookies, redirection, and multipage forms. You will learn more from the module documentation examples.

Databases and DBI

The DBI (database interface) module doesn't come with Perl, but it's one of the most popular modules since most people have to connect to a database of some sort. The beauty of DBI is it allows you to use the same interface for almost any common database, from comma-separated value files to big database servers like Oracle. It has ODBC drivers, and some of its drivers are supported by vendors. To get the full details, get *Programming the Perl DBI* (O'Reilly). You can check out the DBI web site, *http://dbi.perl.org/*.

Once you install DBI, you also have to install a DBD (database driver). You can get a long list of DBDs from CPAN Search. Install the right one for your database server, and ensure you get the version that goes with the version of your server.

The DBI is an OO module, but you don't have to know everything about OO programming to use it; just follow the examples in the documentation. To connect to a database, you use the DBI module and call its connect method.

```
use DBI;

$dbh = DBI->connect($data_source, $username, $password);
```

The $data_source contains information particular to the DBD you want to use, so you'll get that from the DBD. For PostgreSQL, the driver is DBD::Pg, and the $data_source is something like:

```
my $data_source = "dbi:Pg:dbname=name_of_database";
```

Once you connect to the database, you will go through a cycle of preparing, executing, and reading queries.

```
$sth = $dbh->prepare("SELECT * FROM foo WHERE bla");
$sth->execute();
@row_ary  = $sth->fetchrow_array;
$sth->finish;
```

When you are finished, you disconnect from the database.

```
$dbh->disconnect();
```

See DBI's documentation for more details.

Exercise

See Appendix A for answers to the following exercise:

1. [15] Install the Module::CoreList module from CPAN. Print a list of all of the modules that came with Perl 5.006. To build a hash whose keys are the names of the modules that came with a given version of Perl, use this line:

   ```
   my %modules = %{ $Module::CoreList::version{5.006} };
   ```

2. [15] Get a list of filenames in the current directory. Use the C<Cwd> module to get the current directory, then use the C<File::Spec> module to join the directory name with the filenames to get an absolute path. Print the list of paths to standard outout with one path per line. Your solution should be portable to other operating systems.

3. [15] Using the output from the previous exercise, read in a list of paths and use the C<File::Basename> module to extract the filename from each path. Print each name on a line by itself. Your solution should be portable to other operating systems.

## CHAPTER 16

Some Advanced Perl Techniques

What we've put in this book so far is the core of Perl, the part that every Perl user should understand. A few other techniques, while not obligatory, are still valuable tools to have in your toolbox. We've gathered the most important of those in this chapter.

Don't be misled by the title of the chapter; these techniques aren't more difficult to understand than the rest of the book. They are only "advanced" in the sense that they aren't necessary for beginners. The first time you read this book, you may want to skip (or skim) this chapter so you can get right to using Perl. Come back to it later when you're ready to get more out of Perl. Consider this entire chapter a huge footnote.[*]

Trapping Errors with eval

Sometimes, your ordinary, everyday code can cause a fatal error in your program. Each of these typical statements could crash a program:

```
$barney = $fred / $dino;        # divide-by-zero error?

print "match\n" if /^($wilma)/;  # illegal regular expression error?

open CAVEMAN, $fred              # user-generated error from die?
  or die "Can't open file '$fred' for input: $!";
```

You could go to some trouble to catch some of these, but it's hard to get them all. (How could you check the string $wilma from that example to ensure it makes a valid regular expression?) Fortunately, Perl provides a way to catch fatal errors: wrap the code in an eval block:

```
eval { $barney = $fred / $dino } ;
```

---

[*] We contemplated doing that in one of the drafts but were firmly rejected by O'Reilly's editors.

Even if $dino is zero, that line won't crash the program. The eval is an expression (not a control structure, like while or foreach), so the semicolon is required at the end of the block.

When a normally fatal error happens during the execution of an eval block, the block is done running, but the program doesn't crash. Right after an eval finishes, you'll be wanting to know if it exited normally or caught a fatal error for you. The answer is in the special $@ variable. If the eval caught a fatal error, $@ will hold what would have been the program's dying words, perhaps something like: Illegal division by zero at my_program line 12. If there was no error, $@ will be empty. That means that $@ is a useful Boolean (true/false) value (true if there was an error), so you'll sometimes see code like this after an eval block:

```
print "An error occurred: $@" if $@;
```

The eval block is a true block, so it makes a new scope for lexical (my) variables. This piece of a program shows an eval block hard at work:

```
foreach my $person (qw/ fred wilma betty barney dino pebbles /) {
  eval {
    open FILE, "<$person"
      or die "Can't open file '$person': $!";

    my($total, $count);

    while (<FILE>) {
      $total += $_;
      $count++;
    }

    my $average = $total/$count;
    print "Average for file $person was $average\n";

    &do_something($person, $average);
  };

  if ($@) {
    print "An error occurred ($@), continuing\n";
  }
}
```

How many possible fatal errors are being trapped here? If there is an error in opening the file, that error is trapped. Calculating the average may divide by zero, so that error is trapped. Even the call to the mysteriously named &do_something subroutine is protected against fatal errors because an eval block traps any otherwise fatal errors that occur during the time it's active. (This feature is handy if you have to call a subroutine written by someone else, and you don't know if he has coded defensively enough to avoid crashing your program.)

If an error occurs during the processing of one of the files, we'll get an error message, but the program will go on to the next file without further complaint.

You can nest eval blocks inside other eval blocks. The inner one traps errors while it is running, keeping them from reaching the outer blocks. (After the inner eval finishes, you may wish to re-post any errors by using die, thereby letting the outer eval catch it.) An eval block traps any errors that occur during its execution, including errors that happen during subroutine calls (as in the earlier example).

The eval is an expression, which is why the trailing semicolon is needed after the closing curly brace. Since it's an expression, it has a return value. If there's no error, it's like a subroutine: The return value is the last expression evaluated, or it's returned early with an optional return keyword. Here's another way to do the math without having to worry about dividing by zero:

```
my $barney = eval { $fred / $dino };
```

If the eval traps a fatal error, the return value is undef or an empty list, depending on the context. So, in the previous example, $barney is the correct result from dividing, or it's undef. We don't need to check $@ before we use it further although it's probably a good idea to check defined($barney) before we use it further.

There are four kinds of problems that eval can't trap. The first group is the serious errors that crash Perl, such as running out of memory or getting an untrapped signal. Since Perl isn't running, it can't trap these errors.* Syntax errors inside the eval block are caught at compile time—they're never returned in $@.

The exit operator terminates the program immediately, even if it's called from a subroutine inside an eval block. This correctly implies that when writing a subroutine, you should use die rather than exit to signal when something goes wrong.

The fourth problem an eval block can't trap are warnings: either user-generated ones (from warn) or Perl's internally generated warnings (requested with the -w command-line option or the use warnings pragma). There's a separate mechanism from eval for trapping warnings. See the discussion of the __WARN__ pseudosignal in the Perl documentation for the details.

There's another form of eval that can be dangerous if it's mishandled. Sometimes, you'll meet people who say you shouldn't use eval in your code for security reasons. They're (mostly) right that eval should be used with great care, but they're talking about the other form of eval, sometimes called "eval of a string." If the keyword eval is followed directly by a block of code in curly braces, as we're doing here, there's no need to worry—that's the safe kind of eval.

---

* Some of these errors are listed with an (X) code on the perldiag manpage, if you're curious.

Picking Items from a List with grep

Sometimes you'll only want certain items from a list. Maybe it's the odd numbers selected from a list of numbers, or the lines mentioning Fred from a file of text. As you'll see in this section, picking some items from a list can be done with the grep operator.

Let's try that first one and get the odd numbers from a large list of numbers. We don't need anything new to do that:

```
my @odd_numbers;

foreach (1..1000) {
  push @odd_numbers, $_ if $_ % 2;
}
```

That code uses the modulus operator (%), which you saw in Chapter 2. If a number is even, that number "mod two" gives zero, which is false. But an odd number will give one; since that's true, only the odd numbers will be pushed onto the array.

The code is all right as it stands except that it's a little longer to write and slower to run than it might be since Perl provides the grep operator:

```
my @odd_numbers = grep { $_ % 2 } 1..1000;
```

That line gets a list of 500 odd numbers in one quick line of code. How does it work? The first argument to grep is a block that uses $_ as a placeholder for each item in the list, and returns a Boolean (true/false) value. The remaining arguments are the list of items to search through. The grep operator will evaluate the expression once for each item in the list as our original foreach loop did. For the ones where the last expression of the block returns a true value, that element is included in the list that results from grep.

While the grep is running, $_ is aliased to one element of the list after another. You've seen this behavior before in the foreach loop. It's generally a bad idea to modify $_ inside the grep expression because this will damage the original data.

The grep operator shares its name with a classic Unix utility that picks matching lines from a file by using regular expressions. We can do that with Perl's grep, which is more powerful. Here we pull only the lines mentioning fred from a file:

```
my @matching_lines = grep { /\bfred\b/i } <FILE>;
```

There's a simpler syntax for grep, too. If all you need for the selector is a simple expression (rather than a whole block), you can use that expression, followed by a comma, in place of the block. Here's the simpler way to write that latest example:

```
my @matching_lines = grep /\bfred\b/i, <FILE>;
```

Transforming Items from a List with map

Another common task is transforming items from a list. For example, suppose you have a list of numbers to format as money numbers for output, as with the subroutine &big_money (from Chapter 13). We don't want to modify the original data, and we need a modified copy of the list just for output. Here's one way to do that:

```
my @data = (4.75, 1.5, 2, 1234, 6.9456, 12345678.9, 29.95);
my @formatted_data;

foreach (@data) {
  push @formatted_data, &big_money($_);
}
```

That looks similar in form to the example code used at the beginning of the section on grep, doesn't it? The replacement code resembles the first grep example:

```
my @data = (4.75, 1.5, 2, 1234, 6.9456, 12345678.9, 29.95);

my @formatted_data = map { &big_money($_) } @data;
```

The map operator looks much like grep because it has the same kind of arguments: a block that uses $_ and a list of items to process. It operates in a similar way, evaluating the block once for each item in the list with $_ aliased to a different original list element each time. But the last expression of the block is used differently; instead of giving a Boolean value, the final value becomes part of the resulting list.[*] Any grep or map statement could be rewritten as a foreach loop pushing items onto a temporary array. But the shorter way is typically more efficient and convenient. Since the result of map or grep is a list, it can be passed directly to another function. Here we can print that list of formatted money numbers as an indented list under a heading:

```
print "The money numbers are:\n",
  map { sprintf("%25s\n", $_) } @formatted_data;
```

We could have done that processing all at once without the temporary array @formatted_data:

```
my @data = (4.75, 1.5, 2, 1234, 6.9456, 12345678.9, 29.95);
print "The money numbers are:\n",
  map { sprintf("%25s\n", &big_money($_) ) } @data;
```

As we saw with grep, there's a simpler syntax for map. If all you need for the selector is a simple expression (rather than a whole block), you can use that expression, followed by a comma, in place of the block:

```
print "Some powers of two are:\n",
  map "\t" . ( 2 ** $_ ) . "\n", 0..15;
```

---

[*] One other important difference is the expression used by map is evaluated in a list context and may return any number of items, not necessarily one each time.

Unquoted Hash Keys

Perl offers many shortcuts that can help the programmer, such as omitting the quote marks on some hash keys.

You can't omit the quote marks on every key since a hash key may be any arbitrary string. But keys are often simple. If the hash key only consists of letters, digits, and underscores without starting with a digit, you may be able to omit the quote marks. This kind of simple string without quote marks is called a *bareword* since it stands alone without quotes.

One place you are permitted to use this shortcut is the most common place a hash key appears, which is in the curly braces of a hash element reference. For example, instead of $score{"fred"}, you could write $score{fred}. Since many hash keys are like this, not using quotes is a convenience. But beware: if there's anything inside the curly braces besides a bareword, Perl will interpret it as an expression.

Another place where hash keys appear is when assigning an entire hash using a list of key/value pairs. The big arrow (=>) is especially useful between a key and a value because (if the key is a bareword) the big arrow quotes it for you:

```
# Hash containing bowling scores
my %score = (
  barney    => 195,
  fred      => 205,
  dino      => 30,
);
```

This is the one important difference between the big arrow and a comma; a bareword to the left of the big arrow is implicitly quoted. (Whatever is on the right is left alone.) You don't have to use this feature of the big arrow only for hashes, though that's the most frequent use.

Slices

It often happens that we need to work with a few elements from a given list. For example, the Bedrock Library keeps information about their patrons in a large file.* Each line in the file describes one patron with six colon-separated fields: a person's name, library card number, home address, home phone number, work phone number, and number of items currently checked out. A little bit of the file looks something like this:

```
fred flintstone:2168:301 Cobblestone Way:555-1212:555-2121:3
barney rubble:709918:3128 Granite Blvd:555-3333:555-3438:0
```

---

* It should be a full-featured database rather than a flat file. They plan to upgrade their system, right after the next Ice Age.

One of the library's applications needs the card numbers and number of items checked out; it doesn't use any of the other data. It could use code something like this to get the fields it needs:

```
while (<FILE>) {
  chomp;
  my @items = split /:/;
  my($card_num, $count) = ($itcms[1], $items[5]);
  ... # now work with those two variables
}
```

The array @items isn't needed for anything else though, so it seems like a waste.[*] Maybe it would be better to assign the result of split to a list of scalars, like this:

```
my($name, $card_num, $addr, $home, $work, $count) = split /:/;
```

That avoids the unneeded array @items, but now we have four scalar variables that we didn't need. For this situation, some people used to make up a number of dummy variable names, like $dummy_1, that showed they didn't care about that element from the split. Larry thought that was too much trouble, so he added a special use of undef. If an item in a list being assigned to is undef, that means to ignore the corresponding element of the source list:

```
my(undef, $card_num, undef, undef, undef, $count) = split /:/;
```

Is this any better? Its advantage is having no unneeded variables. Its disadvantage is that you have to count undefs to tell which element is $count. This becomes unwieldy if the list has more elements. For example, some people who wanted just the mtime value from stat were writing code like this:

```
my(undef, undef, undef, undef, undef, undef, undef,
   undef, undef, $mtime) = stat $some_file;
```

If you use the wrong number of undefs, you'll get the atime or ctime by mistake, and that's a tough one to debug. There's a better way. Perl can index into a list as if it were an array. This is a *list slice*. Since the mtime is item 9 in the list returned by stat,[†] we can get it with a subscript:

```
my $mtime = (stat $some_file)[9];
```

Those parentheses are required around the list of items (in this case, the return value from stat). If you wrote it like this, it wouldn't work:

```
my $mtime = stat($some_file)[9];  # Syntax error!
```

A list slice must have a subscript expression in square brackets after a list in parentheses. The parentheses holding the arguments to a function call don't count.

---

[*] It's not much of a waste, but stay with us. All of these techniques are used by programmers who don't understand slices, so it's worthwhile to see all of them here.

[†] It's the tenth item, but the index number is 9 since the first item is at index 0. This is the same kind of zero-based indexing we've used with arrays.

Going back to the Bedrock Library, the list we're working with is the return value from `split`. We use a slice to pull out item 1 and item 5 with subscripts:

```
my $card_num = (split /:/)[1];
my $count = (split /:/)[5];
```

Using a scalar-context slice like this (pulling a single element from the list) isn't bad, but it would be more efficient and simpler if we didn't have to do the `split` twice. So let's not do it twice; let's get both values at once by using a list slice in list context:

```
my($card_num, $count) = (split /:/)[1, 5];
```

The indices pull out elements 1 and 5 from the list, returning those as a two-element list. When that's assigned to the two `my` variables, we get exactly what we wanted. We do the `slice` once, and we set the two variables with a simple notation.

A slice is often the simplest way to pull a few items from a list. Here, we can pull the first and last items from a list, knowing that index `-1` means the last element:[*]

```
my($first, $last) = (sort @names)[0, -1];
```

The subscripts of a slice may be in any order and may even repeat values. This example pulls five items from a list of ten:

```
my @names = qw{ zero one two three four five six seven eight nine };
my @numbers = ( @names )[ 9, 0, 2, 1, 0 ];
print "Bedrock @numbers\n";  # says Bedrock nine zero two one zero
```

Array Slice

That previous example could be simplified. When slicing elements from an array (as opposed to a list), the parentheses aren't needed, so we could have done the slice like this:

```
my @numbers = @names[ 9, 0, 2, 1, 0 ];
```

This isn't merely a matter of omitting the parentheses; this is actually a different notation for accessing array elements: an *array slice*. In Chapter 3, we said that the at sign on `@names` meant "all of the elements." Actually, in a linguistic sense, it's more like a plural marker, much like the letter "s" in words like "cats" and "dogs." In Perl, the dollar sign means there's one of something, but the at sign means there's a list of items.

A slice is always a list, so the array slice notation uses an at sign to indicate that. When you see something like `@names[ ... ]` in a Perl program, you'll need to do as Perl does and look at the at sign at the beginning as well as the square brackets at the end. The square brackets mean you're indexing into an array, and the at sign means

---

[*] Sorting a list to find the extreme elements isn't likely to be the most efficient way. But Perl's sort is fast enough that this is generally acceptable as long as the list doesn't have more than a few hundred elements.

---

you're getting a whole list* of elements. A dollar sign would mean a single one. See Figure 16-1.

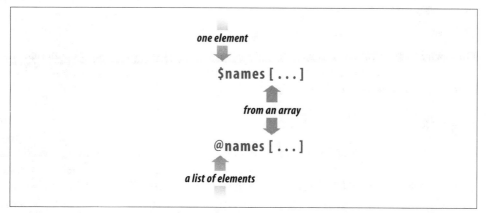

one element

$names [...]

from an array

@names [...]

a list of elements

Figure 16-1. Array slices versus single elements

The punctuation mark at the front of the variable reference (the dollar sign or at sign) determines the context of the subscript expression. If there's a dollar sign in front, the subscript expression is evaluated in a scalar context to get an index. If there's an at sign in front, the subscript expression is evaluated in a list context to get a list of indices.

So we see that @names[2, 5] means the same list as ($names[2], $names[5]) does. If you want that list of values, you can use the array slice notation. Any place you might want to write the list, you can use the array slice.

The slice can be used in one place where the list can't: a slice may be interpolated directly into a string:

```
my @names = qw{ zero one two three four five six seven eight nine };
print "Bedrock @names[ 9, 0, 2, 1, 0 ]\n";
```

If we were to interpolate @names, that would give all of the items from the array, separated by spaces. If we interpolate @names[9, 0, 2, 1, 0], that gives just those items from the array, separated by spaces.† Let's go back to the Bedrock Library for a moment. Maybe our program is updating Mr. Slate's address and phone number in the patron file because he has moved into a large new place in the Hollyrock hills. If

---

* When we say "a whole list," that doesn't necessarily mean more elements than one since the list could be empty, after all.

† More accurately, the items of the list are separated by the contents of Perl's $" variable, whose default is a space. This should not be changed. When interpolating a list of values, Perl internally does join $", @list, where @list stands in for the list expression.

we have a list of information about him in @items, we could do something like this to update those two elements of the array:

```
my $new_home_phone = "555-6099";
my $new_address = "99380 Red Rock West";
@items[2, 3] = ($new_address, $new_home_phone);
```

Once again, the array slice makes a more compact notation for a list of elements. In this case, that last line is the same as an assignment to ($items[2], $items[3]) but more compact and efficient.

Hash Slice

Analogous to an array slice, we can slice some elements from a hash in a *hash slice*. Remember when three of our characters went bowling, and we kept their bowling scores in the %score hash? We could pull those scores with a list of hash elements or with a slice. These two techniques are equivalent, though the second is more concise and efficient:

```
my @three_scores = ($score{"barney"}, $score{"fred"}, $score{"dino"});

my @three_scores = @score{ qw/ barney fred dino/ };
```

A slice is always a list, so the hash slice notation uses an at sign to indicate that.* When you see something like @score{ ... } in a Perl program, you'll need to do as Perl does and look at the at sign at the beginning as well as the curly braces at the end. The curly braces mean that you're indexing into a hash; the at sign means that you're getting a whole list of elements. A dollar sign would mean a single one. See Figure 16-2.

As with the array slice, the punctuation mark at the front of the variable reference (the dollar sign or at sign) determines the context of the subscript expression. If there's a dollar sign in front, the subscript expression is evaluated in a scalar context to get a single key.† If there's an at sign in front, the subscript expression is evaluated in a list context to get a list of keys.

It's normal at this point to wonder why there's no percent sign (%) here, when we're talking about a hash. That's the marker that means there's a whole hash; a hash slice

---

* If it sounds as if we're repeating ourselves, it's because we want to emphasize that hash slices are analogous to array slices. If it sounds as if we're not repeating ourselves, it's because we want to emphasize that hash slices are analogous to array slices.

† There's an exception you're not likely to run across since it isn't used much in modern Perl code. See the entry for $; in the perlvar manpage.

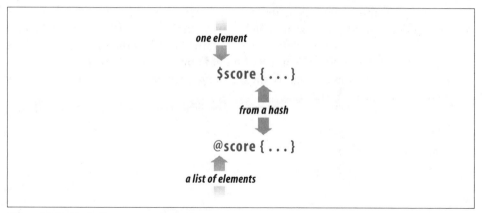

one element

$score { ... }

from a hash

@score { ... }

a list of elements

Figure 16-2. Hash slices versus single elements

(like any other slice) is always a *list* and not a hash.* In Perl, the dollar sign means there's one of something, the at sign means there's a list of items, and the percent sign means there's an entire hash.

As you saw with array slices, a hash slice may be used instead of the corresponding list of elements from the hash, anywhere within Perl. So, we can set our friends' bowling scores in the hash (without disturbing any other elements in the hash) in this way:

```
my @players = qw/ barney fred dino /;
my @bowling_scores = (195, 205, 30);
@score{ @players } = @bowling_scores;
```

That last line does the same thing as if we had assigned to a three-element list: ($score{"barney"}, $score{"fred"}, $score{"dino"}).

A hash slice may be interpolated, too. Here, we print out the scores for our favorite bowlers:

```
print "Tonight's players were: @players\n";
print "Their scores were: @score{@players}\n";
```

Exercise

See Appendix A for an answer to the following exercise:

1. [30] Make a program that reads a list of strings from a file, one string per line, and then lets the user interactively enter patterns that may match some of the strings. For each pattern, the program should tell how many strings from the file matched, then which ones those were. Don't re-read the file for each new pattern; keep the

---

* A hash slice is a slice (not a hash) in the same way that a house fire is a fire (not a house), while a firehouse is a house (not a fire). More or less.

strings in memory. The filename may be hardcoded in the file. If a pattern is invalid (for example, if it has unmatched parentheses), the program should report that error and let the user continue trying patterns. When the user enters a blank line instead of a pattern, the program should quit. (If you need a file full of interesting strings to try matching, try the file *sample_text* in the files from the O'Reilly web site. See the Preface.)

Exercise Answers

This appendix contains the answers to the exercises that appear throughout the book.

Answers to Chapter 2 Exercises

1. Here's one way to do it:

```
#!/usr/bin/perl -w
$pi = 3.141592654;
$circ = 2 * $pi * 12.5;
print "The circumference of a circle of radius 12.5 is $circ.\n";
```

We started this program with a typical #! line; your path to Perl may vary. We also turned on warnings.

The first real line of code sets the value of $pi to our value of π. There are several reasons a good programmer will prefer to use a constant* value like this: it takes time to type 3.141592654 into your program if you ever need it more than once. It may be a mathematical bug if you accidentally used 3.141592654 in one place and 3.14159 in another. There's only one line to check to ensure you didn't accidentally type 3.141952654 and send your space probe to the wrong planet. It's easier to type $pi than π, especially if you don't have Unicode. Maintaining the program also will be easier in case the value of π changes.†. Next, we calculate the circumference, storing it into $circ, and we print it out in a message. The message ends with a newline character because every line of a good program's output should end with a newline. Without it, you might end up with output looking something like this, depending on your shell's prompt:

```
The circumference of a circle of radius 12.5 is
78.53981635.bash-2.01$[ ]
```

---

* If you'd prefer a more formal sort of constants, the constant pragma may be what you're looking for.

† It nearly did change more than a century ago by a legislative act in the state of Indiana. See House Bill No. 246, Indiana State Legislature, 1897, *http://db.uwaterloo.ca/~alopez-o/math-faq/node45.html*.

The box represents the input cursor, blinking at the end of the line, and that's the shell's prompt at the end of the message.* Since the circumference isn't 78.53981635.bash-2.01$, this should probably be construed as a bug. So, use \n at the end of each line of output.

Here's one way to do it:

```
#!/usr/bin/perl -w
$pi = 3.141592654;
print "What is the radius? ";
chomp($radius = <STDIN>);
$circ = 2 * $pi * $radius;
print "The circumference of a circle of radius $radius is $circ.\n";
```

This is like the last one, except now we ask the user for the radius, and then we use $radius in every place where we previously used the hardcoded value 12.5. If we had written the first program with more foresight, we would have had a variable named $radius in that one as well. Note that we chomped the line of input. If we hadn't, the mathematical formula would still have worked because a string like "12.5\n" is converted to the number 12.5 without any problem. But when we print out the message, it would look like this:

```
The circumference of a circle of radius 12.5
 is 78.53981635.
```

The newline character is still in $radius, even though we've used that variable as a number. Since we had a space between $radius and the word "is" in the print statement, there's a space at the beginning of the second line of output. The moral of the story is: chomp your input unless you have a reason not to do it.

2. Here's one way to do it:

```
#!/usr/bin/perl -w
$pi = 3.141592654;
print "What is the radius? ";
chomp($radius = <STDIN>);
$circ = 2 * $pi * $radius;
if ($radius < 0) {
  $circ = 0;
}
print "The circumference of a circle of radius $radius is $circ.\n";
```

Here we added the check for a bogus radius. Even if the given radius was impossible, the returned circumference will at least be nonnegative. You could have changed the given radius to be zero and calculated the circumference. There's more than one way to do it. In fact, that's the Perl motto: There Is More Than One Way To Do It, and that's why each exercise answer starts with "Here's one way to do it."

---

* We asked O'Reilly to spend the extra money to print the input cursor with blinking ink, but they wouldn't do it for us.

Here's one way to do it:

```
print "Enter first number: ";
chomp($one = <STDIN>);
print "Enter second number: ";
chomp($two = <STDIN>);
$result = $one * $two;
print "The result is $result.\n";
```

Notice that we've left off the #! line for this answer. From here on, we'll assume that you know it's there, so you don't need to read it each time.

Perhaps those are poor choices for variable names. In a large program, a maintenance programmer might think $two should have the value of 2. In this short program, it probably doesn't matter; in a large one, we could have called them something more descriptive, with names like $first_response.

In this program, it wouldn't make any difference if we forgot to chomp the two variables $one and $two since we never use them as strings once they've been set. But if next week our maintenance programmer edits the program to print a message like The result of multiplying $one by $two is $result.\n, those pesky newlines will come back to haunt us. Once again, chomp unless you have a reason not to chomp*—like in the next exercise.

3. Here's one way to do it:

```
print "Enter a string: ";
$str = <STDIN>;
print "Enter a number of times: ";
chomp($num = <STDIN>);
$result = $str x $num;
print "The result is:\n$result";
```

This program is almost the same as the last one. We're "multiplying" a string by a number of times. So, we've kept the structure of the previous exercise. In this case, we didn't want to chomp the first input item—the string—because the exercise asked for the strings to appear on separate lines. So, if the user entered fred and a newline for the string and 3 for the number, we'd get a newline after each fred as we wanted.

In the print statement at the end, we put the newline before $result because we wanted to have the first fred printed on a line of its own. That is, we didn't want output like this, with only two of the three freds aligned in a column:

```
The result is: fred
fred
fred
```

At the same time, we didn't need to put another newline at the end of the print output because $result should already end with a newline.

---

* Chomping is like chewing: not always needed, but most of the time it doesn't hurt.

In most cases, Perl won't mind where you put spaces in your program; you can put in spaces or leave them out. But it's important not to spell the wrong thing accidentally. If the x runs up against the preceding variable name $str, Perl will see $strx, which won't work.

Answers to Chapter 3 Exercises

1. Here's one way to do it:

```
print "Enter some lines, then press Ctrl-D:\n"; # or maybe Ctrl-Z
@lines = <STDIN>;
@reverse_lines = reverse @lines;
print @reverse_lines;
```

or, even more simply:

```
print "Enter some lines, then press Ctrl-D:\n";
print reverse <STDIN>;
```

Most Perl programmers would prefer the second one as long as you don't need to keep the list of lines for later use.

2. Here's one way to do it:

```
@names = qw/ fred betty barney dino wilma pebbles bamm-bamm /;
print "Enter some numbers from 1 to 7, one per line, then press Ctrl-D:\n";
chomp(@numbers = <STDIN>);
foreach (@numbers) {
  print "$names[ $_ - 1 ]\n";
}
```

We have to subtract one from the index number so the user can count from 1 to 7 even though the array is indexed from 0 to 6. Another way to accomplish this would be to have a dummy item in the @names array, like this:

```
@names = qw/ dummy_item fred betty barney dino wilma pebbles bamm-bamm /;
```

Give yourself extra credit if you checked to make sure that the user's choice of index was in the range 1 to 7.

Here's one way to do it if you want the output all on one line:

```
chomp(@lines = <STDIN>);
@sorted = sort @lines;
print "@sorted\n";
```

To get the output on separate lines, do it this way:

```
print sort <STDIN>;
```

Answers to Chapter 4 Exercises

1. Here's one way to do it:

```
sub total {
  my $sum;  # private variable
  foreach (@_) {
```

```
        $sum += $_;
    }
    $sum;
}
```

This subroutine uses $sum to keep a running total. At the start of the subroutine, $sum is undef since it's a new variable. Then, the foreach loop steps through the parameter list (from @_) using $_ as the control variable. (There's no automatic connection among @_, the parameter array, and $_, the default variable for the foreach loop.)

The first time through the foreach loop, the first number (in $_) is added to $sum. $sum is undef since nothing has been stored there. Since we're using it as a number, which Perl sees because of the numeric operator +=, Perl acts as if it's already initialized to 0. Perl thus adds the first parameter to 0, and puts the total back into $sum.

Next time through the loop, the next parameter is added to $sum, which is no longer undef. The sum is placed back into $sum and on through the rest of the parameters. Finally, the last line returns $sum to the caller.

There's a potential bug in this subroutine depending on how you think of things. Suppose this subroutine was called with an empty parameter list as we considered with the rewritten subroutine &max in the chapter text. In that case, $sum would be undef which would be the return value. But in this subroutine, it would probably be more correct to return 0 as the sum of the empty list rather than undef. (If you wished to distinguish the sum of an empty list from the sum of, say, (3, -5, 2), returning undef would be the right thing to do.)

If you don't want a possibly undefined return value, though, it's easy to remedy: simply initialize $sum to zero rather than using the default of undef:

```
    my $sum = 0;
```

Now the subroutine will always return a number even if the parameter list were empty.

2. Here's one way to do it:

```
    # Remember to include &total from previous exercise!
    print "The numbers from 1 to 1000 add up to ", &total(1..1000), ".\n";
```

We can't call the subroutine from inside the double-quoted string,[*] so the subroutine call is another separate item being passed to print. The total should be 500500, a nice round number. And it shouldn't take any noticeable time at all to run this program; passing a parameter list of 1,000 values is an everyday task for Perl.

3. Here's one way to do it:

```
    sub average {
        if (@_ == 0) { return }
```

---

[*] We can't do this without advanced trickiness. It's rare to find anything that you *absolutely* can't do in Perl.

```
  my $count = @_;
  my $sum = &total(@_);              # from earlier exercise
  $sum/$count;
}
sub above_average {
  my $average = &average(@_);
  my @list;
  foreach $element (@_) {
    if ($element > $average) {
      push @list, $element;
    }
  }
  @list;
}
```

In average, we return without giving an explicit return value if the parameter list is empty. That gives the caller undef* to report that no average comes from an empty list. If the list wasn't empty, using &total makes it simple to calculate the average. We didn't need to use temporary variables for $sum and $count, but doing so makes the code easier to read.

The second sub, above_average, builds and returns a list of the desired items. (Why is the control variable named $element instead of using Perl's favorite default, $_?) Note that this second sub uses a different technique for dealing with an empty parameter list.

Answers to Chapter 5 Exercises

1. Here's one way to do it:

```
print reverse <>;
```

Well, that's pretty simple! It works because print is looking for a list of strings to print, which it gets by calling reverse in a list context. And reverse is looking for a list of strings to reverse, which it gets by using the diamond operator in list context. So, the diamond returns a list of all of the lines from all of the files of the user's choice. That list of lines is just what cat would print out. Now reverse reverses the list of lines, and print prints them out.

2. Here's one way to do it:

```
print "Enter some lines, then press Ctrl-D:\n";  # or Ctrl-Z
chomp(my @lines = <STDIN>);
print "1234567890" x 7, "12345\n";  # ruler line to column 75
foreach (@lines) {
  printf "%20s\n", $_;
}
```

---

* Or an empty list, if &average is used in a list context.

Here, we start by reading in and chomping all of the lines of text. Then we print the ruler line. Since that's a debugging aid, we'd generally comment out that line when the program is done. We could have typed "1234567890" repeatedly, or copy and pasted to make a ruler line as long as we needed, but we chose to do it this way because it's kind of cool.

Now, the foreach loop iterates over the list of lines, printing each one with the %20s conversion. If you chose to do so, you could have created a format to print the list all at once without the loop:

```
my $format = "%20s\n" x @lines;
printf $format, @lines;
```

It's a common mistake to get 19-character columns. That happens when you say to yourself,* "Hey, why do we chomp the input if we're only going to add the newlines back on later?" So you leave out the chomp and use a format of "%20s" (without a newline).† Mysteriously, the output is off by one space. So, what went wrong?

The problem happens when Perl counts the spaces needed to make the right number of columns. If the user enters **hello** and a newline, Perl sees *six* characters, not five, since newline is a character. So, it prints 14 spaces and a six-character string, sure that it gives the 20 characters you asked for in "%20s". Oops.

Perl isn't looking at the contents of the string to determine the width; it is checking the raw number of characters. A newline (or another special character, such as a tab or a null character) will throw things off.‡

Here's one way to do it:

```
print "What column width would you like? ";
chomp(my $width = <STDIN>);
print "Enter some lines, then press Ctrl-D:\n";  # or Ctrl-Z
chomp(my @lines = <STDIN>);
print "1234567890" x (($width+9)/10), "\n";      # ruler line as needed
foreach (@lines) {
  printf "%${width}s\n", $_;
}
```

This is much like the previous one, but we ask for a column width first. We ask for that first because we can't ask for more input *after* the end-of-file indicator, at least on some systems. In the real world, you'll generally have a better end-of-input indicator when getting input from the user, as we'll see in later exercise answers.

Another change from the previous exercise's answer is the ruler line. We used some math to cook up a ruler line that's at least as long as we need as suggested

---

* Or to Larry if he's standing nearby.

† Unless Larry told you not to do that.

‡ As Larry should have explained to you by now.

as an "extra credit" part of the exercise. Proving that our math is correct is an additional challenge. (Hint: Consider possible widths of 50 and 51, and remember that the right side operand to x is truncated, not rounded.)

To generate the format this time, we used the expression "%${width}s\n", which interpolates $width. The curly braces are required to "insulate" the name from the following s; without the curly braces, we'd be interpolating $widths, which is the wrong variable. If you forgot how to use curly braces to do this, you could have written an expression like '%' . $width . "s\n" to get the same format string.

The value of $width brings up another case where chomp is vital. If the width isn't chomped, the resulting format string would resemble "%30\ns\n". That's not useful.

People who have seen printf before may have thought of another solution. Because printf comes to us from C, which doesn't have string interpolation, we can use the same trick C programmers use. If an asterisk (*) appears in place of a numeric field width in a conversion, a value from the list of parameters will be used:

```perl
printf "%*s\n", $width, $_;
```

Answers to Chapter 6 Exercises

1. Here's one way to do it:

```perl
my %last_name = qw{
   fred flintstone
   barney rubble
   wilma flintstone
};
print "Please enter a first name: ";
chomp(my $name = <STDIN>);
print "That's $name $last_name{$name}.\n";
```

In this one, we used a qw// list (with curly braces as the delimiter) to initialize the hash. That's fine for this simple data set, and it's easy to maintain because each data item is a simple given name and simple family name, with nothing tricky. If your data might contain spaces—for example, if robert de niro or mary kay place were to visit Bedrock—this method wouldn't work as well.

You might have chosen to assign each key/value pair separately, something like this:

```perl
my %last_name;
$last_name{"fred"} = "flintstone";
$last_name{"barney"} = "rubble";
$last_name{"wilma"} = "flintstone";
```

Note that (if you chose to declare the hash with my, perhaps because use strict was in effect) you must declare the hash before assigning any elements. You can't use my on only part of a variable, like this:

```perl
my $last_name{"fred"} = "flintstone";  # Oops!
```

The my operator works only with *entire* variables and never with one element of an array or hash. Speaking of lexical variables, you may have noticed the lexical variable $name is being declared inside of the chomp function call; it is fairly common to declare each my variable as it is needed, like this.

This is another case where chomp is vital. If someone enters the five-character string "fred\n" and we fail to chomp it, we'll be looking for "fred\n" as an element of the hash—and it's not there. chomp alone won't make this bulletproof; if someone enters "fred \n" (with a trailing space), we don't have a way with what we've seen so far to tell that they meant fred.

If you added a check whether the given key exists in the hash, so you'll give the user an explanatory message when he misspells a name, give yourself extra points for that.

2. Here's one way to do it:

```
my(@words, %count, $word);        # (optionally) declare our variables
chomp(@words = <STDIN>);
foreach $word (@words) {
  $count{$word} += 1;             # or $count{$word} = $count{$word} + 1;
}
foreach $word (keys %count) {   # or sort keys %count
  print "$word was seen $count{$word} times.\n";
}
```

In this one, we declared all of the variables at the top. People who come to Perl from a background in languages like Pascal (where variables are declared at the top) may find that way more familiar than declaring variables as they are needed. We're declaring these because we're pretending that use strict may be in effect; by default, Perl won't require such declarations.

Next, we use the line-input operator, <STDIN>, in a list context to read all of the input lines into @words and then we chomp those all at once. So, @words is our list of words from the input if the words were all on separate lines as they should have been.

The first foreach loop goes through all of the words. That loop contains the most important statement of the entire program, the statement that says to add one to $count{$word} and put the result back into $count{$word}. Though you could write it the short way (with the += operator) or the long way, the short way is a little bit more efficient since Perl has to look up $word in the hash only once.* For each word in the first foreach loop, we add one to $count{$word}. If the first word is fred, we add one to $count{"fred"}. Since this is the first time we've seen $count{"fred"}, it's undef. We're treating it as a number (with the numeric

---

* In some versions of Perl, the shorter way will avoid a warning about using an undefined value that may appear with the longer one. The warning can also be avoided by using the ++ operator to increment the variable, though we haven't shown you that operator yet.

+= operator, or with +, if you wrote it the long way), so Perl converts undef to 0 for us, automatically. The total is 1, which is stored back into $count{"fred"}.

The next time through that foreach loop, let's say the word is barney. We add one to $count{"barney"}, bumping it up from undef to 1, as well.

Suppose the next word is fred again. When we add one to $count{"fred"}, which is 1, we get 2. This goes back into $count{"fred"}, meaning that we've seen fred twice.

When we finish the first foreach loop, then we've counted how many times each word has appeared. The hash has a key for each (unique) word from the input, and the corresponding value is the number of times that word appeared.

The second foreach loop goes through the keys of the hash, which are the unique words from the input. In this loop, we'll see each *different* word once. For each one, it says something like "fred was seen 3 times."

If you want the extra credit on this problem, you could put sort before keys to print out the keys in order. If there will be more than a dozen items in an output list, it's generally a good idea to sort them, so that a human being who is trying to debug the program will fairly quickly be able to find the item she wants.

Answers to Chapter 7 Exercises

1. Here's one way to do it:

```
while (<>) {
  if (/fred/) {
    print;
  }
}
```

This is pretty simple. The more important part of this exercise is trying it out on the sample strings. It doesn't match Fred, showing that regular expressions are case-sensitive. (We'll see how to change that later.) It does match frederick and Alfred since both of those strings contain the four-letter string fred. (Matching whole words only, so frederick and Alfred won't match, is another feature we'll see later.)

2. Here's one way to do it: Change the pattern used in the first exercise's answer to /[fF]red/. You could also have tried /(f|F)red/ or /fred|Fred/, but the character class is more efficient.

3. Here's one way to do it: Change the pattern used in the first exercise's answer to /\./. The backslash is needed because the dot is a metacharacter, or you could use a character class: /[.]/.

4. Here's one way to do it: Change the pattern used in the first exercise's answer to /[A-Z][a-z]+/.

5. Here's one way to do it:

```
while (<>) {
  if (/wilma/) {
    if (/fred/) {
      print;
    }
  }
}
```

This tests /fred/ after we find /wilma/ matches, but fred could appear before or after wilma in the line; each test is independent of the other.

If you wanted to avoid the extra nested if test, you might have written something like this:*

```
while (<>) {
  if (/wilma.*fred|fred.*wilma/) {
    print;
  }
}
```

This works because we'll either have wilma before fred or fred before wilma. If we had written /wilma.*fred/, that wouldn't have matched a line like fred and wilma flintstone though that line mentions them both.

We made this an extra-credit exercise because many folks have a mental block here. We showed you an "or" operation (with the vertical bar, |), but we never showed you an "and" operation. That's because there isn't one in regular expressions.† If you want to know if two patterns are both successful, just test both of them.

Answers to Chapter 8 Exercises

1. There's one easy way to do it, and we showed it back in the chapter body. If your output isn't saying before<match>after as it should, you've chosen a hard way to do it.

2. Here's one way to do it:

```
/a\b/
```

(That's a pattern for use inside the pattern test program.) If your pattern mistakenly matches barney, you probably needed the word-boundary anchor.

---

* Folks who know about the logical-and operator (see Chapter 10), could do both tests of /fred/ and /wilma/ in the same if conditional. That's more efficient and scalable and an all-around better way than the ones given here. But we haven't seen logical-and yet.

† There are some tricky and advanced ways of doing what some folks would call an "and" operation. These are generally less efficient than using Perl's logical-and depending upon what optimizations Perl and its regular expression engine can make.

3. Here's one way to do it:

```
#!/usr/bin/perl
while (<STDIN>) {
  chomp;
  if (/(\b\w*a\b)/) {
    print "Matched: |$`<$&>$'|\n";
    print "\$1 contains '$1'\n";          # The new output line
  } else {
    print "No match: |$_|\n";
  }
}
```

This is the same test program (with a new pattern), except that the one marked line has been added to print out $1.

The pattern uses a pair of \b word-boundary anchors* inside the parentheses though the pattern works the same way when they are placed outside. That's because anchors correspond to a place in the string but not to any characters in the string: anchors have "zero width."

4. Here's one way to do it:

```
m!
  (\b\w*a\b)          # $1: a word ending in a
  (.{0,5})            # $2: up to five characters following
!xs                   # /x and /s modifiers
```

(Don't forget to add code to display $2 now that you have two memory variables. If you change the pattern to have just one again, you can simply comment out the extra line.) If your pattern doesn't match wilma anymore, perhaps you require one or more characters instead of zero or more. You may have omitted the /s modifier since there shouldn't be newlines in the data. (If there are newlines in the data, the /s modifier could make for different output.)

5. Here's one way to do it:

```
while (<>) {
  chomp;
  if (/\s+$/) {
    print "$_#\n";
  }
}
```

We used the pound sign (#) as the marker character.

Answers to Chapter 9 Exercises

1. Here's one way to do it:

```
/($what){3}/
```

---

* Admittedly, the first anchor isn't really needed due to details about greediness that we won't go into here. It may help efficiency. It certainly helps with clarity, and in the end, that one wins out.

Once $what has been interpolated, this gives a pattern resembling /(fred|barney){3}/. Without the parentheses, the pattern would be something like /fred|barney{3}/, which is the same as /fred|barneyyy/. So, the parentheses are required.

Here's one way to do it:

```
my $in = $ARGV[0];
unless (defined $in) {
  die "Usage: $0 filename";
}
my $out = $in;
$out =~ s/(\.\w+)?$/.out/;
unless (open IN, "<$in") {
  die "Can't open '$in': $!";
}
unless (open OUT, ">$out") {
  die "Can't write '$out': $!";
}
while (<IN>) {
  s/Fred/Larry/gi;
  print OUT $_;
}
```

This program begins by naming its only command-line parameter and complaining if it didn't get it. It copies that to $out and does a substitution to change the file extension, if any, to .out. (It would be sufficient to append .out to the filename.)

Once the filehandles IN and OUT are opened, the real program can begin. If you didn't use the /g and /i options, take off half a point since *every* fred and every Fred should be changed.

2. Here's one way to do it:

```
while (<IN>) {
  chomp;
  s/Fred/\n/gi;        # Replace all FREDs
  s/Wilma/Fred/gi;     # Replace all WILMAs
  s/\n/Wilma/g;        # Replace the placeholder
  print OUT "$_\n";
}
```

This replaces the loop from the previous program. To do this swap, we need to have some "placeholder" string that doesn't appear in the data. By using chomp (and adding the newline back for the output), we ensure that a newline (\n) can be the placeholder. (You could choose some other unlikely string as the placeholder. Another good choice would be the NUL character, \0.)

3. Here's one way to do it:

```
$^I = ".bak";          # make backups
while (<>) {
  if (/^#!/) {          # is it the shebang line?
    $_ .= "## Copyright (C) 20XX by Yours Truly\n";
  }
}
```

Invoke this program with the filenames you want to update. For example, if you've been naming your exercises *ex01-1*, *ex01-2*, etc., so they all begin with ex..., you would use:

```
./fix_my_copyright ex*
```

4. To keep from adding the copyright twice, we have to make two passes over the files. First, we make a "set" with a hash where the keys are the filenames and the values don't matter though we'll use 1 for convenience:

```
my %do_these;
foreach (@ARGV) {
  $do_these{$_} = 1;
}
```

Next, we'll examine the files and remove any file from our to-do list that contains the copyright. The current filename is in $ARGV, so we can use that as the hash key:

```
while (<>) {
  if (/^## Copyright/) {
    delete $do_these{$ARGV};
  }
}
```

Finally, it's the same program as before once we've reestablished a reduced list of names in @ARGV:

```
@ARGV = sort keys %do_these;
$^I = ".bak";              # make backups
while (<>) {
  if (/^#!/) {             # is it the shebang line?
    $_ .= "## Copyright (c) 20XX by Yours Truly\n";
  }
}
```

Answer to Chapter 10 Exercise

1. Here's one way to do it:

```
my $secret = int(1 + rand 100);
# This next line may be un-commented during debugging
# print "Don't tell anyone, but the secret number is $secret.\n";
while (1) {
  print "Please enter a guess from 1 to 100: ";
  chomp(my $guess = <STDIN>);
  if ($guess =~ /quit|exit|^\s*$/i) {
    print "Sorry you gave up. The number was $secret.\n";
    last;
  } elsif ($guess < $secret) {
    print "Too small. Try again!\n";
  } elsif ($guess == $secret) {
    print "That was it!\n";
    last;
  } else {
```

```
        print "Too large. Try again!\n";
    }
}
```

The first line picks out our secret number from 1 to 100, and here's how it works. First, rand is Perl's random number function, so rand 100 gives us a random number in the range from 0 up to (but not including) 100. That is, the largest possible value of that expression is something like 99.999.* Adding one gives a number from 1 to 100.999, and the int function truncates that, giving a result from 1 to 100, as we needed.

The commented-out line can help during development and debugging, or if you like to cheat. The main body of this program is the infinite while loop. That will keep asking for guesses until we execute last.

It's important that we test the possible strings before the numbers. If we didn't, do you see what would happen when the user types quit? That would be interpreted as a number (probably giving a warning message if warnings were turned on); since the value as a number would be zero, the poor users would get the message that their guess was too small. We might never get to the string tests in that case.

Another way to make the infinite loop here would be to use a naked block with redo. It's no more or less efficient; merely another way to write it. If you expect to loop most of the time, write while since that loops by default. If looping will be the exception, a naked block may be a better choice.

Answers to Chapter 11 Exercises

1. Here's one way to do it:
```
foreach my $file (@ARGV) {
  my $attribs = &attributes($file);
  print "'$file' $attribs.\n";
}
sub attributes {
  # report the attributes of a given file
  my $file = shift @_;
  return "does not exist" unless -e $file;
  my @attrib;
  push @attrib, "readable" if -r $file;
  push @attrib, "writable" if -w $file;
  push @attrib, "executable" if -x $file;
  return "exists" unless @attrib;
  'is ' . join " and ", @attrib;  # return value
}
```

---

* The actual largest possible value depends upon your system. See *http://www.cpan.org/doc/FMTEYEWTK/ random* if you need to know.

In this one, it's convenient to use a subroutine. The main loop prints one line of attributes for each file, perhaps telling us that 'cereal-killer' is executable or that 'sasquatch' does not exist.

The subroutine tells us the attributes of the given filename. If the file doesn't exist, there's no need for the other tests, so we test for that first. If there's no file, we'll return early.

If the file does exist, we'll build a list of attributes. (Give yourself extra credit points if you used the special _ filehandle instead of $file on these tests to keep from calling the system separately for each new attribute.) It would be easy to add additional tests like the three we show here. But what happens if none of the attributes is true? Well, if we can't say anything else, at least we can say that the file exists, so we do. The unless clause uses the fact that @attrib will be true (in a Boolean context, which is a special case of a scalar context) if it has any elements.

If we have some attributes, we'll join them with " and " and put "is " in front, to make a description like is readable and writable. This isn't perfect however; if there are three attributes, it will say that the file is readable and writable and executable, which has too many ands, but we can get away with it. If you wanted to add more attributes to the ones this program checks for, you should probably fix it to say something like is readable, writable, executable, and nonempty. Do this if it matters to you.

If you didn't put any filenames on the command line, this produces no output. This makes sense because if you ask for information on zero files, you should get zero lines of output. But let's compare that to what the next program does in a similar case, in the discussion below.

2. Here's one way to do it:

```
die "No file names supplied!\n" unless @ARGV;
my $oldest_name = shift @ARGV;
my $oldest_age = -M $oldest_name;
foreach (@ARGV) {
  my $age = -M;
  ($oldest_name, $oldest_age) = ($_, $age)
    if $age > $oldest_age;
}
printf "The oldest file was %s, and it was %.1f days old.\n",
  $oldest_name, $oldest_age;
```

This one starts by complaining if it didn't get any filenames on the command line. That's because it's supposed to tell us the oldest filename, and there isn't one if there aren't any files to check.

Once again, we're using the "high-water-mark" algorithm. The first file is certainly the oldest one seen so far. We have to keep track of its age as well, so that's in $oldest_age.

For each of the remaining files, we'll determine the age with the -M file test as we did for the first one (except that here, we'll use the default argument of $_ for the file test). The last-modified time is generally what people mean by the "age" of a file, though you could make a case for using a different one. If the age is more than $oldest_age, we'll use a list assignment to update the name and age. We didn't have to use a list assignment, but it's a convenient way to update several variables at once.

We stored the age from -M into the temporary variable $age. What would have happened if we had used -M each time rather than using a variable? Unless we used the special _ filehandle, we would have been asking the operating system for the age of the file each time, which is a potentially slow operation (not that you'd notice unless you have hundreds or thousands of files and maybe not even then). More importantly, we should consider what would happen if someone updated a file while we were checking it. That is, we see the age of some file, and it's the oldest one so far. But before we can get back to use -M a second time, someone modifies the file and resets the timestamp to the current time. Now, the age that we save into $oldest_age is actually the *youngest* age possible. The result would be that we'd get the oldest file among the files tested from that point on rather than the oldest overall; this would be a tough problem to debug.

At the end of the program, we use printf to print out the name and age, with the age rounded off to the nearest tenth of a day. Give yourself extra credit if you went to the trouble to convert the age to a number of days, hours, and minutes.

Answers to Chapter 12 Exercises

1. Here's one way to do it, with a glob:

```
print "Which directory? (Default is your home directory) ";
chomp(my $dir = <STDIN>);
if ($dir =~ /^\s*$/) {          # A blank line
  chdir or die "Can't chdir to your home directory: $!";
} else {
  chdir $dir or die "Can't chdir to '$dir': $!";
}
my @files = <*>;
foreach (@files) {
  print "$_\n";
}
```

First, we show a prompt and read the desired directory, chomping it as needed. (Without a chomp, we'd be heading for a directory that ends in a newline, which is legal in Unix and therefore cannot be presumed to be extraneous by the chdir function.)

If the directory name is nonempty, we'll change to that directory, aborting on a failure. If empty, the home directory is selected instead.

Finally, a glob on "star" pulls up all the names in the (new) working directory, automatically sorted to alphabetical order, and the names are printed one at a time.

2. Here's one way to do it:

```
print "Which directory? (Default is your home directory) ";
chomp(my $dir = <STDIN>);
if ($dir =~ /^\s*$/) {          # A blank line
  chdir or die "Can't chdir to your home directory:
$!";
} else {
  chdir $dir or die "Can't chdir to '$dir': $!";
}
my @files = <.* *>;        ## now includes .*
foreach (sort @files) {    ## now sorts
  print "$_\n";
}
```

Two differences from previous one: first, the glob now includes "dot star," which matches all the names that *do* begin with a dot. Second, we must sort the resulting list because some of the names that begin with a dot must be interleaved appropriately before or after the list of things without a beginning dot.

3. Here's one way to do it:

```
print "Which directory? (Default is your home directory) ";
chomp(my $dir = <STDIN>);
if ($dir =~ /^\s*$/) {          # A blank line
  chdir or die "Can't chdir to your home directory:
$!";
} else {
  chdir $dir or die "Can't chdir to '$dir': $!";
}
opendir DOT, "." or die "Can't opendir dot: $!";
foreach (sort readdir DOT) {
  # next if /^\./; ##   if we were skipping dot files
  print "$_\n";
}
```

Again, here is the same structure as the previous two programs, but now we've chosen to open a directory handle. Once we've changed the working directory, we want to open the current directory, which is the DOT directory handle.

Why DOT? If the user asks for an absolute directory name, like /etc, there's no problem opening it. But if the name is relative, like fred, watch what would happen. We chdir to fred and we want to use opendir to open it. That would open fred in the new directory, not fred in the original directory. The only name we can be sure will mean "the current directory" is ., which always has that meaning (on Unix and similar systems, at least).

The readdir function pulls up all the names of the directory, which are sorted and displayed. If we had done the first exercise this way, we would have skipped over the dot files, and that's handled by uncommenting the commented-out line in the `foreach` loop.

You may find yourself asking, "Why did we `chdir` first? You can use `readdir` and friends on any directory, not merely on the current directory." Primarily, we wanted to give the user the convenience of being able to get to her home directory with a single keystroke. But this could be the start of a general file management utility program. The next step might be to ask the user which of the files in this directory should be moved to offline tape storage.

4. Here's one way to do it:

```
unlink @ARGV;
```

or, if you want to warn the user of any problems:

```
foreach (@ARGV) {
  unlink $_ or warn "Can't unlink '$_': $!, continuing...\n";
}
```

Here, each item from the command-invocation line is placed individually into `$_`, which is used as the argument to `unlink`. If something goes wrong, the warning gives the clue why.

5. Here's one way to do it:

```
use File::Basename;
use File::Spec;
my($source, $dest) = @ARGV;
if (-d $dest) {
  my $basename = basename $source;
  $dest = File::Spec->catfile($dest, $basename);
}
rename $source, $dest
  or die "Can't rename '$source' to '$dest': $!\n";
```

The workhorse in this program is the last statement, but the remainder of the program is necessary when we are renaming into a directory. First, after declaring the modules we're using, we name the command-line arguments sensibly. If $dest is a directory, we need to extract the basename from the $source name and append it to the directory ($dest). Once $dest is patched up, if needed, the rename does the deed.

6. Here's one way to do it:

```
use File::Basename;
use File::Spec;
my($source, $dest) = @ARGV;
if (-d $dest) {
  my $basename = basename $source;
  $dest = File::Spec->catfile($dest, $basename);
}
link $source, $dest
  or die "Can't link '$source' to '$dest': $!\n";
```

As the hint in the exercise description said, this program is much like the previous one. The difference is that we'll link rather than rename. If your system doesn't support hard links, you might have written this as the last statement:

```
print "Would link '$source' to '$dest'.\n";
```

7. Here's one way to do it:

```perl
use File::Basename;
use File::Spec;
my $symlink = $ARGV[0] eq '-s';
shift @ARGV if $symlink;
my($source, $dest) = @ARGV;
if (-d $dest) {
  my $basename = basename $source;
  $dest = File::Spec->catfile($dest, $basename);
}
if ($symlink) {
  symlink $source, $dest
    or die "Can't make soft link from '$source' to '$dest': $!\n";
} else {
  link $source, $dest
    or die "Can't make hard link from '$source' to '$dest': $!\n";
}
```

The first few lines of code (after the two use declarations) look at the first command-line argument, and if it's -s, we're making a symbolic link, so we note that as a true value for $symlink. If we saw -s, we would need to get rid of it in the next line. The next few lines are cut and pasted from the previous exercise answers. Finally, based on the truth of $symlink, we'll create a symbolic link or a hard link. We updated the dying words to make it clear which kind of link we were attempting.

8. Here's one way to do it:

```perl
foreach (<.* *>) {
  my $dest = readlink $_;
  print "$_ -> $dest\n" if defined $dest;
}
```

Each item resulting from the glob ends up in $_ one by one. If the item is a symbolic link, then readlink returns a defined value, and the location is displayed. If not, then the condition fails, and we can skip over it.

Answers to Chapter 13 Exercises

1. Here's one way to do it:

```perl
my @numbers;
push @numbers, split while <>;
foreach (sort { $a <=> $b } @numbers) {
  printf "%20g\n", $_;
}
```

That second line of code is confusing, isn't it? We did that on purpose. Though we recommend you write clear code, some people like writing code that's as hard to understand as possible,* so we want you to be prepared for the worst. Someday, you'll need to maintain confusing code like this.

Since that line uses the `while` modifier, it's the same as if it were written in a loop like this:

```
while (<>) {
  push @numbers, split;
}
```

That's better but maybe still unclear. (Nevertheless, we don't have a quibble about writing it this way. This one is on the correct side of the "too hard to understand at a glance" line.) The `while` loop is reading the input a line at a time (from the user's choice of input sources, as shown by the diamond operator). The `split` is, by default, splitting that on whitespace to make a list of words, or in this case, a list of numbers. The input is just a stream of numbers separated by whitespace, after all. Either way you write it, that `while` loop will put all of the numbers from the input into `@numbers`.

The `foreach` loop takes the sorted list and prints each one on its own line, using the `%20g` numeric format to put them in a right-justified column. You could have used `%20s` instead. What difference would that make? That's a string format, so it would have left the strings untouched in the output. Did you notice that our sample data included both 1.50 and 1.5, and both 04 and 4? If you printed those as strings, the extra zero characters will still be in the output; but `%20g` is a numeric format, so equal numbers will appear identically in the output. Either format could potentially be correct, depending upon what you want to do.

2. Here's one way to do it:

```
    # don't forget to incorporate the hash %last_name,
    # either from the exercise text or the downloaded file
    my @keys = sort {
      "\L$last_name{$a}" cmp "\L$last_name{$b}"  # by last name
        or
      "\L$a" cmp "\L$b"                          # by first name
    } keys %last_name;
    foreach (@keys) {
      print "$last_name{$_}, $_\n";              # Rubble,Bamm-Bamm
    }
```

---

* We don't recommend it for *normal* coding purposes, but it can be a fun game to write confusing code, and it can be educational to take someone else's obfuscated code examples and spend a weekend or two figuring out just what they do. If you want to see some fun snippets of such code and maybe get a little help with decoding them, ask around at the next Perl Mongers' meeting. Or search for JAPHs on the Web, or see how well you can decipher the example obfuscated code block near the end of this chapter's answers.

There's not much to say about this one. We put the keys in order as needed, and printed them out. We chose to print them in last-name-comma-first-name order just for fun; the exercise description left that up to you.

3. Here's one way to do it:

```
print "Please enter a string: ";
chomp(my $string = <STDIN>);
print "Please enter a substring: ";
chomp(my $sub = <STDIN>);
my @places;
for (my $pos = -1; ; ) {                    # tricky use of three-part for loop
  $pos = index($string, $sub, $pos + 1);    # find next position
  last if $pos == -1;
  push @places, $pos;
}
print "Locations of '$sub' in '$string' were: @places\n";
```

This one starts out simply enough, asking the user for the strings and declaring an array to hold the list of substring positions. But once again, as we see in the for loop, the code seems to have been "optimized for cleverness," which should be done only for fun, never in production code. This actually shows a valid technique that could be useful in some cases, so let's see how it works.

The my variable $pos is declared private to the scope of the for loop, and it starts with a value of -1. So as not to keep you in suspense about this variable, we'll tell you right now that it's going to hold a position of the substring in the larger string. The test and increment sections of the for loop are empty, so this is an infinite loop. (We'll eventually break out of it, in this case with last).

The first statement of the loop body looks for the first occurrence of the substring at or after position $pos + 1. That means that on the first iteration, when $pos is still -1, the search will start at position 0, the start of the string. The location of the substring is stored back into $pos. If that is -1, we're done with the for loop, so last breaks out of the loop in that case. If it isn't -1, then we save the position into @places and go around the loop again. This time, $pos + 1 means we start looking for the substring after the previous place where we found it. So, we get the answers we wanted and the world is again a happy place.

If you didn't want that tricky use of the for loop, you could accomplish the same result as shown here:

```
{
  my $pos = -1;
  while (1) {
    ... # Same loop body as the for loop used above
  }
}
```

The naked block on the outside restricts the scope of $pos. You don't have to do that, but it's often a good idea to declare each variable in the smallest possible scope. This means we have fewer variables "alive" at any given point in the program, making it less likely that we'll accidentally reuse the name $pos for some new purpose. For the same reason, if you don't declare a variable in a small scope, you should give it a longer name that's less likely to be reused by accident. Maybe something like $substring_position would be appropriate in this case.

On the other hand, if you were wanted to obfuscate your code (shame on you), you could create a monster like this (shame on us):

```
for (my $pos = -1; -1 !=
  ($pos = index
    +$string,
    +$sub,
    +$pos
    +1
  );
push @places, (((((+$pos))))) {
    'for ($pos != 1; # ;$pos++) {
      print "position $pos\n";#;';#' } pop @places;
}
```

That trickier code works in place of the original tricky for loop. You should be able to decipher that one or obfuscate code to amaze your friends and confound your enemies. Use these powers only for good, never for evil.

Oh, and what did you get when you searched for t in This is a test.? It's at positions 10 and 13. It's not at position 0. Since the capitalization doesn't match, the substring doesn't match.

Answers to Chapter 14 Exercises

1. Here's one way to do it:

```
chdir "/" or die "Can't chdir to root directory: $!";
exec "ls", "-l" or die "Can't exec ls: $!";
```

The first line changes the current working directory to the root directory as our particular hardcoded directory. The second line uses the multiple-argument exec function to send the result to standard output. We could have used the single-argument form, but it doesn't hurt to do it this way.

2. Here's one way to do it:

```
open STDOUT, ">ls.out" or die "Can't write to ls.out: $!";
open STDERR, ">ls.err" or die "Can't write to ls.err: $!";
chdir "/" or die "Can't chdir to root directory: $!";
exec "ls", "-l" or die "Can't exec ls: $!";
```

The first and second lines reopen STDOUT and STDERR to a file in the current directory before we change directories. After the directory change, the directory listing command executes, sending the data back to the files opened in the original directory.

Where would the message from the last die go? Why, it would go into *ls.err* since that's where STDERR is going at that point. The die from chdir would go there, too. But where would the message go if we can't re-open STDERR on the second line? It goes to the old STDERR. For the three standard filehandles, STDIN, STDOUT, and STDERR, if re-opening them fails, the old filehandle is still open.

3. Here's one way to do it:

```
if (`date` =~ /^S/) {
  print "go play!\n";
} else {
  print "get to work!\n";
}
```

Since both Saturday and Sunday start with an S and the day of the week is the first part of the output of the date command, this is fairly simple. Check the output of the date command to see if it starts with S. There are many harder ways to do this program, and we've seen most of them in our classes.

If we had to use this in a real-world program, we'd probably use the pattern /^(Sat|Sun)/. It's a tiny bit less efficient, but that hardly matters; besides, the maintenance programmer can understand it more easily.

Answer to Chapter 15 Exercise

1. Here's one way to do it.

```
#!/usr/bin/perl
use Module::CoreList;
my %modules = %{ $Module::CoreList::version{5.006} };
print join "\n", keys %modules;
```

This answer uses a hash reference (which you'll have to read about in Alpaca, but we gave you the part to get around that. You don't have to know how it all works as long as you know it does work. You can get the job done and learn the details later.)

2. There are a couple ways to approach this problem. For our solution, we used the C<Cwd> (current working directory) module to find out where we were in the file-system. We used a glob to get the list of all the files in the current directory; the names don't have the directory information, so we have to add that. You could have used C<opendir> too, but C<glob> is less typing. Our glob pattern includes C<.*> to get the Unix hidden files, which don't match the C<*> pattern.

Once we have all the filenames, we go through them with C<foreach>. For every name, we call C<File::Spec->catfile()> just like that module shows in its documentation. We save the result in C<$path>, then print that to standard output:

```
#!/usr/bin/perl

use Cwd;          # Current Working Directory
use File::Spec;
```

```
my $cwd = getcwd;
my @files = glob ".* *";

foreach my $file ( @files )
{
my $path = File::Spec->catfile( $cwd, $file );
print "$path\n";
}
```

3. This answer is much easier than the previous one, even though you had to write
the last program to use this one. The work happens in the C<while> loop. For
every line of input, we call the C<basename> function from C<File::Basename>. We
cribbed directly from the C<File::Basename> documentation. We pass the line of
input directly to C<basename> and save the result in C<$name>. Since we didn't
C<chomp> the line, C<$name> still has the trailing newline, so we can simply print
the name to get one filename per line:

```
#!/usr/bin/perl

use File::Basename;

while( <STDIN> )
{
my $name = basename( $_ );

print $name;
}
```

Answer to Chapter 16 Exercise

1. Here's one way to do it:

```
my $filename = 'path/to/sample_text';
open FILE, $filename
  or die "Can't open '$filename': $!";
chomp(my @strings = <FILE>);
while (1) {
  print "Please enter a pattern: ";
  chomp(my $pattern = <STDIN>);
  last if $pattern =~ /^\s*$/;
  my @matches = eval {
    grep /$pattern/, @strings;
  };
  if ($@) {
    print "Error: $@";
  } else {
    my $count = @matches;
    print "There were $count matching strings:\n",
      map "$_\n", @matches;
  }
  print "\n";
}
```

This one uses an eval block to trap any failure that might occur when using the regular expression. Inside that block, a grep pulls the matching strings from the list of strings.

Once the eval is finished, we can report either the error message or the matching strings. We "unchomped" the strings for output by using map to add a newline to each string.

Beyond the Llama

We've covered a lot in this book, but there's more. In this appendix, we'll explain a little more about what Perl can do, and give some references on where to learn the details. Some of what we mention here is on the bleeding edge and may have changed by the time you're reading this book, which is one reason why we frequently send you to the documentation for the full story. We don't expect many readers to read every word of this appendix, but we hope you'll at least skim the headings so that you'll be prepared to fight back when someone tells you, "You just can't use Perl for project X because Perl can't do Y."

So as not to repeat ourselves in every paragraph: the important part of what we don't cover here is covered in the Alpaca. Read the Alpaca, especially if you'll be writing programs that are longer than 100 lines (alone or with other people). Especially if you're tired of hearing about Fred and Barney, and you want to move on to another fictional universe featuring seven people* who got to spend a lot of time on an isolated island after a cruise!

Further Documentation

The documentation that comes with Perl may seem overwhelming at first. Fortunately, you can use your computer to search for keywords in the documentation. When searching for a particular topic, it's often good to start with the perltoc (table of contents) and perlfaq (frequently asked questions) sections. On most systems, the perldoc command should be able to track down the documentation for Perl, installed modules, and related programs (including perldoc itself).

---

* Call them "castaways."

Regular Expressions

Yes, there's more about regular expressions than we mentioned. *Mastering Regular Expressions* by Jeffrey Friedl (O'Reilly) is one of the best technical books we've ever read.* It's half about regular expressions in general, and half about Perl's regular expressions. It goes into detail about how the regular expression engine works internally and why one way of writing a pattern may be much more efficient than another. Anyone who is serious about Perl should read this book. See the `perlre` manpage (and its companion manpages `perlretut` and `perlrequick` in newer versions of Perl). And, there's more about regular expressions in the Alpaca as well.

Packages

Packages† allow you to compartmentalize namespaces. Imagine you have ten programmers all working on one big project. If you use the global names `$fred`, `@barney`, `%betty`, and `&wilma` in your part of the project, what happens when I accidentally use one of those same names in my part? Packages keep them separate; I can access your `$fred`, and you can access mine but not by accident. Packages are needed to make Perl scalable, so we can manage large programs. The Alpaca discusses packages in detail.

Extending Perl's Functionality

One of the most common pieces of good advice heard in the Perl discussion forums is that you shouldn't reinvent the wheel. Other folks have written code you can put to use. The most frequent way to add to what Perl can do is by using a library or module. Many come with Perl and others are available from CPAN. You can even write your own libraries and modules.

Libraries

Many programming languages offer support for libraries much as Perl does. Libraries are collections of (mostly) subroutines for a given purpose. In modern Perl, though, it's more common to use modules than libraries.

---

* And we're not just saying that because it's also published by O'Reilly. It's a great book.

† The name "package" is perhaps an unfortunate choice in that it makes many people think of a packaged-up chunk of code (in Perl, that's a module or a library). All that a package does is define a namespace (a collection of global symbol names, like `$fred` or `&wilma`). A namespace is *not* a chunk of code.

Modules

A module is a "smart library." A module will typically offer a collection of subroutines that act as if they were built-in functions, for the most part. Modules are smart in that they keep their details in a separate package, only importing what you request. This keeps a module from stomping on your code's symbols.

Though many useful modules are written in pure Perl, others are written using a language like C. For example, the MD5 algorithm is like a high-powered checksum.* It uses a lot of low-level bit twiddling that could be done in Perl but hundreds of times more slowly;† it's an algorithm that was designed to be efficiently implemented in C. So, the Digest::MD5 module is made to use the compiled C code. When you use that module, it's as if your Perl had a built-in function to calculate MD5 digests.

Finding and Installing Modules

Maybe your system already has the module you need. But how can you find out which modules are installed? You can use the program *inside*, which should be available for download from CPAN in the directory *http://www.cpan.org/authors/id/P/PH/PHOENIX/*.

If none of the available modules on your system suit your needs, you can search for Perl modules on CPAN at *http://search.cpan.org/*. To install a module on your system, see the perlmodinstall manpage.

When using a module, you'll generally put the required use directives at the top of your program. That makes it easy for someone who is installing your program on a new system to see at a glance which modules it needs.

Writing Your Own Modules

In the rare case that there's no module to do what you need, an advanced programmer can write a new one, in Perl or in another language (often C). See the perlmod and perlmodlib manpages for more information. The Alpaca covers how to write, test, and distribute modules.

---

* It's not a checksum, but that's good enough for this explanation.

† The module Digest::Perl::MD5 is a pure Perl implementation of the MD5 algorithm. Though your mileage may vary, we found it to be about 280 times slower than the Digest::MD5 module on one sample dataset. Many of the bit twiddling operations in the C algorithm compile down to a *single* machine instruction; thus, entire lines of code can take a mere handful of clock cycles to run. Perl is fast, but let's be realistic.

Some Important Modules

We describe some of the most important features[*] of the most important modules[†] in this section. The modules that we discuss here should be found on every machine that has Perl except where noted otherwise. You can get the latest ones from CPAN.

The CGI and CGI_Lite Modules

Many people use Perl to write programs that a web server will run, called *CGI programs*. The CGI module comes with Perl, and the CGI_Lite module is available separately from CPAN. We showed an example in Chapter 15, and you can read more in the section "The Common Gateway Interface (CGI)" later in this appendix.

The Cwd Module

Sometimes you need to know what the current working directory's name is. (You could use ., but maybe you need to save the name so you can change back to this directory later.) The Cwd module, which comes with Perl, provides the cwd function, which you can use to determine the current working directory.

```
use Cwd;

my $directory = cwd;
```

The Fatal Module

If you get tired of writing "or die" after every invocation of open or chdir, then maybe the Fatal module is for you. Tell it which functions to work with, and those will be automatically checked for failure as if you'd written or die and a suitable message after each one. This won't affect such calls in someone else's package (code contained within a module you're using, for example), so don't use this to fix poorly written code. It's a timesaver for simple programs in which you don't need direct control over the error message itself. For example:

```
use Fatal qw/ open chdir /;

chdir '/home/merlyn';  # "or die" is now supplied automatically
```

---

[*] We're including the most important features of each module. See the module's own documentation to learn more.

[†] To be sure, there are other important modules whose use is too complex for most readers of this book, typically because using the module requires understanding Perl's references or objects.

The File::Basename Module

We covered this module in Chapter 15. Its primary uses are to portably pull the basename or directory name from a full filename:

```
use File::Basename;

for (@ARGV) {
  my $basename = basename $_;
  my $dirname = dirname $_;
  print "That's file $basename in directory $dirname.\n";
}
```

The File::Copy Module

When you need to copy or move files, the File::Copy module is for you. (It's often tempting to call a system program to do these things, but that's not portable.) This module provides the functions move and copy, which may be used much as the corresponding system programs would be used:

```
use File::Copy;

copy("source", "destination")
  or die "Can't copy 'source' to 'destination': $!";
```

The File::Spec Module

When you need to manipulate a filename (more formally called a "file specification"), it's generally more portable and reliable to use the File::Spec module than to do the work yourself from Perl. For example, you can use the catfile function to put together a directory name and a filename to produce a long filename (as we saw in Chapter 15), but you don't have to know if the system your program is running on uses a forward slash or some other character to separate those. You could use the curdir function to get the name of the current directory (. on Unix systems).

The File::Spec module is object-oriented, but you don't need to understand objects to use it. Call each function ("method," really) by using File::Spec and a small arrow before the function's name, like this:

```
use File::Spec;

my $current_directory = File::Spec->curdir;
opendir DOT, $current_directory
  or die "Can't open current directory '$current_directory': $!";
```

The Image::Size Module

When you have an image file, you may want to know what its height and width are. (This is handy for making programs that write HTML if you wish for an IMG tag to indicate the image's dimensions.) The `Image::Size` module, which is available from CPAN, understands the common GIF, JFIF (JPEG), and PNG image types, and some others. For example:

```
use Image::Size;

# Get the size of fred.png
my($fred_height, $fred_width) = imgsize("fred.png");
die "Couldn't get the size of the image"
  unless defined $fred_height;
```

The Net::SMTP Module

If you want your program to be able to send email through an SMTP server (which is the way most of us send email these days), you may use the `Net::SMTP` module to do the work.* This module, available from CPAN, is OO, but you may simply follow the syntax to use it. You will need to change the name of your SMTP host and the other items to make this work on your system. Your system administrator or local expert can tell you what to use. For example:

```
use Net::SMTP;

my $from = 'YOUR_ADDRESS_GOES_HERE';        # maybe fred@bedrock.edu
my $site = 'YOUR_SITE_NAME_GOES_HERE';      # maybe bedrock.edu
my $smtp_host = 'YOUR_SMTP_HOST_GOES_HERE'; # maybe mail or mailhost
my $to = 'president@whitehouse.gov';

my $smtp = Net::SMTP->new($smtp_host, Hello => $site);

$smtp->mail($from);
$smtp->to($to);
$smtp->data( );

$smtp->datasend("To: $to\n");
$smtp->datasend("Subject: A message from my Perl program.\n");
$smtp->datasend("\n");
$smtp->datasend("This is just to let you know,\n");
$smtp->datasend("I don't care what those other people say about you,\n");
$smtp->datasend("I still think you're doing a great job.\n");
$smtp->datasend("\n");
$smtp->datasend("Have you considered enacting a law naming Perl \n");
$smtp->datasend("the national programming language?\n");

$smtp->dataend( );                          # Not datasend!
$smtp->quit;
```

---

* Yes, this means you are now able to use Perl to send spam. Please don't.

The POSIX Module

If you need access to the POSIX (IEEE Std 1003.1) functions, the POSIX module is for you. It provides many functions that C programmers may be used to, such as trigonometric functions (asin, cosh), general mathematical functions (floor, frexp), character-identification functions (isupper, isalpha), low-level I/O functions (creat, open), and some others (asctime, clock). You'll probably want to call each of these with its "full" name; that is, with POSIX and a pair of colons as a prefix to the function's name:

```
use POSIX;

print "Please enter a number: ";
chomp(my $str = <STDIN>);

$! = 0;  # Clear out the error indicator
my($num, $leftover) = POSIX::strtod($str);

if ($str eq '') {
  print "That string was empty!\n";
} elsif ($leftover) {
  my $remainder = substr $str, -$leftover;
  print "The string '$remainder' was left after the number $num.\n";
} elsif ($!) {
  print "The conversion function complained: $!\n";
} else {
  print "The seemingly-valid number was $num.\n";
}
```

The Sys::Hostname Module

The Sys::Hostname module provides the hostname function, which will be the network name of your machine if that can be determined. If it can't be determined, perhaps because your machine is not on the Internet or not properly configured, the function will die automatically; there's no point in using or die here. For example:

```
use Sys::Hostname;
my $host = hostname;
print "This machine is known as '$host'.\n";
```

The Text::Wrap Module

The Text::Wrap module supplies the wrap function, which lets you implement simple word-wrapping. The first two parameters specify the indentation of the first line and the others; the remaining parameters make up the paragraph's text:

```
use Text::Wrap;

my $message = "This is some sample text which may be longer " .
  "than the width of your output device, so it needs to " .
```

```
    "be wrapped to fit properly as a paragraph. ";
$message x= 5;

print wrap("\t", "", "$message\n");
```

The Time::Local Module

If you have a time (for example, from the time function) that needs to be converted to a list of year, month, day, hour, minute, and second values, you can do that with Perl's built-in localtime function in a list context.[*] (In a scalar context, that gives a formatted string representing the time, which is more often what you'd want.) If you need to go in the other direction, you may use the timelocal function from the Time::Local module instead. The value of $mon and $year for January 2004 are not 1 and 2004 as you might expect, so read the documentation before you use this module. For example:

```
use Time::Local;

my $time = timelocal($sec, $min, $hr, $day, $mon, $year);
```

Pragmas

Pragmas are special modules that come with each release of Perl and tell Perl's internal compiler something about your code. You've used the strict pragma. The pragmas available for your release of Perl should be listed in the perlmodlib manpage.

You use pragmas with a use directive, much like you'd use ordinary modules. Some pragmas are lexically scoped, like lexical (my) variables are, and so apply to the smallest enclosing block or file. Others may apply to the entire program or to the current package. If you don't use any packages, the pragmas apply to your entire program. Pragmas should usually appear near the top of your source code. The documentation for each pragma should tell you how it's scoped.

The constant Pragma

If you've used other languages, you've probably seen the ability to declare constants in one way or another. Constants are handy for making a setting once, near the beginning of a program, but that can be updated if the need arises. Perl can do this with the package-scoped constant pragma, which tells the compiler that a given identifier has a constant value, which may be optimized wherever it appears as in this example:

```
use constant DEBUGGING => 0;
use constant ONE_YEAR => 365.2425 * 24 * 60 * 60;
```

---

[*] The return value of localtime in a list context is different than you might expect. See the documentation.

```
if (DEBUGGING) {
  # This code will be optimized away unless DEBUGGING is turned on
  ...
}
```

The diagnostics Pragma

Perl's diagnostic messages often seem cryptic, at least the first time you see them. You can always look them up in the perldiag manpage to find what they mean, and often a little about what's likely to be the problem and how to fix it. You can save yourself the trouble of searching that manpage if you use the diagnostics pragma, which tells Perl to track down and print out the related information for any message. Unlike most pragmas, this one is *not* intended for everyday use, as it makes your program read the entire perldiag manpage just to get started. This is potentially a significant amount of overhead in terms of time and memory. Use this pragma only when you're debugging *and* expecting to get an error message you don't yet understand. It affects your entire program. The syntax is:

```
use diagnostics;
```

The lib Pragma

It's nearly always best to install modules in the standard directories, so they're available for everyone, but only the system administrator can do that. If you install your own modules, you'll have to store them in your own directories, so how will Perl know where to find them? That's what the lib pragma is all about. It tells Perl that the given directory is the first place to look for modules. (That means it's also useful for trying out a new release of a given module.) It affects all modules loaded from this point on. The syntax is:

```
use lib '/home/rootbeer/experimental';
```

Use a nonrelative pathname as the argument since there's no telling what the current working directory will be when your program is run. This is especially important for CGI programs (that is, programs run by a web server).

The strict Pragma

You've been using use strict without having to understand that it's a pragma. It's lexically scoped, and it enforces some good programming rules. See its documentation to learn what restrictions are available in your release of Perl. The Alpaca talks about other things that the strict module performs.

The vars Pragma

In the rare case that you need a global variable when use strict is in effect, you may declare it with the vars pragma.* This package-scoped pragma tells Perl you are intentionally using one or more global variables:

```
use strict;
use vars qw/ $fred $barney /;

$fred = "This is a global variable, but that's all right.\n";
```

This is covered in detail in the Alpaca.

The warnings Pragma

Starting in Perl Version 5.6, you may choose to have lexically scoped warnings with the warnings pragma.† Rather than using the -w option crudely to turn warnings on or off for the entire program at once, you may specify that you want no warnings about undefined values in one section of code, but want other warnings to be available. This signals the maintenance programmer, "I know that this code would produce warnings, but I know what I'm doing anyway." See the documentation for this pragma to learn about the categories of warnings available in your release of Perl.

Databases

If you've got a database, Perl can work with it. This section describes some of the common types of databases. We've seen the DBI module briefly in Chapter 15.

Direct System Database Access

Perl can directly access some system databases, sometimes with the help of a module. These are databases like the Windows Registry (which holds machine-level settings), or the Unix password database (which lists which username corresponds to which number, and related information), as well as the domain-name database (which lets you translate an IP number into a machine name, and vice versa).

Flat-File Database Access

If you'd like to access your own flat-file databases from Perl, there are modules to help you do that (seemingly a new one every month or two, so any list here would be out of date).

---

* If your program will never be used with a version of Perl prior to 5.6, you should use the our keyword instead of the vars pragma.

† If your program may be used with a version of Perl prior to 5.6, you shouldn't use the warnings pragma.

Other Operators and Functions

Yes, there are more operators and functions than we can fit here, from the scalar `..` operator to the scalar `,` operator, from `wantarray` to `goto(!)`, from `caller` to `chr`. See the `perlop` and `perlfunc` manpages.

Transliteration with tr///

The `tr///` operator looks like a regular expression, but it's really for transliterating one group of characters into another. It can also efficiently count selected characters. See the `perlop` manpage.

Here Documents

Here documents are a useful form of multiline string quoting. See the `perldata` manpage.

Mathematics

Perl can do just about any kind of mathematics you can dream up.

Advanced Math Functions

All of the basic mathematical functions (square root, cosine, logarithm, absolute value, and many others) are available as built-in functions. See the `perlfunc` manpage for details. Some others (like tangent or base-10 logarithm) are omitted, but those can be created from the basic ones or loaded from a module. (See the `POSIX` module for many common math functions.)

Imaginary and Complex Numbers

Though the core of Perl doesn't directly support them, modules are available for working with complex numbers. These overload the normal operators and functions, so you can multiply with `*` and get a square root with `sqrt` even when using complex numbers. See the `Math::Complex` module.

Large and High-Precision Numbers

You can do math with arbitrarily large numbers with an arbitrary number of digits of accuracy. For example, you could calculate the factorial of 2,000, or determine π to 10,000 digits. See the `Math::BigInt` and `Math::BigFloat` modules.

Lists and Arrays

Perl has a number of features that make it easy to manipulate an entire list or array.

map and grep

In Chapter 16, we mentioned the map and grep list-processing operators. They can do more than we could include here. See the perlfunc manpage for more information and examples, and check out the Alpaca for more ways to use map and grep.

The splice Operator

With the splice operator, you can add items to the middle of an array or remove them, letting the array grow or shrink as needed. (Roughly, this is like what substr lets you do with strings.) This effectively eliminates the need for linked lists in Perl. See the perlfunc manpage.

Bits and Pieces

You can work with an array of bits (a *bitstring*) with the vec operator, setting bit number 123, clearing bit number 456, and checking the state of bit 789. Bitstrings may be of arbitrary size. The vec operator can work with chunks of other sizes as long as the size is a small power of two, so it's useful if you need to view a string as a compact array of nybbles. See the perlfunc manpage.

Formats

Perl's formats are an easy way to make fixed-format template-driven reports with automatic page headers. In fact, they are one of the main reasons Larry developed Perl in the first place, as a Practical Extraction and *Report* Language. But, alas, they're limited. The heartbreak of formats happens when someone discovers that he or she needs more than what formats provide. This usually means ripping out the program's entire output section and replacing it with code that doesn't use formats. Still, if you're sure that formats do what you need, *all* that you'll need, and all that you'll *ever* need, they are pretty cool. See the perlform manpage.

Networking and IPC

If there's a way that programs on your machine can talk with others, Perl can probably do it. This section shows some common ways.

System V IPC

The standard functions for System V IPC (interprocess communication) are all supported by Perl, so you can use message queues, semaphores, and shared memory. An array in Perl isn't stored in a chunk of memory in the same way* that an array is stored in C, so shared memory can't share Perl data as is. But there are modules that will translate data, so you can pretend that your Perl data is in shared memory. See the perlfunc manpage and the perlipc module.

Sockets

Perl has full support for TCP/IP sockets, which means that you could write a web server in Perl, or a web browser, Usenet news server or client, finger daemon or client, FTP daemon or client, SMTP or POP or SOAP server or client, or either end of pretty much any other kind of protocol in use on the Internet. You don't need to get into the low-level details because there are modules available for all of the common protocols. For example, you can make a web server or client with the LWP module and one or two lines of additional code.† The LWP module (a tightly integrated set of modules, which implement nearly everything that happens on the Web) is a great example of high-quality Perl code, if you'd like to copy from the best. For other protocols, search for a module with the protocol's name.

Security

Perl has a number of strong security-related features that can make a program written in Perl more secure than the corresponding program written in C. Probably the most important of these is data-flow analysis, better known as *taint checking*. When this is enabled, Perl keeps track of which pieces of data seem to have come from the user or environment and are therefore untrustworthy. If any such piece of so-called "tainted" data is used to affect another process, file, or directory, Perl will prohibit the operation and abort the program. It's not perfect, but it's a powerful way to prevent security-related mistakes. There's more to the story; see the perlsec manpage.

Debugging

There's a debugger that comes with Perl and supports breakpoints, watchpoints, single-stepping, and most things you'd want in a command-line Perl debugger. It's

---

* It would be a lie to say that a Perl array is stored in "a chunk of memory" at all as it's almost certainly spread among many separate chunks.

† Though LWP makes it easy to make a "web browser" that pulls down a page or image, rendering that to the user is another problem. You can drive an X11 display with Tk or Gtk widgets or use curses to draw on a character terminal. It's all a matter of downloading and installing the right modules from CPAN.

written in Perl, so if there are bugs in the debugger, we're not sure how they get those out. In addition to all of the usual debugger commands, you can run Perl code from the debugger—calling your subroutines, changing variables, even redefining subroutines—while your program is running. See the perldebug manpage for the latest details. The Alpaca gives a detailed walkthrough of the debugger.

Another debugging tactic is to use the B::Lint module, which is still preliminary as of this writing.

The Common Gateway Interface (CGI)

One of the most popular uses for Perl on the Web is in writing CGI programs. These run on a web server to process the results of a form, perform a search, produce dynamic web content, or count the number of accesses to a web page.

The CGI module, which comes with Perl, provides an easy way to access the form parameters and to generate some HTML in responses. (If you don't want the overhead of the full CGI module, the CGI_Lite module provides access to the form parameters without all the rest.) It may be tempting to skip the module and copy and paste one of the snippets of code that purport to give access to the form parameters, but nearly all of these are buggy.* When writing CGI programs, there are several big issues to keep in mind. These make this topic too broad to fully include in this book:†

Security, security, security
> We can't overemphasize security. Somewhere around half of the successful attacks on computers around the world involve a security-related bug in a CGI program.

Concurrency issues
> It's easy to have several processes concurrently trying to access a single file or resource.

Standards compliance
> No matter how hard you try, you probably won't be able to test your program thoroughly with more than about 1% or 2% of the web browsers and servers in use today‡ because thousands of programs are available, with new ones popping

---

* There are some details of the interface that these snippets don't support. Trust us; it's better to use a module.

† Several of the reviewers who looked over a draft of this book for us wished we could cover more about CGI programming. We agree, but it wouldn't be fair to the reader to give just enough knowledge to be dangerous. A proper discussion of the problems inherent in CGI programming would probably add at least 50% to the size (and cost) of this book.

‡ Every new release of each browser on each different platform counts as a new one that you're probably not going to be able to test. We chuckle when we hear someone tested a web site with "both browsers" or when they say "I don't know if it works with the other one."

up every week. The solution is to follow the standards, so your program will work with all of them.[*]

Troubleshooting and debugging

Since the CGI program runs in a different environment than you're likely to be able to access directly, you'll have to learn new techniques for troubleshooting and debugging.

Security, security, security!

There, we've said it again. Don't forget security. It's the first and last thing to think about when your program is going to be available to everyone in the world who wants to try breaking it.

That list didn't mention URI-encoding, HTML entities, HTTP and response codes, Secure Sockets Layer (SSL), Server-Side Includes (SSIs), here documents, creating graphics on the fly, programmatically generating HTML tables, forms, widgets, hidden form elements, getting and setting cookies, path info, error trapping, redirection, taint checking, internationalization and localization, embedding Perl into HTML (or the other way around), working with Apache and mod_perl, and using the LWP module.[†] Most or all of those topics should be covered in any good book on using Perl with the Web. *CGI Programming with Perl* by Scott Guelich, et al. (O'Reilly) is mighty nice here, as is Lincoln Stein's *Network Programming with Perl* (Addison-Wesley).

Command-Line Options

Many different command-line options are available in Perl; many let you write useful programs directly from the command line. See the perlrun manpage.

Built-in Variables

Perl has dozens of built-in variables (like @ARGV and $0), which provide useful information or control the operation of Perl itself. See the perlvar manpage.

Syntax Extensions

There are more tricks you could do with Perl syntax, including the continue block and the BEGIN block. See the perlsyn and perlmod manpages.

---

[*] At the very least, following the standards lets you put the blame squarely on the other programmer, who didn't.

[†] Do you see why we didn't try to fit all of that into this book?

References

Perl's references are similar to C's pointers, but in operation, they're more like what you have in Pascal or Ada. A reference "points" to a memory location, but because there's no pointer arithmetic or direct memory allocation and deallocation, you can be sure that any reference you have is a valid one. References allow OO programming and complex data structures, among other tricks. See the `perlreftut` and `perlref` manpages. The Alpaca covers references in great detail.

Complex Data Structures

References allow us to make complex data structures in Perl. For example, suppose you want a two-dimensional array. You can do that,[*] or you can do something much more interesting, like have an array of hashes, a hash of hashes, or a hash of arrays of hashes.[†] See the `perldsc` (data-structures cookbook) and `perllol` (lists of lists) manpages. The Alpaca covers this thoroughly, including techniques for complex data manipulation, like sorting and summarizing.

Object-Oriented Programming

Yes, Perl has objects—it's buzzword-compatible with all of those other languages. OO programming lets you create your own user-defined datatypes with associated abilities, using inheritance, overriding, and dynamic method lookup.[‡] Unlike some object-oriented languages, Perl doesn't force you to use objects. (Many object-oriented modules can be used without understanding objects.) But if your program is going to be larger than *N* lines of code, it may be more efficient for the programmer (a tiny bit though slower at runtime) to make it OO. No one knows the precise value of *N*, but we estimate it's around a few thousand or so. See the `perlobj` and `perlboot` manpages for a start, and Damian Conway's excellent *Object-Oriented Perl* (Manning Press) for more advanced information. The Alpaca book covers objects thoroughly as well.

Anonymous Subroutines and Closures

Odd as it may sound at first, it can be useful to have a subroutine without a name. Such subroutines can be passed as parameters to other subroutines, or they can be accessed via arrays or hashes to make jump tables. Closures are a powerful concept

---

[*] Well, not really, but you can fake it so well that you'll hardly remember that there's a difference.

[†] Actually, you can't make any of these things because these are verbal shorthands for what's happening. What we call "an array of arrays" in Perl is really an array of *references to* arrays.

[‡] OO has its own set of jargon words. Terms used in one OO language will typically not match those in a different OO language.

that comes to Perl from the world of Lisp. A closure is (roughly speaking) an anonymous subroutine with its own private data. Again, this is covered in the Alpaca book.

Tied Variables

A tied variable may be accessed like any other but it uses your own code behind the scenes. So, you could make a scalar that is really stored on a remote machine or an array that always stays sorted. See the perltie manpage.

Operator Overloading

You can redefine operators like addition, concatenation, comparison, or even the implicit string-to-number conversion with the overload module. For example, this is how a module implementing complex numbers can let you multiply a complex number by 8 to get a complex number as a result.

Dynamic Loading

The basic idea of dynamic loading is that your program decides at runtime that it needs more functionality than what's currently available, so it loads it up and keeps running. You can always dynamically load Perl code, but it's more interesting to dynamically load a binary extension.* This is how non-Perl modules are made.

Embedding

The reverse of dynamic loading (in a sense) is embedding.

Suppose you want to make a cool word processor, and you start writing it in (say) C++.† You decide you want the users to be able to use Perl's regular expressions for an extra-powerful search-and-replace feature, so you embed Perl into your program. Then you realize you could open up some of the Perl's power to your users. A power user could write a subroutine in Perl that could become a menu item in your program. Users can customize the operation of your word processor by writing a little Perl. So, you open up a little space on your website where users can share and exchange these Perl snippets, and you've got thousands of new programmers extending what your program can do at no extra cost to your company. And how much do

---

* Dynamic loading of binary extensions is available if your system supports that. If it doesn't, you can compile the extensions statically, meaning you can make a Perl binary with the extension built-in, ready for use.

† That's probably the language we'd use for writing a word processor. Hey, we love Perl, but we didn't swear an oath in blood to use no other language. When language X is the best choice, use language X. But often, X equals Perl.

you have to pay Larry for all this? Nothing. Check the licenses that come with Perl. Larry is a nice guy. You should send him a thank-you note. .

Though we don't know of such a word processor, some folks have used this technique to make other powerful programs. One such example is Apache's mod_perl, which embeds Perl into a powerful web server. If you're thinking about embedding Perl, you should check out mod_perl; since it's all open source, you can see how it works.

Converting Other Languages to Perl

If you've got old *sed* and *awk* programs that you wish were written in Perl, you're in luck. Not only can Perl do everything that those can do, it has a conversion program, and it's probably installed on your system. Check the documentation for *s2p* (for converting from *sed*) or *a2p* (for converting from *awk*).* Since programs don't write programs as well as people do, the results won't be the best Perl, but it's a start and it's easy to tweak. The translated program may be faster or slower than the original, too. After you've fixed up any gross inefficiencies in the machine-written Perl code, it should be comparable.

Do you have C algorithms you want to use from Perl? Luck is on your side; it's not too hard to put C code into a compiled module that can be used from Perl. In fact, just about any language that compiles to make object code can be used to make a module. See the perlxs manpage and the Inline module, as well as the SWIG system.

Do you have a shell script you want to convert to Perl? Your luck has run out. There's no automatic way to convert shell to Perl. That's because the shell hardly does anything by itself; it spends all of its time running other programs. Sure, we could make a program that would mostly call system for each line of the shell, but that would be slower than letting the shell do things in the first place. It takes a human level of intelligence to see how the shell's use of *cut, rm, sed, awk*, and *grep* can be turned into efficient Perl code. It's better to rewrite the shell script from scratch.

Converting find Command Lines to Perl

A common task for a system administrator is to recursively search the directory tree for certain items. On Unix, this is typically done with the find command. We can do that directly from Perl, too.

---

* If you're using *gawk* or *nawk* or some other variant, *a2p* may not be able to convert it. Both of these conversion programs were written long ago and have had few updates except when needed to keep working with new releases of Perl.

The find2perl command, which comes with Perl, takes the same arguments that find does. Instead of finding the requested items, however, the output of find2perl is a Perl program that finds them. Since it's a program, you can edit it for your own needs. (The program is written in a somewhat odd style.)

One useful argument that's available in find2perl but not in the standard find is the -eval option. This says that what follows it is Perl code to be run each time that a file is found. When it's run, the current directory will be the directory in which an item is found, and $_ will contain the item's name.

Here's an example of how you might use find2perl. Suppose that you're a system administrator on a Unix machine, and you want to find and remove all of the old files in the /tmp directory.* Here's the command that writes the program to do that:

```
$ find2perl /tmp -atime +14 -eval unlink >Perl-program
```

That command says to search in /tmp (and recursively in subdirectories) for items whose atime (last access time) is at least 14 days ago. For each item, the program should run the Perl code unlink, which will use $_ by default as the name of a file to remove. The output (redirected to go into the file Perl-program) is the program that does all of this. Now you merely need to arrange for it to be run as needed.

Command-Line Options in Your Programs

If you'd like to make programs that take command-line options (like Perl's -w for warnings, for example), there are modules that let you do this in a standard way. See the documentation for the Getopt::Long and Getopt::Std modules.

Embedded Documentation

Perl's own documentation is written in *Pod* (plain-old documentation) format. You can embed this documentation in your own programs to be translated to text, HTML, or many other formats as needed. See the perlpod manpage. The Alpaca book covers this, too.

More Ways to Open Filehandles

There are other modes to use in opening a filehandle. See the perlopentut manpage.

---

* This is a task typically done by a *cron* job at some early-morning hour each day.

Locales and Unicode

It's a small world, after all. To work properly in places where the alphabet is different, Perl has support for locales and Unicode.

Locales tell Perl how things are done locally. For example, does the character æ sort at the end of the alphabet or between Š and Œ? And what's the local name for the third month? See the perllocale manpage (not to be confused with the *perllocal* manpage).

See the perlunicode manpage for the latest on how your version of Perl deals with Unicode. As of this writing, each new release of Perl has many new Unicode-related changes, but we hope things will settle down soon.

Threads and Forking

Perl has support for threads. Though this is experimental, it can be a useful tool for some applications. Using fork (where it's available) is better supported. See the perlfork and perlthrtut manpages.

Graphical User Interfaces (GUIs)

A large and powerful module set is Tk, which lets you make on-screen interfaces that work on more than one platform. See *Mastering Perl/Tk* by Nancy Walsh and Steve Lidie (O'Reilly).

And More…

If you check out the module list on CPAN, you'll find modules for more purposes, from generating graphs and other images to downloading email, and from figuring the amortization of a loan to figuring the time of sunset. New modules are added all the time, so Perl is even more powerful today than when we wrote this book. We can't keep up with it all, so we'll stop here.

Larry says he no longer keeps up with all of the development of Perl because the Perl universe is big and keeps expanding. And he can't get bored with Perl because he can always find another corner of this ever-expanding universe. And we suspect, neither will we. Thank you, Larry!

Index

Symbols

@ (at sign), array referencing, 43
| (bar), regular expressions, 103
=~ (binding operator), 111
   m// and, 123
^ (caret), character classes, 105
$_ default variable, 47
<> diamond operator, 70
#! line, portability, 14
.. (range operator), 41

A

access
   array elements, 39
   databases, 264
   hash elements, 91
algorithms, high-water mark, 61
ampersand, subroutines, 65
anchors
   regular expressions, 110
   word anchors, 110
answers to exercises, 229–254
arguments
   invocation, 70, 72
   subroutines, 57
     passing, 57
@ARGV array, 72
array slices, 224–226
arrays, 38
   @ sign, 43
   @ARGV, 72

bits, 266
elements, 38
   access, 39
foreach control, 46
grep and, 266
indices, 40, 88
interpolation to string, 45
keys, 88
map and, 266
pop operator, 44
printf and, 77
push operator, 44
reverse operator, 47
shift operator, 45
sort operator, 48
splice operator, 266
unshift operator, 45
assigning hashes, 93
   keys, 94
   values, 94
assignment
   binary assignment operators, 27
   list values to variables, 42
   scalar variables, 27
associativity, operators, 29
at sign (@), array referencing, 43
autodecrement operator, 140
autoincrement operator, 140
   preincrements, 141
automatic match variables, 115

We'd like to hear your suggestions for improving our indexes. Send email to *index@oreilly.com*.

J

join function, 125

K

keys, 88
  hash assignment, 94
  hashes
    expressions, 92
    unquoted, 222
  multiple, sorting by, 190
keys function, hashes, 95
keywords
  else, 32
  for, 144
  foreach, 144
  sub, 54

L

labeled loop blocks, 148
large numbers, 265
last operator, 145
lexical variables, 59
  blocks, 62
lib pragma, 263
libraries, 256
  modules and, 257
links, directories, 171–176
  symbolic links, 174
list context
  backquotes and, 200
  m// in, 126
list-producing expressions, scalar context, 49
lists, 38
  assign values to variables, 42
  context, 48
    scalar-producing expressions, 50
    <STDIN> operator, 51
  empty parameters, 61
  grep and, 220
  literals, 40
  map and, 221
  qw shortcut, 41
  slices, 222–224
literals
  double-quoted string, 22
  floating-point, 19
  integer, 19
  list, 40
  single-quoted string, 21
locales, support, 274
localtime function, 160

logical operators, 148
  short-circuit operators, 149
loops
  blocks, labeled, 148
  control structures, 144
lstat function, file tests, 158

M

m//
  list context and, 126
  regular expressions and, 107
map
  arrays and, 266
  list items and, 221
match variables, 113
  automatic, 115
  persistence, 114
matches, regular expressions
  binding operator, 111
  case-insensitive, 108
  m//, 107
  multiline text, 129
  /s, 108
  word anchors, 110
matching patterns, 102
math
  complex numbers, 265
  imaginary numbers, 265
  large numbers, 265
math functions
  advanced, 265
  high-precision numbers, 265
metacharacters, 102
modifiers in expressions, 137
modules
  CGI, 258
  CGI_Lite, 258
  CGI.pm, 214
  Cwd, 258
  DBI, 215
  documentation, 208
  Fatal, 258
  File::Basename, 211, 259
  File::Copy, 259
  File::Spec, 213, 259
  functions
    import list, 212
    limiting, 212
  Image::Size, 259
  installation, 209, 257
  libraries and, 257
  Net::SMTP, 260

S

T

About the Authors

Randal L. Schwartz is one of the bestselling Perl authors of all time, having been fortunate enough to coauthor two of the seminal books on learning Perl. In addition to writing *Programming Perl* and *Learning Perl*, Randal has been the Perl columnist for *UNIX Review*, *Web Techniques*, *Sys Admin*, and *Linux Magazine*.

Tom Phoenix has been working in the field of education since 1982. After more than 13 years of dissections, explosions, work with interesting animals, and high-voltage sparks during his work at a science museum, he started teaching Perl classes for Stonehenge Consulting Services, where he's worked since 1996. Since then, he has traveled to many interesting locations, so you might see him soon at a Perl Mongers meeting. When he has time, he answers questions on Usenet's *comp.lang.perl.misc* and *comp.lang.perl.moderated* newsgroups and contributes to the development and usefulness of Perl. In addition to his work with Perl, Perl hackers, and related topics, Tom spends his time on amateur cryptography and speaking Esperanto. He lives in Portland, Oregon.

brian d foy has been an instructor for Stonehenge Consulting Services since 1998, a Perl user since he was a physics graduate student, and a die-hard Mac user since he first owned a computer. He founded the first Perl user group, the New York Perl Mongers, as well as the Perl advocacy nonprofit Perl Mongers, Inc., which helped form more than 200 Perl user groups across the globe. He maintains the *perlfaq* portions of the core Perl documentation, several modules on CPAN, and some stand-alone scripts. He's the publisher of *The Perl Review*, a magazine devoted to Perl, and is a frequent speaker at conferences that include the Perl Conference, Perl University, MarcusEvans BioInformatics '02, and YAPC. His writings on Perl appear in The O'Reilly Network, *The Perl Journal*, *Dr. Dobbs*, *The Perl Review*, *use.perl.org*, and in several Perl usenet groups.

Colophon

Our look is the result of reader comments, our own experimentation, and feedback from distribution channels. Distinctive covers complement our distinctive approach to technical topics, breathing personality and life into potentially dry subjects.

The animal on the cover of *Learning Perl*, Fourth Edition is a llama, a relation of the camel native to the Andean range. Also included in this llamoid group is the domestic alpaca and their wild ancestors, the guanaco and the vicuna. Bones found in ancient human settlements suggest that domestication of the alpaca and llama dates back 4,500 years. In 1531, when Spanish conquistadors overran the Inca Empire in the high Andes, they found both animals present in great numbers. These llamas are suited for high mountain life; their hemoglobin can take in more oxygen than that of other mammals.

Llamas can weigh up to 300 pounds and are mainly used as beasts of burden. A packtrain may contain several hundred animals and can travel up to 20 miles per day. Llamas will carry loads up to 50 pounds, but have a tendency to be short-tempered and resort to spitting and biting to demonstrate displeasure. To the people of the Andes, llamas also provide meat, wool for clothing, hides for leather, and fat for candles. Their wool can also be braided into rope and rugs, and their dried dung is used for fuel.

Matt Hutchinson was the production editor for *Learning Perl*, Fourth Edition. GEX, Inc. provided production services. Genevieve d'Entremont, Sarah Sherman, and Colleen Gorman provided quality control.

Edie Freedman designed the cover of this book. The cover image is a 19th-century engraving from the Dover Pictorial Archive. Karen Montgomery produced the cover layout with Adobe InDesign CS using Adobe's ITC Garamond font.

David Futato designed the interior layout. This book was converted by Joe Wizda to FrameMaker 5.5.6 with a format conversion tool created by Erik Ray, Jason McIntosh, Neil Walls, and Mike Sierra that uses Perl and XML technologies. The text font is Linotype Birka; the heading font is Adobe Myriad Condensed; and the code font is LucasFont's TheSans Mono Condensed. The illustrations that appear in the book were produced by Robert Romano, Jessamyn Read, and Lesley Borash using Macromedia FreeHand MX and Adobe Photoshop CS.

Better than e-books

Buy *Learning Perl,* Fourth Edition, and access
the digital edition FREE on Safari for 45 days.

Go to www.oreilly.com/go/safarienabled
and type in coupon code MYPA-0BBO-CQH9-9HOM-H4M1

Search
over 2000 top
tech books

Download
whole chapters

Cut and Paste
code examples

Find
answers fast

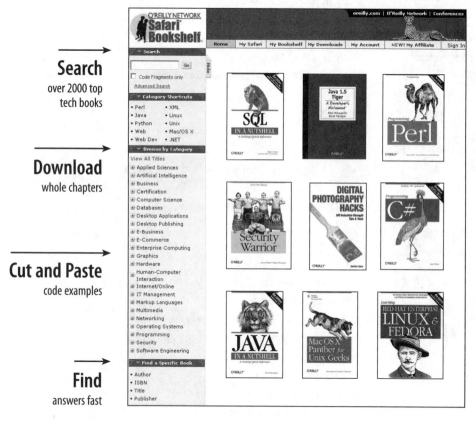

Search Safari! The premier electronic reference
library for programmers and IT professionals

Related Titles from O'Reilly

Perl

Advanced Perl Programming, *2nd Edition*

CGI Programming with Perl, *2nd Edition*

Computer Science & Perl Programming: The Best of the Perl Journal

Embedding Perl in HTML with Mason

Games, Diversions, & Perl Culture: The Best of the Perl Journal

Learning Perl, *4th Edition*

Learning Perl Objects, References and Modules

Mastering Algorithms with Perl

Mastering Perl/Tk

Mastering Regular Expressions, *2nd Edition*

Perl & LWP

Perl & XML

Perl 6 and Parrot Essentials, *2nd Edition*

Perl Best Practices

Perl CD Bookshelf, *Version 4.0*

Perl Cookbook, *2nd Edition*

Perl Debugger Pocket Reference

Perl for System Administration

Perl Graphics Programming

Perl in a Nutshell, *2nd Edition*

Perl Pocket Reference, *4th Edition*

Perl Template Toolkit

Perl Testing: A Developer's Notebook

Practical mod_perl

Programming the Perl DBI

Programming Perl, *3rd Edition*

Programming Web Services with Perl

Regular Expression Pocket Guide

RT Essentials

Web, Graphics & Perl/Tk: The Best of the Perl Journal

XML Publishing with AxKit

O'REILLY®

Our books are available at most retail and online bookstores.

To order direct: 1-800-998-9938 • *order@oreilly.com* • *www.oreilly.com*

Online editions of most O'Reilly titles are available by subscription at *safari.oreilly.com*

Keep in touch with O'Reilly

Download examples from our books

To find example files from a book, go to: *www.oreilly.com/catalog* select the book, and follow the "Examples" link.

Register your O'Reilly books

Register your book at *register.oreilly.com* Why register your books? Once you've registered your O'Reilly books you can:

- Win O'Reilly books, T-shirts or discount coupons in our monthly drawing.
- Get special offers available only to registered O'Reilly customers.
- Get catalogs announcing new books (US and UK only).
- Get email notification of new editions of the O'Reilly books you own.

Join our email lists

Sign up to get topic-specific email announcements of new books and conferences, special offers, and O'Reilly Network technology newsletters at:

elists.oreilly.com

It's easy to customize your free elists subscription so you'll get exactly the O'Reilly news you want.

Get the latest news, tips, and tools

www.oreilly.com

- "Top 100 Sites on the Web"—PC Magazine
- CIO Magazine's Web Business 50 Awards

Our web site contains a library of comprehensive product information (including book excerpts and tables of contents), downloadable software, background articles, interviews with technology leaders, links to relevant sites, book cover art, and more.

Work for O'Reilly

Check out our web site for current employment opportunities:

jobs.oreilly.com

Contact us

O'Reilly Media, Inc.
1005 Gravenstein Hwy North
Sebastopol, CA 95472 USA
Tel: 707-827-7000 or 800-998-9938
    (6am to 5pm PST)
Fax: 707-829-0104

Contact us by email

For answers to problems regarding your order or our products:
order@oreilly.com

To request a copy of our latest catalog:
catalog@oreilly.com

For book content technical questions or corrections: **booktech@oreilly.com**

For educational, library, government, and corporate sales: **corporate@oreilly.com**

To submit new book proposals to our editors and product managers:
proposals@oreilly.com

For information about our international distributors or translation queries:
international@oreilly.com

For information about academic use of O'Reilly books:
adoption@oreilly.com
or visit:
academic.oreilly.com

For a list of our distributors outside of North America check out:
international.oreilly.com/distributors.html

Order a book online

www.oreilly.com/order_new
